MARCH 5, - T.W. MANSON (ED.) THE COMPANION
to The BIBLE

C.H. DODO, "THE ... F

B.P.I.

JESUS" PP 373 - 389

P 114 -130

P 114 -130

AN INTRODUCTION TO
THE NEW TESTAMENT

AN INTRODUCTION TO
THE NEW TESTAMENT

BY

RICHARD HEARD
M.A., M.B.E., M.C.

FELLOW OF PETERHOUSE, CAMBRIDGE
UNIVERSITY LECTURER IN DIVINITY, CAMBRIDGE

HARPER & BROTHERS PUBLISHERS
NEW YORK

CONTENTS

v

PART III

THE ACTS OF THE APOSTLES AND THE GROWTH OF THE CHURCH

INTRODUCTION

MODERN Introductions to the New Testament for the most part confine themselves to providing introductions to the separate books, their authorship, contents, and problems, with discussions of text and canon, and of the inspiration and value of the New Testament as a whole. While this method of treatment has considerable advantages, it has, especially for the uninstructed reader, the disadvantage of introducing him to the detailed study of the New Testament without focusing his attention on the religious problems involved.

The importance of the application of modern methods of criticism to the New Testament for the ordinary Christian man and woman lies in their influence upon our attitude to some of the cardinal tenets of our religion. Once we have lost our unquestioning belief in the truth and authority of every word in the New Testament—and few persons can study the results of the last century's work upon the New Testament and retain such a belief—both those doctrines which divide the Christian Churches and those which they share in common have to be justified again in the light of our new attitude to those documents which support them. To take one example out of many, the different doctrines of Baptism and Confirmation held in different Churches were worked out and established largely on the basis of a true and authoritative New Testament; to-day many New Testament scholars would hesitate to accept any of the three commands in the gospels to baptise (Mt. xxviii 19, Mk. xvi 16, Jn. iii 5) as having been spoken by Jesus, and their interpretations of the baptismal references in Acts would be influenced by the degree of historical accuracy which they were willing to ascribe to the author of Acts. This is not to say, of course, that any large number of competent critics would deny the dominical institution of Baptism, but only that the establishment of such doctrines must rest upon a revised treatment of the New Testament evidence.

It is here that the ordinary Christian reader has both great difficulties to face and a great reward to win. The difficulties arise from the lack of certainty inherent in historical criticism : historical judgements are seldom unanimous, and must often be qualified ; where the evidence is scanty and confused, as is often the case in the New Testament, the historian can attain to no more than a disputed probability. The ordinary reader can expect help and guidance for drawing his own conclusions, but not the help and guidance of infallible authority. On the other hand he can hope, by studying the results and probabilities that have been achieved, to gain for himself a truer knowledge of how Christianity came into the world, and a truer understanding of the life and teaching of Jesus Christ, the Son of God.

In the pages that follow an attempt is made to introduce the reader to the relevance of the separate books of the New Testament, in the light of their authorship, circumstances of composition, and teaching, to some of the great religious issues of the New Testament. Four of these issues have been selected as having each of them a particular—though not exclusive—connection with one of the four types of book to be found in the New Testament, the Gospels, the Acts of the Apostles, the Epistles, and the Revelation of John, and as providing a framework for the discussion of the problems connected with them.

The first of these issues, and to most Christians by far the most important, is that of the historical value of the Gospels. If they are not free from error and inconsistency, do they still enable us to form a generally reliable and trustworthy picture of Jesus' life and teaching on earth ?

The second issue is primarily, but not exclusively, concerned with the historical value and the interpretation of the Acts of the Apostles. How far can we reconstruct the earliest history of the Christian Church, and trace developments in its order, worship, etc.?

The questions that arise about the authorship and teaching of the Epistles are clearly of importance for this second issue, as the Gospels and the speeches in Acts are for the third, which is concerned with the value of the Epistles for reconstructing what the Apostles preached about the significance of Jesus' life, death, and resurrection, and what they taught about the Christian life.

The fourth issue concerns the place of apocalyptic expectation in the New Testament. While it is treated here in connection with the value of the Revelation of John, the discussion inevitably involves both the message of the Apostolic Church and that of Jesus himself, and the ultimate problem is the place of such expectation in the message of Jesus.

Each of these questions is discussed in the pages that follow. No more is claimed for these discussions than that they suggest one out of many possible Christian solutions to the problems. Their purpose is to concentrate the attention of the reader on the religious implications of modern New Testament criticism and to encourage him to follow up the evidence for himself with the more intensive study of the text and the important books and commentaries to which it is the function of an Introducion to lead him.

BOOKS FOR READING

The first essential for the serious study of the New Testament, if the student cannot read Greek, is a good modern translation. The Revised Version, with marginal references and with alternative readings at the foot of the page, has the advantage of being a good translation of a Greek text which has more claim to represent the original wording than that followed by the Authorised Version. Much can be learnt, however, about the meaning of diffi-cult passages, especially in the epistles, by comparing this translation with some of the more recent ones, such as Moffatt or, perhaps the best translation of all, the new American Revised Standard Version (cf. p. 20). Of the

Commentaries that cover the whole Bible in one volume the three best are the *Abingdon Commentary* (Abingdon Press, New York), *Peake's Commentary* (Jack) and *A New Commentary*, edited by Gore, Goudge, and Guillaume (S.P.C.K.). The New Testament section of this last is sold separately. These standard works provide introductions and commentaries to each book, a series of general articles on Biblical history and religion, and useful bibliographies for further reading. Up to date bibliographies are contained in two book-lists published jointly by the Lutterworth Press, S.C.M. and S.P.C.K., *A Popular Bibliography of the Christian Faith*, and, for more advanced works, *A General Bibliography of Christian Theology, History, and Apologetic.*

Of modern Introductions to the New Testament those of K. and S. Lake (Christophers) and of Sir E. C. Hoskyns and N. Davey, *The Riddle of the New Testament* (Faber), may be mentioned, and for advanced study those of A. H. McNeile (Oxford) and J. Moffatt (Clark).

PART I

THE NEW TESTAMENT AS A WHOLE

I

CHAPTER I

THE CRITICAL STUDY OF
THE NEW TESTAMENT

CHRISTIANS agree in regarding the books of the New Testament as possessing a special authority. They differ as to the nature of this authority and in their interpretation of the contents of the books. The purpose of the critical study of the New Testament, if it is also religious, is to use all the available methods of applying human knowledge to discover how the authority of the New Testament is to be understood, and to set the revelation which it contains as far as possible in its original historical context. The central fact that God has revealed himself to men through Jesus Christ is in the last resort based for Christians on faith and experience and not on knowledge alone. It can be accepted or rejected, but, for those who accept it, it becomes as the act of God no longer a matter for human argument, but the supreme event of history. The final aim of Christian study of the New Testament is the better understanding of the revelation which it contains, and here the resources of human knowledge can be fitly employed, because the books of the New Testament were written and copied by men who were fallible like ourselves and under the influence of their human environment.

This fallibility becomes evident as soon as we undertake the necessary preliminary examination of the text of the New Testament and of the way in which the books of the New Testament were gathered into one authoritative collection. There are a great many places where the wording of our oldest Greek manuscripts differs, and a considerable number where it is impossible to decide with certainty exactly what the original authors wrote. A study of the history of the early Church reveals disagreements as to the books which should be reckoned as of special authority, and it took centuries of dispute before the final selection received general agreement.   The detailed study of the books themselves provides further evidence that this fallibility extended to the authors themselves and to the sources which they used.   'We have this treasure in earthen vessels' (2 Cor. iv 7).

When once we have come to see that the early disciples did not have perfect memories and that their understanding of Jesus was influenced at many points by the mental and religious background of their time, the purpose of the modern critical and scientific approach to the contents of the New Testament becomes clear.   It is to establish as far as possible the historical truth as to what Jesus said and did, how the Church grew and developed, and the historical circumstances in which Christians came to write the books of the New Testament.   We cannot, of course, achieve more than a very limited reconstruction of the New Testament events and teaching, and on many important points there will continue to be great disagreement.   Yet for all the uncertainties that follow in its train, the critical study of the New Testament provides us with a picture of Christian origins that gives a new focus to certain aspects of Jesus' teaching and the development of the Church and a truer understanding of the mode of God's revelation than that which derives from a complete and uncritical acceptance of the New Testament as uniformly and verbally inspired.

THE PROGRESS OF CRITICISM

It was only by slow degrees over a period of centuries that the Church settled which books were to be included in the New Testament and given a place side by side with the Old Testament.   The ancient Church contained some acute and learned scholars who raised many of the critical questions that are discussed to-day.   Thus Irenaeus at the close of the second century noted the different numbers given to the Beast in his texts of Rev. xiii 18, and preferred the reading ' 666 ', as modern scholars do, on the ground that it was contained in the oldest copies known to him. In the third century Origen expressed doubts as to the Pauline authorship of the Epistle to the Hebrews on the grounds of the epistle's style and thought, and Dionysius of Alexandria on similar grounds distinguished between the author of the fourth gospel and the author of Revelation. Such instances of critical acumen could be multiplied, but for the most part members of the Church lacked a scholarly knowledge of Greek and by the end of the fourth century the text of the chosen books was received unquestioningly as of apostolic authority; a series of revisions produced an ' official ' Greek text which was to remain of great influence from the fifth to the nineteenth century, but which we now see in the light of further knowledge to have been based on wrong principles.

The attribution to this New Testament text—as to that of the Old Testament—of verbal inerrancy was associated with methods of exegesis which often disregarded the literal meaning of a passage for an allegorical interpretation which gave it a meaning of more present significance. Such methods had been employed by the New Testament writers themselves in their interpretation of Old Testament passages (e.g. 1 Cor. x 1-2, Heb. vii 1-17) and for the same reason, the desire to gain the authority of infallible scripture for purposes of controversy or instruction; they could only be justified when the original meaning of the passage had been taken into account, and even in the New Testament this had often not been done. In the later Church this type of exegesis sometimes led to fantastic misinterpretations, e.g. the view held by both Origen and Jerome that Peter and Paul had only pretended to quarrel at Antioch (Gal. ii 11 ff.). Even when the New Testament was literally interpreted, the conception of the equal authority of all passages in it led to distorted ideas of what was the teaching of Christ : the literal interpretation of the Revelation, for example, with its material and temporal picture of Christ's reign (Rev. xx) has sometimes obscured the spiritual nature of Jesus' teaching on the kingdom.

The effect of such a mechanical doctrine of inspiration and of such inadequate methods of interpretation was to rob the New Testament of much of its true force and to make it the handmaid of ecclesiastical tradition for more than a thousand years. The Reformation saw the re-emergence of some true principles of criticism, but they were only slowly to influence the now widespread reading of the New Testament. Thus Erasmus' publication in 1516 of a Greek text based on the comparison of manuscripts marked the beginning of a new era in the determination of the correct text, but progress in the examination and classification of manuscripts was slow, and three centuries were to pass before the textual criticism of the New Testament was firmly based on scientific principles. Luther himself distinguished between the value of different parts of the New Testament (p. 18), and Calvin declared it as the first business of an interpreter, to let his author say what he does say, instead of attributing to him what we think he ought to say ', but neither reformer fully lived up to his own precepts, and it was only gradually that scholars began to adopt a truly historical approach to the documents of the New Testament.

There is no one moment at which ' modern ' methods of criticism can be said to have come into existence, but the first half of the nineteenth century saw their adoption on a wide scale in the universities of Germany. The rationalism of the eighteenth century had led to the widespread abandonment of belief in the infallibility of the Bible and to the rejection e.g. of the miraculous elements of the Old Testament narratives. The application of scientific methods of source-criticism and textual criticism to the writings of Greek and Latin authors had also begun. When men trained in such scientific methods and dominated by philosophical preconceptions which left no room for the miraculous in human life turned to the study of the New Testament, they started a revolution in New Testament criticism. The philosophical bases of thought changed, and are still changing, and the Lives of Jesus and Histories of the Early Church which were written under their influence have each yielded place in turn to a new interpretation, but in the process of controversy the documents of the New Testament have been subjected to such a continuous and minute scrutiny that their scientific study is now established on firm and stable foundations. Perhaps the most important pioneer in the early nineteenth century was the great scholar Lachmann who applied to the New Testament methods which he had learnt from his study of the Classics. It was he who in 1830 laid the foundations of modern textual criticism of the New Testament by rejecting the authority of the traditional 'textus receptus' (p. 21) in favour of the witness of the oldest Greek and Latin manuscripts, and his declaration in 1835 that the gospels of Matthew and Luke presuppose the Marcan order of the gospel-narrative pointed the way to what is now the accepted basis of any comparative study of the gospels.

The priority of Mark, however, was not generally acknowledged for many years, and only when every possible explanation of the similarities between the gospels, e.g. that Matthew used Luke, that Luke used Matthew, that a common oral tradition alone accounts for the similarities, had been put forward and examined in great detail, did it become finally clear that Mark was the earliest of our gospels. In the process of controversy that led to this conclusion it became widely recognised that a second document, largely composed of sayings of Jesus, was also used by Matthew and Luke, although controversies still continue as to the nature and extent of this source, which is normally designated as Q (from the German *Quelle* = source).

When once Mark had been acknowledged as the 'foundation' gospel, the implications of such a belief were seen to be important. The Matthaean authorship of the first gospel was no longer defended by the majority of critics, and both the apostolic authorship and the historical value of the fourth gospel were matters of dispute. On the other hand there was widespread agreement at the end of the century that Mark provided a generally trustworthy account of the ministry of Jesus, although in the prevailing liberal temper of the time critics tended to question the historicity of the miracles recorded in the gospel and also to disregard the apocalyptic nature of e.g. Mk. xiii. The authority of Mark was claimed in support of the view that Jesus was first and foremost a great human ethical teacher, whose teaching had been altered by the early Church, and especially by Paul, into a system of theological and sacramental belief.

The problem of reconciling a merely human view of Jesus with the emergence of the Catholic Church was, of course, much older, and the theories of the Tübingen school of critics, which had first been put forward in the eighteen-thirties by F. C. Baur, exercised a wide influence on men's conceptions of the early history of the Church for most of the nineteenth century and spread a distorted view of the circumstances in which Acts and the epistles were written. Under the influence of the philosopher Hegel's theory that history proceeds by thesis, antithesis, and synthesis, Baur and his followers proclaimed that the early Church was rent asunder by conflict between Jewish (Petrine) and Gentile (Pauline) factions, and that Acts represented an attempt of later Catholicism to veil these differences. To support these views Baur denied the Lucan authorship of Acts, whose historical value he impugned, and left to Paul the authorship only of Romans, 1 and 2 Corinthians, and Galatians; the other ' Pauline ' epistles were products of the Christian struggle against Gnosticism. It was fifty years before the traditional authorship of Acts and of most of Paul's epistles were again re-established in the favour of the leading German scholars.

The nineteenth century was above all a period in which new knowledge was gained, systematised, and made available for effective use. In the textual field thousands of manuscripts were examined, collated, and classified, and it was the new availability of adequate material that made possible the establishment of the New Testament text on scientific principles (p. 22). Archaeological finds threw new light on the accuracy of many of the details in Acts, e.g. the Asiarchs of xix 31 and the 'chief man' of Malta xxviii 7, and papyri dug up in Egypt helped to elucidate the language of the New Testament. The knowledge of the New Testament background was immensely increased both by archaeological discoveries and by the scientific assessment of new sources of evidence. The effect of the accumulation of this knowledge was to make possible a much fuller understanding of the New Testament writers as men of their own time; there is hardly a verse in the New Testament where the application of this knowledge does not bring out some new aspect of the original meaning.

The early years of the twentieth century saw the rise of two new schools of thought which have each made a permanent contribution to the understanding of Jesus and the early Church, although not in the form in which it was originally made.

The 'eschatological' interpretation of Jesus was a protest against the liberal misinterpretation of him as primarily an ethical teacher. In the last years of the century J. Weiss had shown that such a picture of Jesus was incompatible with the presentation of him in Mark as proclaiming the imminence of the Day of Judgment and the setting up of the Kingdom of God. Weiss, and after him A. Schweitzer in a book, *The Quest of the Historical Jesus*, which made a great impression on English scholars, interpreted Jesus as primarily a prophet of the approaching world-catastrophe who stood in the succession of Jewish apocalyptists. Such a theory, however, has proved too one-sided for acceptance as a satisfactory explanation of Jesus' life, although it has brought out the undoubted apocalyptic element in the gospels and has forced all subsequent critics to offer an explanation of it.

Of even greater influence has been the 'sceptical' approach to the gospels of a succession of German critics. The 'Christ-myth' theory that Jesus never existed [1] was

---

[1] Cf. A. Drews, *The Christ-Myth*; J. M. Robertson, *Pagan Christs*.

an aberration of thought that could never be taken seriously, but the view that we can know very little about him because the gospels are the creation of the Christian community has received unexpected support in the last fifty years. The starting-point of the movement was the publication by Wrede in 1901 of a book [1] in which he challenged the genuineness of the Marcan outline of Jesus' ministry. The book made little stir at the time, but was to have great influence, especially upon the advocates of ' Form Criticism', a new method of gospel criticism that arose in the years succeeding the first World War.

The Form critics treated the gospels as ' Folk literature ' compiled out of the beliefs of a community, and broke down the gospel material into separate incidents and pieces of teaching which had had a separate existence before being collected together and ultimately formed into a gospel. They drew on parallel folk traditions to show that such isolated stories obey certain laws of development, and that they often lose their original point in the telling. The result of the application of such principles of criticism to Mark by sceptical scholars was to change ' the memoirs of Peter ' into an anonymous compilation of material, the historical value of which could not be determined with any certainty. The methods of form criticism have a certain value, and the employment of them opens up new possibilities of understanding how the gospels were composed, but the majority of critics to-day would separate the employment of such methods from the adoption of the sceptical standpoint which used them to such a negative effect.

For all those who hold that the early Christians misunderstood Jesus there arises the necessity of accounting for the misunderstanding and for the development of the earliest community into the Church as we know it in the second century. The breakdown of the Tübingen theory was followed by the development of other theories which attempted to solve the same problem without disregarding

[1] *Das Messiasgeheimnis in den Evangelien* (= The Messianic Secret in the Gospels). Significantly enough the book has not appeared in an English translation.

so much of the evidence of Acts and the epistles. Attempts were made to show that Paul was responsible for the transformation of a simple Jewish cult in which Jesus was thought of as Messiah into a Hellenistic mystery-religion, and some scholars tried to push the Hellenisation of Christianity even farther back and to associate it with the introduction of title ' Lord ' (Greek, *kyrios*) for Jesus in early Syrian-Christian circles. Against such theories the ' eschatological school maintained the essentially Jewish nature of Paul's teaching and held that his conceptions, e.g. of baptism and the eucharist, were based on eschatological expectation and not on any ' magical ' regard for them ; the Hellenisation of Christianity was due not to Paul but to his Gentile converts.

This sketch of the development of ' tendencies ' in modern New Testament criticism has been confined for the most part to work done by German scholars. This is not accidental, for the Germans have been the outstanding pioneers, not only in the production of new theories about the New Testament, but in the accumulation of knowledge. Yet it would be wrong to ascribe too much importance to the emergence of ' new schools of thought ' in the progress of New Testament studies. Such developments have played a useful and valuable part in increasing our understanding of the New Testament, but even more valuable has been the patient sifting of each new theory as it has appeared, the elimination of what is unsound, and the retention for permanent profit of what has proved to be of worth when tested by the New Testament documents themselves.

It is in this field that scholars in England, America and elsewhere, as well as in Germany, have made their most important contributions. The progress of criticism in England, for example, has not been by violent swings of opinion but by gradual steps, in which the conception of a verbally inerrant New Testament has yielded slowly but surely to that of a collection of books, imperfect in all kinds of ways, but containing very much that is historically trustworthy and offering still a sure witness to the truth of the revelation which it contains.

The present position of New Testament criticism cannot be easily defined, although the later chapters of this book attempt to summarise some of the more generally accepted views, and to indicate the main issues of present controversy. There are many important points on which critical opinion is likely to continue divided, but there are good grounds for thinking that we can still get from the New Testament a knowledge of Jesus and of his Church different in some respects from that of earlier days but with the same power to inspire men to follow him in their lives.

BOOKS FOR READING

W. F. HOWARD. *The Romance of New Testament Scholarship* (Epworth Press).

M. JONES. *The New Testament in the Twentieth Century* (Macmillan).

A. SCHWEITZER. *The Quest of the Historical Jesus* (Black).

A. SCHWEITZER. *Paul and His Interpreters* (Black).

M. J. LAGRANGE. *The Meaning of Christianity according to Luther and his Followers* (Longmans).

S. L. CAIGER. *Archaeology and the New Testament* (Cassell).

R. M. GRANT. *The Bible in the Church* (Macmillan).

CHAPTER II

HOW THE BOOKS OF THE NEW TESTAMENT WERE SELECTED

THE CANON OF THE NEW TESTAMENT

THE phrases ' canonical books ' and ' canon of scripture ' are often used for the books which are recognised as authoritative for Christian doctrine, i.e. the books of our Bible. The Greek word ' canon ', which originally meant a bar or measuring rod, came to mean a rule or standard, or even a list. The Christians early came to speak of the formulated profession of their faith, e.g. in the baptismal creed, as ' the canon of faith ', and although the use of ' canon ' and ' canonical ' in connection with the books of the Bible probably came originally from the meaning of ' list ' it naturally acquired also a sense of ' authoritative standard '. It is in this sense that to-day we speak of the books of our New Testament as ' canonical ' or belonging to the Canon of the New Testament, because of the authority that has been attached to them by the Church. A great German scholar [1] has written :

> ' Many Christians have caught hold of the word Canon and think that in the first half of the second century in some mysterious way the Spirit of God collected the whole of the New Testament in a single book—and that since that time the whole Christian Church has stood by that book. The facts are very different.'

The process by which the books of our New Testament came to acquire their canonical authority was a long one, and in the case of such books as 2 Peter and Revelation involved much controversy. There were two main stages in the growth of the canon, first a period extending from the writing of the books to about A.D. 200 when most of the New Testament books had been collected and had acquired

[1] C. R. Gregory, *Canon and Text of the N.T.*, p. 294.

a position of authority side by side with that of the Old Testament, and then a further period of two centuries and more in which the bounds of the New Testament were finally fixed with very general agreement.

THE COLLECTION OF THE NEW TESTAMENT

The earliest Christians had at first no sacred books other than those of the Old Testament, which they, like their Jewish neighbours, regarded as the word of God. The books of our New Testament were written over a period of not much less than a hundred years, the earliest being perhaps the Epistle of James (*c.* A.D. 45 ?) and the Pauline epistles, the latest probably the pseudonymous 2 Peter (between A.D. 100 and 150). Most of the epistles were ' occasional writings ', written in the first place to deal with particular situations and problems, and it is clear that Paul, for example, though he claimed to write with authority, never dreamt that some of his letters would later be collected and venerated as of universal application and of permanent authority. In the same way both Luke and ' Matthew ' did not hesitate to treat Mark's gospel with considerable freedom, and to amend his narrative in many particulars.

Our knowledge of the early history of our canonical New Testament books is slender, but it is clear that most of them were preserved by the person or community for whom they were written, and that their circulation by means of copies must have originally been as separate units and comparatively slow. Their authority, too, was at first by no means undisputed, and from two early second-century writers we hear of people who preferred the authority of the Old Testament and of living witnesses respectively. Ignatius, writing to the Philadelphians *c.* A.D. 110 recalls that :

' I heard some say, Unless I find it in the Charters (i.e. the Old Testament) I believe it not in the gospel. And when I said to them, It is written, they answered me, That is the question.'

Papias, writing about ten years later, also in Asia Minor, gives as his own opinion

> 'I did not think that I could profit so much from the contents of books as from the utterances of a living and abiding voice.'

With the passage of time, however, the prestige of these Christian writings increased, as the first and second generations of disciples passed away, and men turned instinctively for information to the written documents which preserved so many details of the ministry and teaching of Jesus and of what his apostles had taught.   Readings from such writings must from an early period have played an important part in the services of the different churches, side by side with readings from the Old Testament; yet such readings were at first largely governed, not by any conscious conception of the ecclesiastical authority of these 'new' writings, but by what was available and edifying.   We know that many books not in our New Testament were read in churches in the second century, e.g. accounts of martyrs and their sufferings, and the first epistle of Clement, written from the Church of Rome to that of Corinth and read in church there long after the occasion for its writing had passed away; we even hear of a Bishop of Antioch c. A.D. 190 visiting the church at Rhossus in Cilicia and approving the reading there of a gospel of Peter, only to withdraw his approval when he had later been informed of its heretical nature.

The epistles of Paul seem to have been formed within a generation of his death into a separate collection which enjoyed a wide circulation.   The author of 2 Peter, writing in the first half of the second century, refers to 'Paul . . . in all his epistles' (iii 15-16), and Polycarp of Smyrna soon after A.D. 110 shows knowledge of at least eight of them. The Gospels, too, supplementing each other as they did, came to be grouped together, although the evidence suggests that their collection was later, and at first sometimes only partial; thus Justin Martyr, writing after the middle of the century, speaks of the 'memoirs of the apostles' as being read with the prophets in the weekly services

(Apol. lxviii), but does not seem to include John's gospel with the others.

Round these two main groups of writings collected other books, e.g. Acts and 1 Peter, but even in a large church not all our New Testament books would be known in the second century, while others not included in our New Testament seem often to have been collected and used as of comparable value and authority. The difficulties of circulation were very real, and it is by no means surprising that the Epistle of James, for example, is unmentioned by name in any Christian writing that has survived, up to the time of Origen in the third century.

It was not until the middle of the second century that the Church began consciously to erect a ' canon ' of Christian writings, which could be reckoned (at least in a wide sense, e.g. Mark's gospel based on Peter's teaching) as apostolic, and the impulse to do so came from the heretics. The great heretical leaders in the second century supported their perversions of Christian doctrine by appealing to private traditions handed down by apostles, or even by forging or adapting gospels and epistles. Thus the followers of Basilides (fl. c. A.D. 130) claimed that he had been taught by one Glaucias, ' the interpreter of Peter ', and they used also a kind of gospel that claimed to be ' the Traditions of Matthias the Apostle ', while the great heretic Marcion established his own canon of scripture, rejecting the Old Testament and accepting as the only authoritative books carefully edited versions of Luke's gospel and of ten of Paul's epistles. The second century, too, saw a spate of gospels, acts, and apocalypses, to which apostolic names were attached, but which contained little of historic value and much of legend and false doctrine. It was in the face of such developments that the Church was driven to make a clear distinction between those works which could be vouched for as of apostolic authority and the others.

By the close of the second century this process had advanced sufficiently for there to be general agreement within the Church on the acceptance as authoritative of our four gospels and thirteen epistles of Paul, and the refusal to accord the same veneration to such a non-apostolic work as e.g. the Shepherd of Hermas. In a list drawn up, perhaps at Rome, towards the end of the century, the late date of Hermas is stressed, and that

> ' It ought also to be read ; but it cannot be publicly read in the church to the people, either among the prophets, as their number is complete, or among the apostles, to the end of the time.'

Of the remaining books of our New Testament some were not yet in general circulation, e.g. James, Jude, 2 and 3 John; the apostolic authorship of others was not yet universally admitted, e.g. Hebrews and 2 Peter, and in the case of Revelation, with its material picture of heaven and of the thousand year reign of Christ before the end, the Eastern churches as a whole were still unwilling to accept its authority. The Christian Church, it must be remembered, was still only loosely organised, and although all of our New Testament books are continually quoted, and often quoted as authoritative, by Christian writers from the third century on, it was not until the close of the fourth and beginning of the fifth century that the Canon of the New Testament, as we know it, can be said to have obtained almost [1] universal acceptance.

THE VALUE OF THE CANON

The Canon of the New Testament was fixed in accordance with two criteria, that the writings which it contains were apostolic, and that the words of these writings consequently had an authority which could not be given to other Christian writings, however edifying. How far can the books of the New Testament still claim such an especial authority ?

Before discussing the effects of recent biblical criticism

---

[1] The Syriac-speaking churches continued to hesitate for centuries about accepting 2 Peter, 2 and 3 John, Jude and Revelation, and their doubts about Revelation were long shared by the Greek Church generally.

2

on our estimation of the value of the canon, it is well to
remember that, even in the days when the authority of
scripture was accepted on the traditional grounds, not all
Christians have accorded an equal authority to all the books.
Thus Luther could say of the Epistle of James that 'it has
no character of the gospel in it', and refuse to count the
Epistle to the Hebrews and the Epistle of Jude among the
books necessary to lay the foundation of faith.   Calvin, too,
significantly omitted the Book of Revelation from the number
of New Testament books which he furnished with a commentary.

But it is within the last century that the whole conception
of canonicity has been subjected to criticism on the basis of
our new knowledge.   The general rejection of the apostolic
authorship of e.g. the Gospel of Matthew, the Epistle to
the Hebrews, and the Book of Revelation, has changed
the basis on which authority can truthfully be claimed for
the New Testament.   The whole conception, too, of the
absolute authority of every word of the New Testament has
itself been undermined.   Thus an Archbishop of Canter-
bury has felt able to withdraw the ban on women coming
bare-headed to church, in spite of the words of Paul in
1 Cor. xi 5-16.   While this is in itself, of course, a minor
matter, it illustrates a very important principle, that the
words even of Paul must be weighed by the teaching of
Christ before they can be accepted as fully authoritative.

This is not to say that once the traditional principles
on which the canon was established have been challenged,
the whole idea of an authoritative canon must be abandoned.
A truer estimate of the results of modern criticism would be
that it has substituted for the traditional principles new
ones which establish the authority of our New Testament on
sounder and abiding foundations.

While the New Testament can now be regarded as
'apostolic' only partially, and in a very wide sense, it remains
true that the New Testament does contain substantially all
that has survived of those first-century Christian writings
which preserved the knowledge of the early ministry of

Christ and the teaching of the first Christian generation. As such it is of unique authority for Christians. None of the other Christian writings which survive from the first and second centuries can rank as serious competitors for inclusion; neither in information about Jesus nor in the formulation of Christian doctrine do they add anything that is at once important and primitive. Only in the New Testament itself can we still have confidence that the essential truths proclaimed by the apostles are preserved, even if we now must add that the books of the New Testament are not free from faults and errors. The true significance of canonicity lies not in the inerrancy of scripture, but in the fact that it ' containeth all things necessary to salvation '.

BOOKS FOR READING

A. SOUTER. *The Text and Canon of the New Testament* (Duckworth).
The article, 'The Bible in the Church', by Bishop Gore in *The New Commentary* (S.P.C.K.) gives a short but interesting account of the growth of the idea of canonicity.
C. R. GREGORY. *Canon and Text of the New Testament* (Clark).
A. HARNACK. *The Origin of the New Testament* (Williams and Norgate).

CHAPTER III

THE TEXT OF THE NEW TESTAMENT

THE New Testament claims from its readers an unique authority, and the reliability of its text is therefore of great importance. We wish to be assured that, when we read it, even in translation, we are reading essentially what the original authors wrote, and not a corrupted version of their work. In one sense it is true that no translation can correctly render the nuances and subtleties of thought of the original, but for practical purposes the ordinary reader will be content if he can be reasonably certain of the fidelity of the translation which he reads to a Greek text which can claim to be substantially that of the original works.

If the Authorised Version of 1611, still by far the most widely read of all English translations of the New Testament, is compared with later authoritative translations, such as the Revised Version of 1881, or the American Revised Standard Version of 1946, it is at once clear that there are numerous differences, but that the sum of all these differences amounts to very little. In the words of one of the latest revisers—

> ' It will be obvious to the careful reader that still in 1946, as in 1881 and in 1901, no doctrine of the Christian faith has been affected by the revision, for the simple reason that, out of the thousands of variant readings in the manuscripts, none has turned up thus far that requires a revision of Christian doctrine.' [1]

While the general reliability of the Authorised Version has thus been confirmed by recent scholarship, there is no doubt that the modern translations bring the reader in hundreds of small instances nearer to the words and meaning of the original writers. The Authorised Version is not altogether free from mistranslations, e.g. Mk. xiv 8 ' being before instructed ' for ' being put forward ', or

[1] *An Introduction to the Revised Standard Version of the N.T.*, p. 42.

1 Cor. iv 4 'I know nothing by myself' for 'I know nothing against myself', but its most serious defect, and one which requires it to be corrected in more than a thousand places —most of them, of course, of trivial importance—is that it is a translation of a Greek text which we now know to be comparatively late and inaccurate. Two examples will illustrate this. A comparison between the Authorised and Revised Versions of the Lord's Prayer in Lk. xi 2-4 shows that in the Revised Version the prayer is much abbreviated; the abbreviation often strikes with a shock the reader who is familiar with the Lord's Prayer as it is said in church services, and yet the shorter version is certainly nearer to what Luke wrote; the additions, mostly from Matthew's form of the prayer, crept into later manuscripts which were employed for the earliest printed Greek texts on which the Authorised Version is based. Again the reader will look in vain in the Revised Version for the Three Heavenly Witnesses of 1 Jn. v 7 in the Authorised Version; when Erasmus published the first printed Greek text of the New Testament in 1516, he left out the words because they were not to be found in any Greek manuscript known to him, promising to insert the clause if it could be shown to exist in a simple Greek manuscript. The clause is in fact a late gloss which crept into the Latin Vulgate in the sixth century; unfortunately, however, it was shown to Erasmus in a sixteenth century Greek manuscript which had been assimilated to the Latin Vulgate text; Erasmus kept his promise, and the translators of the Authorised Version followed the erroneous text.

Between the Authorised and Revised Versions there stand two and a half centuries of progress in the science of textual criticism and of the collection and study of manuscripts. In the nineteenth century especially, the scientific study of the text developed apace, and the Revisers included in their number the two great scholars Westcott and Hort, whose theories as to the history of the New Testament text played then, as they have done since for other translators, a large part in determining the text to be followed.

Westcott and Hort were able to utilise a mass of new knowledge that their predecessors had brought to light. Thousands of Greek manuscripts of the New Testament, as well as versions in numerous other languages, had been examined by scholars, dated, and grouped into ' families '. The older and more important manuscripts had been minutely studied and exactly reproduced in printed editions. The chief textual variants had been grouped in the ' apparatus criticus ' of critical texts, notably in the later editions of Tischendorf's Greek New Testament.

On the basis of this accumulated knowledge and of their own painstaking studies, Westcott and Hort made a great step forward in the search for the true text. They divided the readings of manuscripts into four great groups. The great mass of readings of later manuscripts they regarded as deriving from a Syrian revision of the text, which took place in the fourth century, and as largely worthless for the reconstruction of the true text. A number of readings found especially, but not exclusively, in manuscripts from the West, and termed ' Western ', they regarded as early but as generally due to a corruption of the apostolic texts. Another type of text, the ' Alexandrian ', supported largely by writers and manuscripts associated with Alexandria, was to be suspected as likely to have been the result of correction by literary scribes. Finally, a ' Neutral ' text was constructed containing readings that were pre-Syrian but neither ' Western ' nor ' Alexandrian ' and proclaimed as the purest. No manuscript, version, or Father preserved this text in its original purity, but the great fourth century manuscript B (preserved in the Vatican Library) comes nearest to doing so, often with the support of ℵ (the fourth or fifth century Codex Sinaiticus, then in St. Petersburg and now in the British Museum).

Since the time of Westcott and Hort textual criticism of the New Testament has made great strides. New manuscripts and papyrus fragments have come to light, notably a fourth or fifth century Syriac ' Gospels ' from Sinai which has preserved a very old translation from the Greek, the Chester Beatty Papyri from Egypt of the third century, our oldest witness by a century for the text of much of the New Testament, and a small fragment of papyrus from Egypt (now in the John Rylands Library at Manchester) which contains Jn. xviii 31-33, 37-38 and is dated by experts within the first half of the second century, or within half a century of the original writing of the gospel.

Side by side with this acquisition of new material have gone new developments in textual theory. The ' Western ' text, which is now seen from newly utilised evidence to have been more widespread than Westcott and Hort perceived, has been given by some scholars greater weight than before (in Acts especially the ' Western ' text contains many interesting variations from the ' Neutral ' text, some of which are mentioned on p. 141 below). New problems, too, have come to light as our knowledge of the early text has grown. At present, indeed, there is a widespread inclination among scholars to doubt whether we can ever pierce through the period of ' variations ' in the first three centuries to any certain knowledge of the original text. Yet it must be remembered that these ' variations ' are comparatively small, and of little religious significance. It is also perhaps significant that the translators of the latest American Revised Standard Version of 1946, who preferred an eclectic principle in determining the text which they should follow in place of adherence to such a theory as that of the ' Neutral Text ', found that—

> ' It is really extraordinary how often, with the fuller apparatus of variant readings at our disposal, and with the eclectic principle now more widely accepted, we have concurred in following Westcott and Hort.' [1]

The reader of any of the standard modern translations, such as the Revised Version, the new American Version, or Moffatt, can have confidence that he will nowhere be seriously misled on important points of Christian doctrine in his reading.

[1] *Op. cit.* p. 41.

BOOKS FOR READING

H. W. ROBINSON. *Ancient and English Versions of the Bible* (Oxford).

F. KENYON. *Our Bible and the Ancient Manuscripts* (Eyre and Spottiswoode).

G. MILLIGAN. *The New Testament and its Transmission* (Hodder and Stoughton).

An Introduction to the Revised Standard Version of the New Testament (International Council of Religious Education) explains briefly the principles on which this recent new Version is based.

For more advanced study :

K. and S. LAKE. *The Text of the New Testament* (Rivington).

F. KENYON. *The Textual Criticism of the New Testament* (Macmillan).

PART II

THE GOSPELS AND THE LIFE OF JESUS

CHAPTER IV

THE STUDY OF THE GOSPELS

THE gospels are for Christians of great value and authority, but they have not the supreme importance of Jesus himself. The critical study of the gospels can be justified only by its aim of obtaining a truer picture of Jesus and his teaching than that given by the gospels in their present form. To the superficial reader the gospels appear to furnish a uniformly consistent representation of Jesus' life and message, but closer examination reveals that there are in fact serious inconsistencies in the accounts both of what Jesus did and said. To account for these inconsistencies involves the most detailed and painstaking study of the circumstances in which the gospels came to be written and of the value that is to be attached to the material which they contain.

Of the problems which confront the student of the gospels two are of overriding importance. The first is that of the *apostolicity* of the gospels. In the light of recent criticism it is no longer possible to accept the Matthaean authorship of the first gospel in its present form, and both the Marcan authorship of the second gospel and the Johannine authorship of the fourth gospel are matters of dispute. Yet, if the traditional authorship of these gospels is abandoned, the authority of the gospels is in some ways shaken. An apostle may well have made mistakes in his recollection of Jesus' words and actions, and his own interpretation of Jesus' teaching may not always have been faithful to Jesus' intention, but he is unlikely to have distorted Jesus' teaching outside certain narrow limits and we can confidently assume that he would not deliberately have falsified his reports of what Jesus had done. On the other hand an anonymous tradition that cannot be checked by the witness of an apostle such as Peter, Matthew, or John, may not be trusted to have preserved the memory of Jesus' words and actions without serious distortion. The problem of apostolicity is, therefore, a serious one for the historical value of the gospels.

The second problem is that of Jesus' own consistency. He is represented in the gospels as teaching in very different ways. In the fourth gospel he proclaims his Sonship of God openly from the beginning of his ministry, speaks of his Kingdom almost always in spiritual terms, makes discipleship dependent on the use of sacraments not yet established, and promises the coming of the Holy Spirit. In Mark, Jesus reveals his Messiahship only towards the end of his ministry, speaks of his Kingdom now as present and now as future, uses apocalyptic language, says little of the Spirit and nothing of baptism. Even when allowance has been made for the distortion of Jesus' teaching by the evangelists the evidence permits of more than one interpretation of Jesus' teaching, and there is a final residue of inconsistency which may be attributed either to Jesus or to Christian tradition. The question is of particular importance in relation to the place of apocalyptic in Jesus' message side by side with so much that is of a purely spiritual nature.

Answers are suggested to both these questions in the pages that follow, but no claim is made that different answers are not possible. The reader must ultimately make his own decisions in the consciousness that his answers will determine his understanding of the Jesus of history.

BOOKS FOR READING

Of the many good commentaries available on the gospels, the following are some of the most useful for those who do not know Greek :

MARK : 　A. W. F. BLUNT (Clarendon Bible). Brief but good.

　　　　A. E. J. RAWLINSON (Westminster). More advanced.

MATTHEW : B. T. D. SMITH (Cambridge Bible). A small but important work.

　　　　T. H. ROBINSON (Moffatt).

LUKE : H. BALMFORTH (Clarendon Bible).
W. MANSON (Moffatt).

JOHN : R. H. STRACHAN (S.C.M.).
G. H. C. MACGREGOR (Moffatt).
SIR E. C. HOSKYNS (Faber).

The Four Gospels: MAJOR, MANSON and WRIGHT. *The Mission, Message and Teaching of Jesus* (Nicholson and Watson). This is a very valuable book, if only for its arrangement of the gospel material, with a running commentary, by sources. Part of this book has been re-issued as T. W. MANSON. *The Sayings of Jesus.*

On the problems of literary and form criticism.

V. TAYLOR. *The Gospels* (Epworth Press). An excellent short introduction to the study of the gospels.

E. B. REDLICH. *A Student's Introduction to the Synoptic Gospels* (Longmans).

V. TAYLOR. *The Formation of the Gospel Tradition* (Macmillan). A more detailed examination of the methods of Form criticism.

M. DIBELIUS. *From Tradition to Gospel* (Nicholson and Watson). The English translation of one of the original German expositions of the methods of Form criticism.

B. H. STREETER. *The Four Gospels* (Macmillan) Parts II and III. A detailed study of the problems of authorship and of Source-criticism.

W. F. HOWARD. *The Fourth Gospel in Recent Criticism and Interpretation* (Epworth Press). A survey of recent critical work on John.

R. H. LIGHTFOOT. *History and Interpretation in the Gospels* (Hodder and Stoughton). This work applies the methods of Form criticism to the gospels.

On the Life and Teaching of Jesus.

M. GOGUEL. *The Life of Jesus* (Allen and Unwin).
G. DUNCAN. *Jesus, Son of Man* (Nisbet).
C. H. DODD. *The Parables of the Kingdom* (Nisbet).
C. H. DODD. *History and the Gospel* (Nisbet).
J. MOFFATT. *The Theology of the Gospels* (Duckworth).
V. TAYLOR. *Jesus and His Sacrifice* (Macmillan).
W. MANSON. *Jesus the Messiah* (Hodder and Stoughton).
A. E. J. RAWLINSON. *Christ in the Gospels* (Oxford).

CHAPTER V

THE ORAL TRADITION

IT can be taken for granted that the earliest Christian preaching contained as two of its most important elements a number of facts about Jesus, with the interpretation to be placed upon them, and numerous sayings of Jesus, with their application to the needs of believers. These elements correspond to the two great divisions of Christian evangelism, the Proclamation or Kerygma (from the Greek *Keryssein*, to proclaim) that Jesus is the Christ of God, and the Teaching or Didache (from the Greek *Didaskein*, to teach) which those who believe in him must follow.

THE KERYGMA AND DIDACHE

It was essential in the proclamation of the Good News to let all hearers know HOW Jesus had been shown to be in truth the Messiah who was to come again. In the speeches that are scattered through the Acts of the Apostles, and in the Pauline epistles, a skeleton pattern can be traced, which indicates the lines on which Christian missionaries answered this question. Jesus of Nazareth, of the seed of David, was ' approved of God unto you by mighty works and wonders and signs, which God did by him in the midst of you ' (Acts ii, 22). He suffered, as had been foretold by the prophets, and after his crucifixion in Jerusalem God raised him from the dead on the third day, and he appeared to witnesses from among his disciples. He is exalted to the right hand of God, and will return again to judge the quick and the dead. What Luke adopts as a short and summary pattern for the missionary speeches which he puts into the mouths of Peter and Paul has to be considered in the light of literary exigencies and of the fuller details which he has already given to Theophilus in his gospel. Paul, although

he probably had not himself seen Jesus in the flesh (yet cf.
2 Cor. v 15), from time to time makes it clear, not only
that the outlines of such a pattern were familiar to him,
but that he can supplement it with much fuller details, as
when he wishes to support his message to the Corinthians
with appeals to the institution of the Eucharist at the Last
Supper (1 Cor. xi) and to Resurrection appearances
(1 Cor. xv).[1]

Once the hearer of the Kerygma had been converted
he had to be instructed more perfectly as to the implications
of the new life. This involved not only the teaching of what
Jesus had laid down on particular subjects, e.g. on Marriage
or on Swearing, but the illustration from Jesus' words of the
great new principles involved in his message, e.g. the nature
of the Kingdom of God, the imminence of the Second
Coming and the Judgement, the fundamental nature of the
two great commandments. In the process of such teaching
examples of Jesus' teaching were employed which often
involved the narration of some scene in Jesus' ministry.
It is probable indeed that most of the facts about Jesus,
apart from the great and significant narratives, were
handed down almost incidentally as part of the necessary
background for the sayings of Jesus which were of supreme
authority for guiding the lives of the early Christians.

As the Christian mission spread, so both Kerygma and
Didache inevitably expanded, changed their emphasis, and
tended to crystallise in form. Papias quotes an Elder as
saying of Peter that he used to suit his teachings to the needs
(of his hearers), and the needs of Gentile converts were
often very different from those of Jewish converts. Jews
could understand without difficulty the implications of the
title Christ, and much of Christian morality is in fact
Jewish morality informed by the Holy Spirit; for Gentiles
on the other hand the title of Christ needed explanation
and interpretation, and much of Christian moral teaching
was new and difficult. Sayings of Jesus that had special
reference to Jewish ceremonial customs, such as those on

[1] Cf. C. H. Dodd, *The Apostolic Preaching and its Developments.*

the washing of hands contained in Mark vii, were of little interest to Gentiles and are omitted by Luke from his gospel; Matthew has preserved two sayings connected with the Temple altar (Mt. v 23, xxiii 18) which had a special significance for Jewish Christians, but which would lose much of their effectiveness for Gentile Christians. On the other hand, ever new problems arose for the solution of which the authority of a saying of Jesus, originally uttered in a different context, was sometimes legitimately, sometimes illegitimately claimed, and at times even perhaps invented. Thus we have Jesus' teaching on divorce preserved in three forms. In what seems to be the earliest and best form (preserved in Luke xvi 18) Jesus says that a man who divorces his wife and marries another, or who marries a woman who has been divorced, commits adultery. This is in accord with conditions in Jewish Palestine in the first century A.D.; divorce was a prerogative of the husband and the wife had no similar rights. Mark gives a similar saying of Jesus (Mk. x 11-12) which condemns divorce initiated by the husband or wife; this seems to be a—legitimate—adaptation of the principle laid down by Jesus for Gentile conditions under which the woman was in many places able to divorce her husband. Matthew preserves the reference to men alone (Mt. v 32, xix 9), but inserts the clause ' except for fornication ', which is widely regarded as a later weakening of what Jesus actually said.

LACK OF BIOGRAPHICAL INTEREST

While both Kerygma and Didache involved incidental references to the ministry and sayings of Jesus, there seems to have been comparatively little biographical interest in the minor details of his life. This should not surprise us overmuch. The modern interest in detailed biography was not marked in the ancient world, and Professor Burkitt has claimed the Gospel of Mark as the earliest biography. There can be no doubt that the apostles and the family of Jesus in fact told much more of the life

of Jesus than has been preserved, but with the passing of the
earliest Christian generation, and with the catastrophe of the
Jewish War and the destruction of Jerusalem in A.D. 70,
which largely severed the communications between the
Christians in Palestine and those of the Gentile world,
most of this information, preserved only orally and temporarily, was lost to posterity.   Here and there an incident in
the gospels, such as that of the young man who fled away
naked at Jesus' arrest (Mk. xiv 51-52), or that of the friendly
Pharisees who warned Jesus of Herod's plot to kill him
(Lk. xiii 31), or the connection of Jesus with Nazareth and
his approximate age, has preserved such incidental knowledge, but the great bulk of gospel material owes its preservation not to biographical interest but to its value for preaching
and teaching.

THE FACTS ABOUT JESUS

1. *Old Testament Prophecies fulfilled*

Expectation of a Messiah (Greek, *Christos* = anointed)
was widespread among the Jews of the first century A.D.
(p. 119).   The Christians, in proclaiming that Jesus was
indeed the Christ, supporting their claim by appealing to
his fulfilment of the prophecies that had been made about
the Christ to come.   The genealogies, differently given
by Matthew and Luke, agree on his legal descent from
David.   Matthew and Luke, in the course of differing
narratives about the birth of Jesus, supported in Matthew
by a series of prophecies from the Old Testament, agree
again on his birth of a virgin at Bethlehem.   Luke prefaces
the ministry of Jesus with Jesus' own summary at Nazareth
of his fulfilment of the prophecy of Isaiah lxi 1-2, and with
the parallel drawn by Jesus between his rejection by his
own people and the missions of Elijah and Elisha to non-
Israelites (iv 24-27).   The reply of Jesus to John the Baptist's
enquiry as to whether he is the Christ (Mt. xi 5-6, Lk.
vii 22-23) is in effect a claim that his words have fulfilled
the prophecies.   The healings of the blind, the lame, the

lepers, the deaf, the raising of the dead, and the evangelising of the poor, are recorded in the gospels in detail not least because they illustrate this claim. The teaching in parables (Mt. xiii 35) and its purpose that ' hearing ye shall hear, and shall in no wise understand ' (Mt. xiii 13 f.) are likewise shown to be in accordance with Old Testament prophecy. So, too, many of the details of the Passion narrative are indicated as fulfilments of the Old Testament, e.g. the entry to Jerusalem on an ass, the price of the betrayal, and the correspondence of many features of the crucifixion with Psalm xxii. Finally the resurrection itself, as the suffering before, is interpreted by the risen Jesus as in accordance with the Scriptures (Lk. xxiv 26-27).

The influence of such Old Testament prophecies in the selection of material for Christian preaching about the life of Jesus is clear. In many points it has been argued that such influence has led to the material alteration of facts to suit prophecies—the two asses of Mt. xxi 2-7, due to a misunderstanding of Zech. ix 9, is a clear case, but it remains true that it also led to the preservation of much valuable material about the teaching and ministry of Jesus.

2. John the Baptist

Another influence which led to the accumulation of a cycle of stories about Jesus was the need felt by Christian preachers to relate the work of Jesus with that of John the Baptist. How far a John the Baptist sect continued after John's death is uncertain, but John's fame was widespread, and probably many of the earliest Christians had first been baptised by John (cf. Jn. i esp. 35-40). The motive for the several references to John that are found in the gospels seems to have been not primarily one of rivalry with later disciples of John, if indeed such disciples continued to proselytise after John's death, but the desire to show that John's place in the scheme of God's revelation as the forerunner of Christ had been expressly confirmed by the Christ

himself.   This interest led at any rate to the preservation
of much important information about John the Baptist and
about Jesus' baptism and later references to John. Here
again the tradition seems later to have gained accretions
of doubtful worth, such as the narrative connecting John's
birth with that of Jesus (Lk. i 5 ff.), the effort to explain away
the baptism of Jesus by John (Mt. iii 14-15), and the highly
coloured account of John's death (Mk. vi 17-29).

3. Turning points in the Ministry

It is possible that the gospels have preserved the narratives of the three incidents, outside the Passion Narrative,
which mark decisive turning points in the ministry of Jesus,
and which were told as such by apostles, although their
original significance has been in part lost by the variations
in the tradition visible in the gospels as they stand.   The
motive in all three of these narratives, if they go back to the
teaching of Peter, as they may well do, is not so much a
biographical one in the ministry of Jesus as an autobio-
graphical one of witness on Peter's part.   The first of these
narratives concerns what is told in Mk. i 16-38 of the call
of Peter, Andrew, James, and John, the casting out of an
unclean spirit in the synagogue at Capernaum, the healing
of Peter's mother-in-law, and of many sick, the departure of
Jesus to pray in a desert place next morning, and his words
to Peter and others who followed him there.   It has sometimes been called ' a day in the life of Jesus ' but could be
even more justly called ' the beginning of the new life of
Peter '.   As such it may well have formed a favourite part
of Peter's preaching, although probably in a less bald form
than that in which Mark gives it.   For us it furnishes, if
this theory is acceptable, a starting point for the Galilean
ministry of Jesus.
   The second of the narratives, the Mission of the Disciples,
is recorded by Mark (vi 7-13) and seems also to have stood
in the now lost document Q (Lk. x 1-20, with parallels
to many verses in Mt. ix 37-38, x 7-16, etc.).   Although

little is told of the actual mission apart from references to
its general success, it clearly marked a memorable stage in
the training of the disciples who were now sufficiently
advanced to be entrusted with authority to heal and to
preach.   It also marks, of course, a stage in the ministry of
Jesus, who had now achieved both some popular success and
a deeper and more enduring task in the instruction of his
disciples.   While the narrative was probably remembered
and passed on as an example and inspiration for later
Christian missionaries, it may well preserve also one of the
significant steps in the ministry of Jesus himself.

It may even be that this mission was the immediate
cause of, and originally connected with, the third narrative,
a cycle containing the account of the feeding of the multitude beyond the lake and the signs of great popular success
(in John vi 15, Jesus, ' perceiving that they were about to
come and take him by force, to make him king, withdrew
again into the mountain himself alone '), a crossing of the
lake, a demand for a sign, and then, after an interval,
Peter's confession at Caesarea Philippi that Jesus was the
Christ (Mk. viii 1-33, cf. Jn. vi 1-69).   The substantial
agreement of John with Mark here appears to be due to
the following of a similar tradition rather than to literary
dependence, and it is at least conceivable that we have here
a series of consecutive narratives, largely altered in detail
during their transmissions, which go back to Peter's recollections.   Peter's reasons for telling of this connected
series of events may well have sprung in part from the memory
of the moment of his avowal as at once his greatest and most
chastening, but the point of the narrative for missionary
preaching lay above all in Jesus' prophetic rejection of the
popular conception of the Messiah-king for the true one of
the suffering Son of Man who would rise again.   To the
student of the life of Jesus the confession of Peter represents
in itself a decisive point in the ministry of Jesus.   If it is
true that we have this confession preserved in its original
historical setting, embroidered but not substantially altered by the vicissitudes of oral transmission, a flood of

light is thrown on the reasons for Herod's suspicions and for Jesus' retirement before his final challenge to authority in Jerusalem.

The treatment of these narratives has been brief and of necessity speculative, yet enough has been said, perhaps, to suggest that the possibility of reconstructing some of the main stages of Jesus' ministry must not be too carelessly dismissed.

4. The Passion Narrative

While Mark and Luke differ considerably in the substance, order, and arrangement of the events of Jesus' ministry, and John shows even wider differences from both, all three of these gospels come together again into substantial agreement, although not without quite considerable variations, when they tell the story of the Passion of Jesus. It is generally held that this agreement indicates the existence of a comparatively trustworthy record of the outlines of the Passion story from the earliest days of the primitive church, a record which has preserved the main outlines of what really happened. That this should be so is only natural, in view of the consuming interest and concern of every Christian in this climax of the life of Jesus. The drama and significance of the events have exercised upon Christians of every generation a special influence, and from the very beginning the story has belonged to the essential core of Christian preaching. Professor C. H. Dodd has summarised the nine chief episodes that seem to have constituted the original pattern of the Passion-narrative as follows : [1]

1. The Last Supper. Forecast of the treachery of Judas.
2. Forecast of Peter's denial, and of the desertion of the disciples.
3. Retirement to a place on or near the Mount of Olives. Betrayal, arrest, desertion of disciples.
4. Examination before the High Priest. Peter's denial.
5. Trial before Pilate. Declaration of innocence. Condemnation as King of the Jews. Release of Barabbas.

[1] *History and the Gospel*, pp. 80 f.

6. Crucifixion at Calvary, with two others.
7. Burial.
8. The Empty Tomb.
9. Appearances to Disciples.

To this we are perhaps entitled to add, in view of Paul's account in 1 Cor. xi and in spite of John's silence, the institution of the Eucharist at the Last Supper. The general sequence of events from the Last Supper up to the Burial presents a coherent picture, self-authenticating in its simplicity and starkness.

Round this central core there tended inevitably to gather, snow-ball fashion, additional material not all of the same value. While the incident of the young man at the arrest in Mark or the trial before Herod in Luke may represent the filling out of the story from the testimony of eye-witnesses, many of the other additions, notably those in Matthew, seem to be of the nature of ' pious embroidery '. Yet, whatever difficulties are raised by the variations in the additional details provided by the evangelists, the main lines of the Passion narrative can be clearly traced.

5. The Resurrection

Paul's list of resurrection appearances in 1 Cor. xv and his emphatic statements as to the central and vital part of the resurrection in Christian faith illustrate the importance attached to such testimony in Christian preaching. It is possible that Mark's gospel did originally end at xvi 8, and hinted only at an appearance or appearances to come in Galilee (Mk. xiv 28, xvi 7). If so, the explanation probably lies in the fact that he wished to include only the ministry of the earthly Jesus in his book, and counted the appearances as of the heavenly Christ. Yet it was inevitable that those who wrote gospels later, if not Mark himself, should include accounts of some at least of the resurrection appearances. That they should include fewer appearances than those mentioned by Paul as having been received by him is not surprising, but the differences that the gospels show between themselves indicate the speed with which the form of the appearances, as distinguished from the fact of the appearances, could change in the course of oral transmission. They witness, too, to the difficulty, once the apostles were scattered abroad, of harmonising the various strands of tradition that developed. If the problems which the gospel accounts present to the modern reader are largely insoluble, they furnish evidence at any rate of the universal Christian conviction that the risen Christ did in fact appear to his disciples after his death and of the strength and power of that conviction in the face of inconsistencies between different forms of the tradition.

The facts of the gospel material so far discussed have the common characteristic that they have each their particular place in the gospel as a whole. There remain to be considered, besides the sayings of Jesus, a number of stories about Jesus, which seem to have been originally told as single stories to illustrate some particular point of preaching by an appeal to an action of Jesus. While many of these stories are of great value for helping to reconstruct the details of Jesus' ministry, and may well have been told originally by eye-witnesses of the events, their preservation is due to the aptness with which they supported the missionary preaching, and in a number of cases the stories appear to have undergone considerable changes in their transmission to enable them to be used with ever greater point. They fall into two main categories, evidences of Jesus' power over disease and nature, and evidences of Jesus' rejection of the Jewish religion of his time and of his authority.

6. Evidences of Jesus' power over disease and nature

The number of healings recorded in the gospels is high, but can only represent a selection from a much larger number that would for a time be remembered. The selection seems to have been made in Mark to illustrate the healing of as many different kinds of affliction as possible—a fever, leprosy, paralysis, a withered hand, madness, an issue, deafness and stuttering, blindness (twice), epilepsy, and even, in the case of Jairus' daughter, death itself. In oral preaching, where the needs of the hearers had to be considered, such a variety of evidence was both necessary and forthcoming, and Christian sufferers would take comfort from the way in which Jesus had healed in the course of his earthly ministry men, women and children with the same afflictions to which they themselves were subject. So, too, for Gentiles, the healing of the Gentile Centurion's servant (Q, Mt. viii 5-13, Lk. vii 2-10) and of the Syro-Phoenician woman's daughter (Mk. vii 25-30) had a special meaning, although in this latter case Luke seems to have omitted the story deliberately because of Jesus' apparent depreciation of the Gentiles. That the stories should often have been 'heightened' in the telling was inevitable, but in the majority of cases recorded in the gospels it is possible to accept without difficulty the nucleus of the healings as a true reminiscence of Jesus' activity.

The nature-miracles are harder to assess. The purpose of their telling is clear, the demonstration of Jesus' mighty powers in stilling the storm, in walking on the water, in feeding great multitudes, in destroying a fig tree, in changing water into wine. The quick growth and wide popularity of such stories in connection with great men in credulous ages serve as a warning against accepting their truth too readily, but that such stories should soon acquire wide currency in Christian circles and be widely employed as evidences of Jesus' powers is easy to understand. It is only surprising, and to the credit of the general trustworthiness of the oral tradition, that these stories are so few in number.

7. Evidence of Jesus' rejection of the religion of his time

While most of the gospel material that deals with Jesus' controversies is contained in his sayings and in stories leading up to sayings, there are a number of incidents which have been preserved whose narration was clearly intended

to establish that Jesus judged differently from the Jewish
religious leaders of his time and acted with authority, e.g.
the call of the publican Levi as his disciple and the cleansing
of the Temple.

8. *Signs of Jesus' Divinity*

Into a similar but different category fall those incidents
where Jesus' authority is made manifest supernaturally,
e.g. at the Baptism, Temptation, and Transfiguration.
The effectiveness for Christian preaching of these triumphs
of Jesus was undoubted. In each case the story would
appear to rest upon what an intimate disciple of Jesus
heard from him or saw for himself, although in each
case too there is clear evidence of development in the form
of the story.

The examples that have been given so far serve to show
how a great deal of our gospel material owes its preservation
to the demands made by Christian Kerygma for illustrations
from the life and ministry of Jesus to support the central
proclamation that Jesus was indeed the Christ. Side by
side with such material and often—as in the case of some
' pronouncement-stories '—overlapping it stands the mass of
sayings of Jesus, often embedded in a small piece of narrative,
whose preservation was primarily due to the need for
supporting the instruction of Christians with authoritative
examples of what Jesus had himself laid down.

THE SAYINGS OF JESUS

1. *Pronouncement Stories*

The gospels contain some thirty or so stories which share
a common form in that their main interest is to illustrate
the setting for a pronouncement of Jesus, and Professor
Vincent Taylor's suggested title of ' Pronouncement-story '[1]
is a suitable and convenient one for them. Typical of such
stories are those of the controversy about plucking the ears

[1] *Formation of the Gospel Tradition*, p. 30.

of corn on the Sabbath, leading up to Jesus' saying about the Sabbath being made for man (Mk. iii 23-28), or the question of the scribe about the greatest commandment, leading up to Jesus' great answer (Mk. xii 28-34).

This and similar classifications must not, however, be pushed too far. Some of the healing stories, e.g. those of the paralytic (Mk. ii 3 ff.) and of the man with the withered hand (Mk. iii 1 ff.), *may* have been told primarily for their illustration of Jesus' healing power and have only incidentally provided examples of Jesus' claim to authority and to do good on the Sabbath. It is impossible to lay down clear-cut definitions in each case. In giving instruction about particular problems, such as the observance of the Sabbath or of fasting, or of regulations about ceremonial purity, or in laying down the great principles of the faith, such as belief in the resurrection, the authority of Jesus, the central commandments, the Christian missionary would drive home his teaching with a suitable story of what Jesus had said in a particular controversy or in answer to a particular question. In the process of such teaching many fragments of the biography of Jesus were preserved, valuable in themselves, though often presenting problems as to their exact setting in his ministry. These problems have been made more difficult, not only by changes introduced into some of the stories to make them more pointed, but by the collection of such stories into artificial groups, such as the collections of Jesus' controversies in Mark ii 1-3, 6 and Mark xi 27-35, xii 13-40. Such collections, in a more or less floating form, may well go back to the oral stage of the tradition.

2. Parables and Sayings

Of less value for the facts of Jesus' life, but of supreme value for his teaching, are the parables and sayings that have been preserved, for the most part in clearly editorial settings and groupings, in the gospels. The parable form, although clearly a favourite one of Jesus himself, was very liable to changes and to incorrect interpretation. A comparison of the parable of the Marriage Feast as it is found in Matthew (xxii 1-14) with the Lucan form of the parable (Lk. xiv 16-24) shows plainly enough that in Matthew another parable of the Wedding Garment has been introduced into an alien context which spoils its point. Some of the interpretations given to parables in the gospels likewise raise doubts as to their authenticity, e.g. Matthew's interpretation of the parable of the Tares (Mt. xiii 36-43).[1]

Even more subject to distortion were the individual sayings of Jesus, once their true context had been forgotten. Thus in the Beatitudes (Mt. v 3-12, Lk. vi 20-23) there is a clear and important difference between the Matthaean emphasis on the kingdom as a reward for spiritual qualities and the Lucan emphasis on the kingdom as a reward for earthly misfortunes. Can Jesus have said both that ' he who is not against us is for us ' (Mk. ix 40) and that ' he who is not with me is against me ' (Q, Mt. xii 30, Lk. xi 23) ? Perhaps the best example of the confusion and error that in oral tradition attack the transmission of sayings is in the Marcan collection of Jesus' apocalyptic sayings (Mk. xiii). Here genuine sayings lie side by side with sayings apparently altered in the tradition (Mk. xiii 9 ?) and with others whose attribution to Jesus involves grave inconsistencies with the words of Jesus in other forms of the tradition (contrast the signs before the end of Mk. xiii 24-26 with the sudden and unexpected coming of the end predicted by Jesus in Q, Mt. xxiv 37-41, Lk. xvii 26-27). The total effect of such an artificial collection of sayings, of which the genuine ones are quite out of their correct context, was to distort the teachings of Jesus under the influence of Jewish apocalyptic expectation.

Yet a process of collection and arrangement was inevitable if individual sayings of Jesus were to be long remembered. Traces of such arrangement made probably in the oral stage of the tradition can still be found in the gospels. Thus, sayings on the same subject tend to be grouped together ; a comparison of the twin parables of the Mustard

---

[1] See Dr. B. T. D. Smith, *The Parables of the Synoptic Gospels*, p. 200.

Seed and Leaven (Q, Mt. xiii 31-33, Lk. xiii 18-21) with
the single parable of the Mustard Seed preserved by Mark
(iv 30-32) indicates the kind of way in which such grouping
came about.   In one case at least (Mk. ix 41-50), the connection appears to be a mnemonic one suggested by a word
or theme in each saying.

FORM CRITICISM

In offering this sketch of the way in which the material
of our gospels can largely be derived from the needs of
early Christian preaching and teaching, little has so far
been directly said of the methods of Form-criticism which
have developed, especially in Germany, since 1918.   In an
attempt to get behind the period of written documents to
the development of the gospel-material in the oral stage
a number of scholars, notable K. L. Schmidt, Bultmann,
and Dibelius on the continent, and at a later stage R. H.
Lightfoot and V. Taylor in England, have drawn on the
analogies with this material presented by other types of
oral tradition.   By showing that such material tends to
observe certain rules of form and to undergo certain normal
processes of development they have endeavoured to trace
the kind of developments that can be expected to have taken
place in the narratives and sayings of the gospels before
the gospels themselves were written.   Such methods have
in fact proved of great value, especially when used by those
who have not been unduly influenced, as Bultmann has, by
a radical scepticism as to the historicity of the main lines
of the gospel narrative.   Yet the rules of oral tradition
are not absolute rules, nor are the forms of oral tradition
fixed in any than the widest sense.   It is significant that
the pioneers of Form-criticism found themselves seriously
at variance in drawing up their categories of ' forms ',
and that more conservative scholars have been satisfied
with very few wide classifications, Vincent Taylor
for   example [1]   using   only   those   of   Passion-narratives,

[1] *The Formation of the Gospel Tradition.*

Pronouncement stories, Sayings and Parables, Miracle-stories and Stories about Jesus.

The value, however, of even such a limited use of the methods of Form-criticism is very real, not least in suggesting the main lines along which the stories and sayings of the gospels tended to 'develop', and in furnishing certain criteria as to their probable origin and worth. What has been written in the last few pages is dependent on the results achieved by modern scholars in this field. Indications have been given of the more important ways in which the material was subject to change, the tendency to shorten stories in a narrative, the inevitable heightening of the miraculous element and the moulding of material to sharpen the point of the moral, the intrusion of false sayings and incidents and of artificial explanations, the shift of meaning that sometimes followed the loss of the true context, and the growth of cycles of stories and of sayings which gave to the material a new and sometimes unnatural setting, but which once committed to writing was to fix within narrow limits the possibilities of further change.

CHAPTER VI

WRITTEN GOSPEL SOURCES

THE EXISTENCE OF WRITTEN SOURCES
BEHIND THE GOSPELS

LUKE begins his gospel by referring to the fact that ' many have taken in hand to draw up a narrative concerning those matters which have been fulfilled among us, even as they delivered them unto us, which from the beginning were eye-witnesses and ministers of the word ' (i 1-2). Among the sources which were used by Luke himself and by Matthew were at least two written documents, one of them the gospel of Mark in substantially its present form, and the other a collection in Greek of sayings of Jesus, incorporating some narrative details, which is nowadays known as Q (from the German *Quelle* = source). The use by Luke and Matthew of these sources can be demonstrated because, in the case of Mark, the source itself is available, and a comparison of the texts of the three gospels leaves no reasonable doubt as to its employment in the other two gospels ; in the case of Q, although the original document has not survived, the occasional verbal agreement in ' non-Marcan ' passages of Matthew and Luke is such as to show that a document existed, although its extent can only partially be established and the possibility always remains that more than one document was used.

Many more written accounts of Jesus' teaching, his controversies, his miracles, and his ministry, may have been in existence when our gospels were written. If so, they have perished, and we can only search for traces of them in our existing gospels. As none of them seems to have been used in more than one of our gospels, the task of reconstructing them is difficult, and none of the theories which have been put forward can be regarded as more than a possible hypothesis.

Yet the question is of such interest and importance that some at least of the theories suggested deserve to be mentioned here, and further discussed in connection with the composition of the individual gospels.

Two types of theory can be distinguished, that which seeks to explain almost the whole of a gospel as compiled from written sources, and that which argues from peculiarities of style, language, and form, that written sources of limited extent were used by the final author of a gospel in conjunction with a mass of oral tradition. This distinction is an important one, as the former type of theory reduces the status of the final author of a gospel almost to that of an editor writing at a late period when trustworthy oral traditions were comparatively scarce; the latter type of theory assumes the existence of smaller, but earlier and more valuable written sources, some of which may even be apostolic, which have been combined with considerable oral tradition, of varying historical value, by the final author.

Mark is generally admitted to be our earliest gospel, but there are difficulties in accepting it, in its present form, as John Mark's transcript of Peter's preaching (cf. p. 55). Attempts to solve this difficulty by source-theories have been along two lines. Some critics have attempted to sketch out one large original Marcan source (often called *Ur-Markus*, from the German= 'Original Mark') which has been later edited, while others have tried to show that Mark or another has employed a number of small sources, collections of Jesus' controversies and sayings, e.g. Mk. iii 20-35, vii 1-23, ix 38-50, xiii, some of them at least already in written form.

That Matthew used both Mark and Q is generally admitted, although some scholars think that he used Q in a different 'edition' from that which lay before Luke. It has been suggested, notably by Streeter,[1] that virtually all remaining sayings of Jesus in this gospel are drawn from one further written source (M), but other scholars

---

[1] *The Four Gospels*, pp. 254-265.

think that Matthew, while employing written sources for some of his Old Testament quotations and for part of the Sermon on the Mount, also drew much of his material from the oral tradition of his own time.

The question of Luke's sources is complicated by Streeter's theory [1] that an earlier edition of this gospel, Proto-Luke, was later enlarged by the incorporation of much of the material of Mark. Proto-Luke itself, according to Streeter, [2] is a combination of two written sources, Q and L, the latter a document compiled by Luke himself, embodying traditions of the Caesarean church. Others would see in L Luke's own collection of information from more extensive oral sources, and others again a series of short written 'fly-sheets' used by Christian missionaries.

In John's gospel the question of written sources is a very difficult one, but amongst the multitude of explanations that have been offered for the problems presented by this gospel are the redaction by a later editor of an earlier gospel or gospel-material, and the use by the author of a number of written sources, e.g. in the prologue, in his collection of 'signs', and in the discourses.

While none of these theories can ever be finally proved, it seems probable that Q was not the only early document about the life and teaching of Jesus which has disappeared, and that our gospels represent the climax of a development in the writing down of the oral tradition. On the other hand there is much to be said for the view that Mark was the first writing that assumed a 'gospel' form, in the sense that it attempted to give an account of the whole period of Jesus' ministry as well as giving examples of his teaching; it is even possible that the ending of Mark's gospel with the appearance of the angel at the empty tomb and the flight of the women (xvi 8 ; the verses that follow were not part of the original gospel) indicates that his pioneer plan was to tell of the earthly ministry of Jesus, and that he regarded the Resurrection appearances as part of the later story of the heavenly Christ.

[1] *Op. cit.* pp. 199-222.   [2] *Op. cit.* pp. 208 ff.

THE DOCUMENT Q

The difficulties of reconstructing this lost writing from the gospels of Matthew and Luke can be illustrated from their treatment of Mark. If we did not possess Mark's gospel, and could only reconstruct it from the agreement in language of Matthew and Luke, our reconstruction would contain less than three-quarters of the actual gospel of Mark. Furthermore Q seems to have been predominantly a collections of sayings, and the possibility cannot be overlooked of the agreement of language between Matthew and Luke being sometimes due to the overlapping of sayings-sources or to the faithfulness of oral tradition. The order in which Matthew and Luke use pieces of Q is often very different, and while it is on the whole probable that Luke has usually preserved the right order, it is impossible to be certain of this.

What can be regarded as a certain nucleus of Q is given below in Luke's order; many other passages from Luke and/or Matthew may well be considered as having belonged to Q, but are here disregarded.

LUKE	MATTHEW	
iii 7b-9, 16b-17	iii 7b-12	John the Baptist's Preaching
iv 1b-12	iv 1-10	The Temptation
vi 41-2	vii 3-5	The Beam and the Mote
vii 6b-9	viii 8-10	The Centurion's Servant
vii 19, 22-3, 24b-28, 31-35	xi 3-11, 16-19	Jesus' Testimony to John
ix 57b-60	viii 19-22	Two Would-be Disciples
x 2-3, 5, 12	ix 37-38, x 11, 15-16a	Mission Discourse
x 13-15	xi 21-23	Woe to Chorazin, etc.
x 21b-22	xi 25-27	Jesus Thanks His Father
x 23b-24	xiii 16-17	The Blessedness of the Disciples
xi 9-13	vii 7-11	The Answer to Prayer

4

LUKE	MATTHEW	
xi 17-18a, 19-20, 23	xii 25-28, 30	The Beelzebub Controversy
xi 24-26	xii 43-45	The Return of the Evil Spirit
xi 29b-32	xii 39-40, 42, 41	The Sign for this Generation
xi 34	vi 22-23a	On Light
xi 39, 42-43, 49-51	xxiii 25, 23, 6, 34-36	Woes to the Pharisees
xii 5-9	x 28b-33	Whom to Fear
xii 22b-31, 34	vi 25-33, 21	On Cares
xii 39-40, 42-46	xxiv 43-51a	Watch and be a Prudent Servant
xiii 18-19, 21	xiii 31b-33	Mustard Seed and Leaven
xiii 28-29	viii 11-12	The Guests in the Kingdom
xiii 34-35	xxiii 37-39	Jerusalem, Jerusalem
xvi 13	vi 24	No one can serve Two Masters
xvi 16-18	v 18, 32, xi 12-13	About the Law and Divorce
xvii 24, 26-27, 30, 37b	xxiv 27, 37-39, 28	The Days of the Son of Man

From this reconstruction of the kernel of Q,[1] it was clearly not a gospel, but a collection of Jesus' teaching, illustrated occasionally by the introduction of events such as the Temptation and the Healing of the Centurion's Servant. Matthew and Luke rarely agree in their wording when they provide introductions to Q sayings, and it seems likely that in the original Q such introductions were usually very short, i.e. ' And Jesus said ', or not present at all.

No attempt to ' reconstitute ' Q has succeeded in making of it a well-arranged ' handbook ', although there are signs of a rough general arrangement by subjects,[2] and these subjects seem to have included those most vital for Christian evangelism, the Substance of the Christian Life, Principles of Christian Missionary Propaganda, Defence of the New

[1] The English text of Q, following Streeter's more extended reconstruction of this source, has been compiled in a handy form by A. Peel, *The Earliest Gospel* (Epworth Press.)

[2] Cf. T. W. Manson in *The Mission and Message of Jesus*, pp. 314 f.

Religion against Jewish Attacks, Expectation of the Judgement. The selection of topics makes it reasonable to assume that the purpose for which Q was written was to furnish a standing record from the sayings and acts of Jesus to support the teaching (Didache) with which early Christian missionaries encouraged and exhorted their converts.

Any selection from the sayings and acts of Jesus was bound to have ' a Jewish and Palestinian horizon ',[1] but there are a number of signs that Q was compiled primarily for the instruction of Gentile Christians. It was known both to Matthew and Luke in Greek, and no conclusive evidence has ever been produced for its translation from an Aramaic original, as distinct from its ultimate derivation from Jesus' teaching in Aramaic ;[2] the Old Testament quotations are few in number and reflect the Greek Septuagint version rather than the Hebrew. The teaching of Q is generally universalist in nature, and the element of polemic with the Jews is comparatively small. The one healing which is given special prominence is that of the Gentile Centurion's servant, and Jesus' attitude to the Gentiles here is in sharp contrast with his address to the Syro-Phoenician women in Mk. vii 27 (cf. Mt. xv 26).

The value of Q as a record of part of Jesus' teaching is shown by its treatment at the hands of Matthew and Luke. Luke in particular often prefers the Q version of a saying to that given in Mark, e.g. Lk. xiii 18-21, xvi 18. Matthew, although he appears to break up his Q material more, and to conflate some Q sayings with those from other sources, seems to treat the sense of Q's teaching with great respect. This respect for Q is shared by the great majority of modern scholars, who see in it a generally faithful record of some of Jesus' teaching.

The date of Q's composition cannot be accurately determined, but clearly lies within 20 or 30 years of the Resurrection. It does not seem to have been known by

---

[1] Harnack, *The Sayings of Jesus*, p. 248.

[2] The view that the differences between Mt. xxiii 26 and Lk. xi 41 are due to a mistranslation of a common Aramaic source is now discredited.

Mark, whose gospel, when it overlaps with Q, e.g. in John the Baptist's teaching, the Temptation, the Beelzebub controversy, follows an independent course. Probably a date between A.D. 50 and 60 would command most general assent for the writing of Q, and the possibility of authorship by one of the original apostles cannot be ruled out. It has sometimes been thought that the tradition of Matthew's authorship of the first gospel, which is not now seriously defended, rests upon the mistaken application to the whole gospel of a tradition which originally referred to one of his sources, Q. Papias (c. A.D. 120) refers to Matthew as having ' composed the oracles in the Hebrew language, and each one interpreted them as he could '. The meaning of this passage is much disputed (cf. p. 64), but could be understood as indicating that Matthew made an arrangement of Jesus' sayings in Aramaic, the interpretation (or translation) of which was left to individuals. It is improbable, however, that Q is based on Matthew's Sayings ; apart from the doubt as to whether Q ever existed in Aramaic, Matthew is traditionally supposed to have written in Palestine for Jewish Christians, and Q, as stated above, is more easily understood as a collection of Jesus' sayings for Gentile Christians.

CHAPTER VII

THE GOSPEL OF MARK

THE EARLIEST CANONICAL GOSPEL

ONE of the greatest achievements of New Testament criticism in the last century has been to establish beyond reasonable doubt that the gospel of Mark formed one of the principal sources used both by Matthew and Luke, and that it is both the earliest and in some ways the most important of our gospels. For centuries Mark had been the least read and regarded of the four gospels for the very reason that both Matthew and Luke contained most of its material, and had the further advantages of better styles and much additional information on the teaching and life of Jesus. We can now see that the main framework of the ministry of Jesus in Matthew and, to a lesser extent, in Luke is dependent on information supplied by Mark, and that in Mark we have an earlier and clearer picture of the course of Jesus' ministry, even if it has to be supplemented from the other gospels, especially John.

This fundamental solution of the relationship of the Synoptic gospels, as the first three gospels are called because of their common view of the life of Jesus (Gr. *synoptikos* = seeing together), has only been reached after the prolonged testing of every possible view, e.g. that Mark is an abbreviation of Matthew, that Mark and Matthew both used Luke, that all three gospels derive from a comparatively fixed oral tradition. Years of patient study have made it certain that the degree of verbal resemblance between the three gospels is too great for explanation on the basis of common oral sources only, and that the one theory which does full justice to the resemblances of language is that both Matthew and Luke used Mark. It is possible that they used Mark in a rather different form to that in which we possess it, or even in two different forms, but the simplest explanation, that they both used substantially our gospel of Mark, is by far the most probable, and is now generally accepted.

The arguments on which this solution is based are worked out in great detail in many books, but their force can be sufficiently expressed in a few brief statistics. Of Mark's 661 verses, some 430 are substantially reproduced in both Matthew and Luke. Of the remaining 231 verses 176 occur in Matthew and the substance of 25 in Luke. Only 30 verses in Mark do not appear in some form in either Matthew or Luke. Moreover, both Matthew and Luke normally follow Mark's order of events, but, when one departs from the Marcan sequence, the other supports Mark's order.

The question of John's use of Mark is a disputed one, but even those who deny that Mark was known to or used by John admit that Mark is the earlier of the two gospels.

THE CONNECTION OF THE GOSPEL WITH
JOHN MARK

The gospel of Mark is traditionally connected with Peter's preaching. Papias (c. A.D. 120) has recorded the following passage about Mark, which, although not explicitly connected with the gospel of Mark, was taken by later authors as referring to the gospel :

'And the Elder said this also : Mark, having become the interpreter of Peter, wrote down accurately everything that he remembered, without, however, recording in order what was either said or done by Christ. For neither did he hear the Lord, nor did he follow him ; but afterwards, as I said, (attended) Peter, who adapted his instructions to the needs (of his hearers) but had no design of giving a connected account of the Lord's oracles. So then Mark made no mistake, while he thus wrote down some things as he remembered them ; for he made it his one care not to omit anything that he heard, or to set down any false statement therein.'[1]

[1] Eusebius, *Hist. Eccl. III* 39. How far the second and third sentences represent what the Elder said, or Papias' own comments, we have no means of knowing.

Just as Papias' statement on Matthew's oracles (cf. p. 64) is not a good description of our first gospel, the statement of the Elder hardly fits our second gospel. This gospel is precisely a recording of what was said and done by Christ ' in order ', and the Marcan ' order ' of events is generally agreed to be clear and intelligible. Attempts have been made to force the meaning of the Greek in the passage, and to explain it as meaning that the Elder preferred the order of the fourth gospel, and was criticising Mark's gospel as not giving events in the right order. This is a desperate remedy, and does not touch the problem of the internal evidence of the second gospel, which contains some things which are hard to reconcile with Marcan authorship, much less with Peter's teaching.

While there is much in the gospel that has a strong claim to rest on Peter's account of events, there is also much that can hardly be attributed to him. In Mk. xiv 12, 16 it is indicated that the Last Supper was the Passover Meal; this identification raises great difficulties, as it places the arrest, the meeting of the Sanhedrin at night, the trial, and the crucifixion, during the feast (the Jewish day began at sunset), when all business was normally suspended. The fourth gospel gives a different account, in which the Last Supper is not the Passover Meal (xiii 1-2), and the Trial and Crucifixion take place before the feast begins (xviii 28, xix 31); this dating of events would appear much the more likely. There can be no certainty here, but, if John's version is right, it is hard to see how Mark, whose home was in Jerusalem (Acts xii 12), could have made such a mistake.

There are other puzzling passages in the gospel, such as the description of Jesus' journey (vii 31) from Tyre to Galilee ' through the midst of the borders of Decapolis ' (S.E. of the Sea of Galilee, and on the other side from both Tyre and Galilee itself), and the highly-coloured account of John the Baptist's death, which bristles with improbabilities; these errors are unlikely to come from the pen of Mark, who was presumably familiar with Palestinian conditions. But the most serious objection against Marcan authorship of the gospel as it stands lies in the 'developed' nature of many of the stories about Jesus and of some of the teaching attributed to him.   Thus in Mk. vi 34–viii 26 two parallel cycles of events can be traced, each of which contains, in the same sequence, a miraculous feeding of a crowd, a voyage by boat, a conflict with Pharisees, and a healing.   It is difficult not to think that these are variant accounts of the same events (to which Jn. vi offers an instructive parallel), and difficult to ascribe both accounts to Peter or to Mark's misunderstanding of his words.   Again the apocalyptic teaching of Mk. xiii, in its present form, suggests an adulteration of Jesus' teaching far beyond that which might be expected of Peter.

It must be admitted that there are grave obstacles in the way of accepting the second gospel, in its present form, as the work of Mark, although there is much in the gospel which clearly comes ultimately from Peter.   On the other hand there is no good reason for doubting the general accuracy of the Elder's statement, as far as it goes.   To account for the tradition there are two alternatives.   Either the author of the gospel has used Mark's notes, and what the Elder said about these has been later applied to the whole gospel, or the Elder's statement was originally made about a document not used in this gospel,[1] but the gospel itself was recognised as containing much of Peter's teaching and was wrongly attributed to Mark, who was known to have been Peter's 'interpreter'.   The meaning of this last word is much disputed, and amongst those suggested are that Mark was literally an interpreter who translated Peter's Aramaic into Greek, that Mark was Peter's 'dragoman' (cf. Acts xiii 5), and that Mark 'interpreted' Peter's teaching by handing it on and explaining it (Papias speaks of himself as handing on what he had learnt from the elders 'with my interpretations').   In any case it must

---

[1] It is noteworthy that Q seems to have fulfilled some of the necessary conditions.   It was 'not in order', it was suited to the needs of early converts, and it carried the authentic ring of genuine reminiscence ; on the other hand there is little specifically 'Petrine' about it.

be remembered that many people besides Mark had heard Peter teach, and that his words would be preserved, at least orally, through many channels.

THE SOURCES OF THE GOSPEL

Many attempts have been made to trace in the gospel a definite written source which can be identified with Mark's record of Peter's preaching, but none of these attempts has gained general approval. Peter may well have been present at most of the scenes recorded in the gospel, and much of the narrative is probably derived ultimately from him. Thus Mk. i 16-38 represents the beginning of Peter's new life (cf. p. 35), and a number of incidents where only the ' inner circle ' of disciples were present are recorded, including the healing of Jairus' daughter, the Transfiguration (followed by a description of the healing of the Epileptic Boy from the standpoint of one of the three named disciples, cf. Mk. ix 14), the forecast of the destruction of the Temple, the agony in Gethsemane. The story of Peter's confession at Caesarea Philippi, and of his denial of Jesus must have formed part of his own teaching. Yet some of these Petrine incidents are told so baldly, e.g. the Call of Peter i 16-18 (cf. Lk. v 1-9), or have acquired so many accretions, e.g. the apocalyptic discourse of xiii, that it is impossible to be certain that all these stories came direct from Peter, and have not in some cases passed from mouth to mouth.

While the question of a direct Petrine source, therefore, can never be fully answered, there are a number of signs that the author of the gospel put together a mass of material, some of which was already in small collections, whether written or oral. It has already been suggested (cf. pp. 35 ff.) that he had, in addition to a more or less fixed form of Passion-narrative, collections of controversies, e.g. ii 1-iii 6, xi 27-33 and xii 13-40, and cycles of narratives, e.g. vi 34-vii 37, viii 1-26 ; it is possible that the bulk of the apocalyptic discourse in xiii also lay before him in written form (cf.

xiii 14), and the sayings of ix 39-50 may have acquired their connection before his time (cf. p. 44). Besides these possible ' larger ' sources he incorporated a number of single incidents, parables, and sayings, which probably circulated orally as examples of Jesus' actions and words.

PLAN OF THE GOSPEL

The part of the final author of the gospel was to give to his sources a narrative framework and to make of his fragments of material a connected whole. He seems to have been the first person to attempt to construct in writing a sketch of the whole ministry of Jesus, although he must have worked on the basis of an oral account such as the skeleton speeches in Acts suggest formed part of Peter's preaching (e.g. Acts x 37-42). His sources of information were limited, and he shows no sign of knowing, for example, that Jesus' ministry had extended to Judaea and Jerusalem even before its close, as John makes clear. The insertion of incidents and pieces of teaching from his sources into his framework seems often to have been made for their suitability to the situation, and not because the author of the gospel knew that they were actually connected with the particular historical situation.

Yet the main plan of the gospel is simple and straight-forward, and contains a number of consecutive historical developments which have a good claim to rest upon a true tradition. The key to the understanding of this plan is the author's conviction that Jesus was from the first, and knew himself to be, the Son of God, but that he chose to reveal the full implications of this by stages. The gospel falls into two main parts, the Ministry in and around Galilee (i-ix), and the Last Week in Jerusalem (xi-xvi), which are joined by a short account of the Journey to Jerusalem (x).

The preparation for the ministry is provided by the teaching of John the Baptist that a mightier than he is coming after him, by Jesus' baptism, and by the temptation in the wilderness. After John had been imprisoned by

Herod, Jesus comes into Galilee, proclaiming that the time
is fulfilled, the kingdom of God is at hand, and men must
repent and believe in the good news. Little is said about
the details of Jesus' preaching, but its success is described,
and attributed in large measure to Jesus' healing powers.
These are the inevitable consequences of Jesus' Sonship, as
is recognised by the evil spirits, but Jesus does not suffer the
spirits to speak and tries as far as possible to prevent news
of his healings from spreading abroad. These healings
arouse opposition from some of the scribes when Jesus claims
the power to forgive sins (ii 6-7), and when he heals on the
Sabbath the Pharisees and Herodians take counsel to destroy him (iii 6); later, scribes from Jerusalem ascribe
his powers to possession of Beelzebub (iii 22). Mean-
while Jesus has from the first been gathering disciples, to
whom he imparts fuller instruction about the parabolic
teaching which he gives to the multitudes; he tells them
that the purpose of this method of teaching is to hide its real
meaning from them that are without (iv 11-12), but that
to the disciples is given the mystery of the kingdom of
God.

Jesus' apparent success continues, except in ' his own
country' (vi 1), and the training of the Twelve advances
sufficiently far for him to send them out two by two to
exorcise evil spirits, to heal the sick, and to call men to
repent. At this stage Herod himself hears of Jesus, and of
the rumours that he is Elijah, who was supposed to return
to earth to herald ' the great and terrible day of the Lord '
(Malachi iv 5), or a prophet, although Herod himself
thinks that he is John the Baptist risen from the dead. On
the return of the Twelve from their mission Jesus brings
them for rest and quiet to a desert place, but the crowds
follow them, and Jesus out of compassion teaches them and
feeds them by a miracle. Mark does not give to this
feeding, or to the parallel account of the feeding of the four
thousand, the special significance that it has in the fourth
gospel (Jn. vi 15), where the motive for Jesus' withdrawal
afterwards is to prevent the crowd taking him by force

' to make him king ' ; yet it marks the height of his popular success in Galilee (cf. vi 53-56).

Between his two parallel sequences of feeding, voyage, controversy with Pharisees, and healing (cf. p. 36) Mark inserts the departure of Jesus to the borders of Tyre and Sidon (vii 24), and his return ' through Sidon unto the sea of Galilee, through the midst of the borders of Decapolis ' (vii 31). This journey has been made the basis of a theory that Jesus deliberately left Galilee to avoid trouble with the authorities, now alarmed at his popular success, and that he deliberately skirted round Galilean territory on his return. But such a motive is not hinted at by the evangelist, who pictures Jesus' withdrawals as being for the purpose of training the disciples in private, and the geographical puzzles presented by his mention of ' the country of the Gerasenes ' (v 1) and ' the parts of Dalmanutha ' (viii 10) suggest that the reference to Decapolis in vii 31 is an error caused by his unfamiliarity with the geography of Northern Palestine.

After the two ' feeding ' cycles is introduced Jesus' question to his disciples on the way to Caesarea Philippi, ' Who say ye what I am ? ', and Peter's reply, ' Thou art the Christ '. Jesus warns them to keep this secret, and explains that he is ' the Son of Man ', but that he has to die and rise again ; to the multitudes he speaks less explicitly, warning them that to reject him is to be rejected by the Son of Man when he comes in glory (viii 38). To the inner circle of disciples is vouchsafed the vision of the Transfiguration and the heavenly assurance that Jesus is the Son of God. Even so the disciples continue to misunderstand the nature of the Kingdom of God (ix 33 ff., x 35 ff.), and fail to comprehend his repeated references to his death and resurrection (ix 32, x 32 ff.)

Jesus' movements from the Confession at Caesarea Philippi take him through Galilee (ix 30,33), into the borders of Judaea and beyond Jordan (x 1), and so to Jericho and Jerusalem. At Jericho he is hailed by Bartimaeus with the Messianic title ' Son of David ', and his entry into Jerusalem

is the scene of a ' Messianic ' ovation from his supporters
(xi 7-10).   At Jerusalem Jesus is heard gladly by the people
(xii 37), but is involved in a series of controversies with
Scribes, Pharisees, Sadducees, and the Chief Priests.   His
opponents plot to get rid of him before the feast (xiv 1-2),
and Judas agrees to betray him.   Jesus is represented as
conscious of all this (xiv 18, 27-30), and prophesies that all
his disciples will forsake him, but that he will rise again and
go before them to Galilee.   He is arrested, condemned by
the high priest, on his own admission that he is the Christ,
the Son of Man, who is to come with the clouds of heaven,
and again condemned as ' King of the Jews ' by Pilate, is
crucified, and dies.   Thirty-six hours later his tomb is found
empty, and a young man in a white robe tells the women
to inform the Twelve and Peter that Jesus goes before them
to Galilee.   The women are too frightened to obey.

The value of this narrative framework can be challenged
on a number of points, e.g. the significance given by Jesus
to his teaching in parables, the uncertainty that surrounds
some of the miraculous events, the length of time between the
Confession of Caesarea Philippi and the Passion ; yet the
honesty of the writer in leaving vague most of the temporal
connections in the narrative gives an added importance to the
consistency of his general picture.   The gradual unfolding
of the Messianic secret, in particular, and Jesus' lack of
immediate success in instructing his disciples as to the true
nature of the Kingdom, have an inherent probability that is
confirmed by the later history of the misinterpretation of his
teaching in the New Testament Church (cf. pp. 247-250).
The second gospel furnishes only an incomplete and at
times a confused record of Jesus' ministry, but its account is
sufficient to establish the main lines on which Jesus conducted the major part of his ministry with some degree
of certainty.

To discredit completely the Marcan framework would
not only leave us in the dark as to the main features of
Jesus' ministry—that is an alternative which the honest
historian must face—but would also leave inexplicable the

fact that one who taught of himself and the Kingdom in such terms as Q, for example, relates, was also crucified as a false Messiah.

THE ENDING OF THE GOSPEL

The MS. evidence makes it clear that ' the longer ending ' found in most Bibles (Mk. xvi 9-20) is in fact an early addition to bring Mark into line with the other gospels in recording Resurrection appearances of Jesus.   It is probable that both Matthew and Luke used Mark in a form which broke off at xvi 8, and this ending, though abrupt and awkward, may well be original (cf. p. 113).   A number of theories, however, have been advanced to account for the loss of a supposed original ending which included Resurrection appearances in Galilee (cf. xvi 7).   It is possible that the gospel was not finished, or that the original copy was accidentally mutilated, and it has even been suggested that an account of Jesus' appearance in Galilee has been suppressed in view of the alternative tradition (witnessed by Luke xxiv) that the appearances of the risen Christ were in the neighbourhood of Jerusalem.

DATE AND PLACE OF WRITING

The use of Mark by Luke and Matthew makes it difficult to date this gospel later than A.D. 70.   On the other hand the present form of the apocalypse of Mark xiii is held by some scholars to indicate its composition in the late fifties, and the emergence of the earliest gospel is widely held to have been most probable at a time when the first generation of Christian teachers was beginning to die out, c. A.D. 60-70.   Such a date would account most satisfactorily for the combination of much valuable and primitive tradition with other less historical material, which we find in Mark, and would allow time for the development of those collections of material whose use in the gospel has been seen to be probable.

The place of writing is more difficult to fix. Traditionally the gospel is associated with Rome, but the tradition may well be due to that which connected Mark and Peter with Rome. The few ' latinisms ' of the gospel are of a kind that would naturally arise in popular Greek wherever Roman influence had been at work, e.g. legion (v 9), scourge (xv 15), centurion (xv 29). The style is rough and such as might be expected of a Jew who thought in Aramaic, but wrote in Greek. He is careful, however, to supply a translation whenever he gives Jesus' words in their original Aramaic, e.g. v 31, vii 38, and to explain Jewish customs, e.g. vii 3-4. He does not appear, as we have seen, to have himself a good knowledge of Palestinian conditions. If he wrote in Syria, the use of his gospel by Matthew and Luke would be perhaps easiest to explain, but this can only be a conjecture.

CHAPTER VIII

THE GOSPEL OF MATTHEW

THE PROBLEM OF THE ATTRIBUTION TO MATTHEW

THE tradition that the apostle Matthew wrote our first gospel, or an Aramaic gospel of which the Greek is a translation, went unchallenged from the middle of the second century to the nineteenth century, but can no longer be defended with any confidence. The main reason for this lies in the fact, now generally accepted, that the first gospel is not a translation from the Aramaic, but was composed originally in Greek on the basis of at least two written Greek sources, Mark and Q. The comparatively few narrative additions made by the evangelist include some more suggestive of legendary accretion than the pen of an apostle (e.g. xvii 24-27, xxvii 51-53), although much of the teaching material peculiar to Matthew is universally recognised as of high value.

An examination of the earliest tradition that has been preserved on Matthew as a writer gives a possible clue as to how the tradition arose of his authorship of the first gospel. Papias has recorded an enigmatic statement that—

> Matthew compiled the Logia in the Hebrew language, and each one interpreted (the Greek word may mean ' translated ') them as he was able.

Most scholars are agreed that ' Hebrew ' here probably means ' Aramaic ', the everyday language of Jews in the first century A.D., but opinion is very divided about the meaning of ' Logia ', which is sometimes rendered as ' oracles ' or ' sacred utterances '. The most widely accepted view is that these ' oracles ' were sayings of Jesus, with perhaps occasional stories about him; some critics, however, hold that they were Old Testament prophecies about Jesus, of which Matthew made a collection. There is a

further division of opinion as to whether these ' oracles '
needed interpretation, to apply them to particular circumstances, or whether they were translated intoGreek by
different people. This question is further discussed (pp. 69,
71) in connection with the question of the sources behind
the gospel.

Two explanations have been suggested for the transference of this tradition to the first gospel in its present form.
It may be that one of the sayings-sources behind the gospel
is Matthew's collection of Logia, and that the name has
been transferred from the part to the whole. There is
also evidence that the first gospel was very early translated
into Aramaic, and it is possible that such a gospel, which
may well have circulated at first anonymously, was soon
wrongly identified with the Aramaic document which
Matthew was known to have written. It is significant
that little seems to have been known of Matthew as a person,
and that such information as the tradition gives about the
writing of his gospel is clearly conjecture spun out of
his apostleship and the fact that he wrote in ' Hebrew '.
Indeed it has even been suggested that the name ' Matthew '
was attached to the gospel because in Mt. ix 9 the tax-
collector is called Matthew instead of Levi, son of Alphaeus,
as in Mk. ii 14; such a reason, however, hardly seems
adequate by itself to explain the attribution of the gospel.

THE CHARACTER OF THE GOSPEL

If Luke's gospel is essentially an attempt to improve and
supplement Mark as an historical account of Jesus' ministry
for the benefit of Gentile Christian readers, Matthew's gospel
is an attempt to improve and supplement Mark as a record
of Jesus' teaching and as a testimony to his Messiahship
for the guidance of Jewish Christians. Matthew adds to the
narrative of Mark, which he shortens but reproduces in
essentials, only an account of Jesus' birth and infancy, a
few incidents from Q, a couple of other stories, a few variations in Mark's narrative, and a Resurrection appearance in

5

Galilee; some of this material is of doubtful historical value, and the author of the first gospel seems to have written at a time when oral tradition in his community could no longer supplement the Marcan history with much of real importance.

On the other hand the first gospel is peculiarly rich in teaching, and has largely for this reason been throughout the centuries the most popular of all gospels with Christian readers. Matthew had a teaching source or sources of great value, whose material he has for the most part combined with that of Mark and Q to form five great discourses, each of which ends with a formula ' and it came to pass when Jesus ended those words, etc.'

Mt. v 3–vii 27	The Sermon on the Mount
x 5-42	The Mission Discourse
xiii 3-52	Parables
xviii 3-35	On a variety of subjects
xxiv 3–xxv 46	Eschatological Discourse

(xxiii 1-39 Woes against the Scribes and Pharisees forms another discourse, but here the closing formula is missing.)

These discourses are clearly composed by the author of the gospel, who sets them in suitable places in the Marcan framework and conflates his various sources with great skill. In the same way he has incorporated most of his remaining teaching material from Q and his special source or sources in other shorter discourses.

The purpose of this editorial collection of the teaching of Jesus was a double one. It had a great practical advantage in making the gospel also a handbook on Christian life and conduct, and there are many signs that this was in Matthew's mind (e.g. vi 1-18, xviii 15-17). It also enabled him to represent Jesus as a new lawgiver, whose law was the true consummation of the law given to Moses (v 17-20), just as in his narrative he stressed his Messiahship in Jewish terms.

The whole gospel is written with the aim of establishing this Messiahship in terms which would have a special

appeal to Jewish Christian readers. In the very first verse
(i 1) Jesus is the ' Son of David, the Son of Abraham ', and
the Messianic title ' Son of David ' is repeatedly given to
him by those who believe in him. A series of fulfilments
of Old Testament prophecies accompany his birth, infancy,
and ministry. There is a special stress on Jesus' teaching
about the Kingdom (usually ' the Kingdom of Heaven '
in Matthew as a periphrasis for the ' Kingdom of God ')
and its eschatological aspect.

This preoccupation with Jesus' Messiahship has led to
the blurring in Matthew's gospel of the outline of the Marcan
framework. Matthew allows himself considerable liberties
with the order of Marcan incidents, and, in his anxiety to
stress the Messiahship of Jesus and the impression made by
Jesus on his hearers, he has often amended Mark's narrative
in such a way as to obliterate the distinctions drawn by
Mark in the stages of Jesus' revelation of his Sonship.
Thus at his baptism John the Baptist recognises him and has
to be persuaded to ' fulfil all righteousness ' by baptising
him (iii 14-15), and Jesus is made to proclaim his Sonship
openly and to be recognised by some men as Messiah quite
early in his ministry, e.g. ix 27, xiv 33.

THE SOURCES OF THE GOSPEL

Of the additions made to Mark's narrative of Matthew
by far the most extensive is his account of the birth and
infancy of Jesus (i-ii) ; these chapters are probably put
together by Matthew himself on the basis of a genealogy
and a series of stories, most of which are presented as the
fulfilment of Old Testament prophecies (i 23, ii 6, 15, 18, 23).
The stories are quite independent of those told by Luke,
and contain features which make it probable that much
of their content is legend rather than history.

It is noteworthy that Matthew does not appear to have
any continuous written narrative source other than Mark,
and that his additions to Mark are either single incidents,
e.g. the Temple Tribute (xvii 24-27) and Judas' death

(xxvii 3-10), or imply the existence of a narrative similar to the Marcan one in which they are embedded, e.g. John's Protest at the Baptism (iii 14-15), Peter Walking on the Water (xiv 28-33) and a number of additions to the Narrative of the Passion and Resurrection (xxvii 19, 24-25, 51-53, 62-66, xxviii 2-4, 8-15). Even Matthew's Resurrection Appearance gives the impression of being founded on the promise of Mk. xiv 28, xvi 7 and an oral tradition that had preserved few details (cf. ' but some doubted ', xxviii 17).

Most of these narrative additions of Matthew are of doubtful historical value. It would seem that the Marcan account of Jesus' ministry was the only written one known to the community in which Matthew lived, but that it had circulated long enough for a number of additions and variations to have grown up, which Matthew in turn incorporates in his gospel. That Matthew should have had so little of real value to add suggests that he wrote at a time when the first generation of disciples were dead and the catastrophes of the Jewish War of A.D. 66-73 had interrupted the channels of genuine oral reminiscence. It also makes it unlikely that he wrote in one of the larger Christian churches like that of Antioch, where much good information to supplement Mark's narrative must still have been available long after A.D. 70.

In striking contrast to the poverty of Matthew's narrative additions is the richness of the teaching material to be found only in his gospel. In view of what has been said above it is probable that he drew much of this material from a written source or sources. The reconstruction of such sources can only be conjectural, but there are some grounds for thinking that the substance of two sources at least can still be discerned in spite of Matthew's skilful editorial conflation.

The first of these sources seems to have been a list of Old Testament ' Testimonies ' to Jesus. Matthew himself normally quotes the Old Testament from the Greek LXX[1]

---

[1] LXX = The Greek version of the Old Testament called the Septuagint. (Latin septuaginta = 70) from a tradition that 70 translators took part in the work.

version, and when he is using Mark he preserves Mark's
versions of Old Testament quotations or brings them slightly
nearer to the LXX text.   There are, however, in Matthew's
gospel eleven quotations, i 23, ii 6, 15, 18, 23, iv 15-16, viii 17,
xii 18-21, xiii 35, xxi 5, xxvii 9, which show significant variations from the LXX text and approach more or less closely
to the Hebrew text of the Old Testament (allowance has to
be made in some of them, e.g. i 23, xii 21, for Matthew's
editorial revision).   Each of these quotations is introduced by the formula ' . . . that it might be fulfilled which
was spoken by the prophet, saying ', or by a similar phrase ;
they are attached to short accounts of incidents connected with Jesus' birth and infancy (i 23, ii 6, 15, 18, 23),
with his settlement at Capernaum (iv 15-16), his healing
powers (viii 17), his meekness (xii 18-21), his teaching in
parables (xiii 35), his entry into Jerusalem (xxi 5), and with
the death of Judas (xxvii 9) ; in the process of incorporation
by Matthew this original context has sometimes been
disturbed or enlarged.

Some have seen in this list of ' Testimonies ', the original
collection of Logia, which Papias ascribes to Matthew with
accompanying ' interpretations ', but against this view is the
artificiality of some of the ' fulfilments ', e.g. ii 15, 18, 23.
It is more probable that the list represents the work of a
Christian of a later generation, who searched his Hebrew
Bible for texts which would fit some of the details of Jesus'
life as it was known to him.

Far more valuable is the collection of Jesus' sayings that
Matthew utilises in the Sermon on the Mount and perhaps
elsewhere.   It has already been noted that Matthew and
Luke sometimes agree so closely in their account of Jesus'
teaching as to make it certain that they both used the Greek
document Q.   There are also a number of places where they
give versions of Jesus' teaching that are in general agreement
but show substantial variations in wording.   This phenomenon has sometimes been interpreted as showing the continued influence of oral tradition, or as indicating that
Matthew used a different and fuller edition of Q.   It is

perhaps more easy to explain this 'agreement with variations' by supposing that Matthew had a second written collection of Jesus' sayings that largely overlapped Q.

In favour of this theory is the high value that Matthew seems to have attributed to this source, and the fact that the first half of his first great discourse, the Sermon on the Mount (v 3–vi 18), only occasionally shows signs of agreement with Q, while the second half of the discourse (vi 19–vii 27) is for the most part clearly composed of material drawn from Q. The first half of the discourse, moreover, has a formal arrangement—7 Beatitudes, 2 parallel similes of Salt and Light, the New Law and the Old under 5 heads, Murder, Adultery, Swearing, Retaliation, Love of One's Enemies ; 3 parallel instructions on Almsgiving, Prayer, and Fasting. There is no such ordered arrangement of the Q material, and while Matthew clearly adopts editorial arrangements and formulas in other parts of his gospel, e.g. in the artificial arrangement of the Genealogy in 3 sections, each of 14 names, it would be curious if he had himself arranged the material in the first half of the Sermon on the Mount and then given up the attempt in the rest of the discourse. It is at least possible that the arrangement here goes back in part to that of a written source which he employed, although allowance must be made for some editorial work and conflation with Q material by Matthew.

Whether this source, if it existed in written form, was more extensive and was used elsewhere by Matthew, can only be conjectured. It is perhaps significant that in his account of Jesus' denunciation of the Scribes and Pharisees (xxiii) Matthew appears to be conflating Q with other material, some of which is very reminiscent of the first half of the Sermon on the Mount (compare xxiii 2 with v 17-18, xxiii 5-7 with vi 5, xxiii 16-22 with v 23, 33-37) ; there is also a sevenfold series of denunciations, and a repetition of the formula, ' Woe unto you, Scribes and Pharisees, hypocrites ', which suggests that Matthew is here following the arrangement of a source other than Q, which in Luke's parallel section (Lk. xi 39 ff.) is differently assembled.

If these two sections of Matthew are largely dependent on a written source, it is apparently an early and valuable one, overlapping Q but containing also much material not found elsewhere, and some which seems to be known in much the same form to James in his epistle (compare v 33-37 with James v 12, v 19 with James ii 10, v 9 with James iii 18). The teaching is more suited for Jewish Christians than that of Q, and lays stress on the keeping of the Law (v 17-20, xxiii 2) as well as referring to the Temple and its sacrifices (v 23-24, xxiii 16-21). It is even possible—although it must be remembered that the very existence of this source as a written document can be only a matter of guesswork—that this source was the apostle Matthew's collection of Logia, and that it provides the answer to the riddle of Matthew's connection with the gospel. In this case Papias' ' interpretation ' may be taken as ' translation ', but more probably means that each man, as is still the case, had to apply the teaching to his own life and circumstances.

There is little to guide us in determining the sources from which come the remaining sayings and parables peculiar to this gospel. Three passages, however, are of special import-ance and deserve individual mention.

In the discourse which Matthew places at the sending out of the Twelve (x 1-42) he has conflated material from Mark and Q with sayings found only in this gospel. In x 5-6, 23, we read—

> Go not into any way of the Gentiles, and enter not into any city of the Samaritans ; but go rather to the lost sheep of the house of Israel. . . . But when they persecute you in this city, flee into the next ; for verily I say unto you, Ye shall not have gone through the cities of Israel, till the Son of Man be come.

These words are clearly not invented by the evangelist, although he echoes them in his account of the healing of the Canaanitish woman's daughter (xv 24) ; he is emphatic in his representation of the universality of the gospel (e.g.

x 18, xxiv 14, xxviii 19) and he must have drawn them from an older source. Dr. Schweitzer [1] has seen in them Jesus' mistaken expectation of the almost immediate coming of the Son of Man and the end of the age, but such an interpretation is in conflict with the general tenor of Jesus' teaching. There is no need to doubt that Jesus may deliberately have limited his disciples' first mission to Jewish territory, but the verse 23 may well be an edited version of his words out of their true context; it seems unlikely that Jesus would have expected his disciples to meet with persecution on their first short mission.

In following Mark's account of Peter's confession at Caesarea Philippi Matthew has inserted three verses (xvi 17-19) which contain a special promise to Peter of the keys of the kingdom of Heaven. These verses have played a significant role in controversies between Christian churches and it has been disputed whether Jesus in fact spoke such words. They are manifestly introduced here by Matthew himself on the basis of tradition, and he shows elsewhere a particular interest in Peter, although at times he associates him with incidents which have legendary features (e.g. Mt. xiv 28-31, xvii 24-27). It is perhaps significant that the word ' church ' occurs in the gospels only twice, here and in Mt. xviii 17, a passage where the words of Jesus as given by Matthew do not ring true.

The discourse in Mt. xviii contains material from Mark and other sources, much of it clearly of great value. In the section 15-17, however, there are traces of editorial work which has distorted or replaced Jesus' original teaching. A rule is given for the treatment of a brother who has sinned against another. If he does not hear the offended person, witnesses are to be taken to hear his words; ' if he refuse to hear them, tell it to the Church; and if he refuse to hear the Church also, let him be unto thee as the Gentile and the publican '. It is only necessary to compare these last words with the reproach levelled at Jesus by the Pharisees when he dined with his new disciple, Matthew, and with

[1] *The Quest of the Historical Jesus*, pp. 283 ff., 357 ff.

Jesus' answer (Mt. ix 11-12), to understand that in xviii 15-17 ecclesiastical practice has been read back into Jesus' mouth.

THE DATE AND PLACE OF THE
WRITING OF THE GOSPEL

The use of Mark and an apparent reference (xxii 7) to the destruction of Jerusalem imply a date for the gospel of Matthew later than A.D. 70; on the other hand the gospel is probably quoted by Ignatius (c. A.D. 110) and by the unknown author of ' The Teaching of the Twelve Apostles ', a document thought by many to have been composed in Syria about the end of the first century or in the first half of the second century. A date between A.D. 80 and 100 would fit the internal evidence of the gospel itself, and would account both for the growth of legendary accretions and for the absence of reliable tradition, other than that provided by written sources, about the course of Jesus' ministry.

Antioch has been suggested as the place of writing,[1] but reasons have been given above for thinking that Matthew was written in a community where the tradition of Jesus' acts was less trustworthy than would have been the case in a church so closely linked in early days with the mother church of Jerusalem. On the other hand the early use of the gospel by Ignatius and the author of ' The Teaching of the Twelve Apostles ' makes the writing of the gospel in a remoter district of Syria more probable. We know next to nothing of the coming of Christianity to Syria, outside Antioch, but it is known that Christianity was well established in many Syrian cities by the middle of the next century, and there are signs that it was among the large Jewish population in these cities that Christianity first took root.

[1] E.g. by Streeter, *op. cit.*, pp. 500 ff., and by McNeile, *Introduction to the New Testament*, p. 38.

CHAPTER IX

THE GOSPEL OF LUKE

AUTHORSHIP

THE Lucan authorship of the third gospel has been occasionally challenged by those critics who find it impossible to accept Luke as the final author of the Acts of the Apostles, which is generally agreed to be the work of the same hand as the gospel. The problems presented by the Acts of the Apostles are discussed later (pp. 135-137), but it may be said here that they are not such as to justify the attribution of Acts to another than Luke, ' the beloved physician' (Col. iv 14) and companion of Paul.

The tradition of Luke's authorship of the gospel remained undisputed till modern times, and can be traced back to the second half of the second century A.D. An early prologue to the gospel survives, which was perhaps written to stress the genuineness of the full gospel against a garbled version which Marcion, a second century heretic, edited to propagate his own views. In this prologue are given a number of details about Luke which may well preserve much genuine tradition.

> Luke is a Syrian of Antioch, a doctor by profession, who was a disciple of apostles, and later followed Paul until his martyrdom. He served the Lord without distraction, unmarried, childless, and fell asleep at the age of 84 in Boeotia, full of the Holy Spirit.
> He, . . . impelled by the Holy Spirit, wrote this whole gospel in the regions of Achaea . . . and afterwards the same Luke wrote the Acts of the Apostles.

The tradition finds confirmation in the Preface to the gospel and the general character of the gospel itself. In the Preface (Lk. i 1-4) the author of the gospel claims to have followed all things from the first, and that he is in a position to let Theophilus know the truth of the instruction which he has received; at the same time he distinguishes himself from those who ' from the beginning were eye-witnesses and ministers of the word '. The most natural interpretation of these statements is that the author of the gospel comes from among those who have been in intimate contact with Christian disciples of the first generation. In the same way the author combines the use of written sources, e.g. Mark and Q, with an attitude, at least towards Mark, of confident independence, which leads him to treat Mark's text with considerable freedom and, in a number of places, to prefer his own version, e.g. of Peter's call, of the rejection of Jesus at Nazareth, of the Anointing of Jesus by a woman that was a sinner.

Two other arguments in favour of Luke's authorship may be mentioned. The gospel has some literary pretensions, and it is at least possible that the author's name was attached to the original copy, as seems to have been the case with most ' literary ' works of antiquity. Nor is Luke's name one which would have been likely to have been attached to the gospel and the acts, unless he was in fact the author; many names that would carry greater weight were available, and Tertullian (c. A.D. 200) goes so far as to depreciate the value of this gospel as being only by the follower of an apostle, and that apostle behind Matthew, Peter, and John in importance.

PROTO-LUKE

The theory has already been mentioned (p. 48) that Luke had composed a gospel before he came into possession of a copy of Mark, and that our present gospel is a revised and enlarged edition of his earlier work. This theory, which is particularly associated with the names of the late Dr. Streeter and of Dr. Vincent Taylor, is based on the fact that in large sections of Luke, Mark is not employed as a source, and that it is possible to reconstruct from Luke, omitting all his borrowings from Mark, a gospel-like document of considerable extent.

Streeter thinks that the passages most probably to be assigned to Proto-Luke are as follows [1]—

iii 1—iv 30	John the Baptist's Preaching, the Baptism of Jesus, Genealogy, Temptation, Arrival in Galilee and Rejection at Nazareth.
v 1-11	The Call of Simon Peter.
vi 14-16	The Names of the Twelve Apostles.
vi 20–viii 3	The Great Sermon, Healing of the Centurion's Servant, Raising of the Young Man at Nain, The Baptist's Question and Jesus' Answer, The Anointing of Jesus, The Women who accompanied Him.
ix 51–xviii 14	Jesus' Journey towards Jerusalem, the Sending Out of the 70, the Good Samaritan, Martha and Mary, the Lord's Prayer, the Beelzebub Charge, the Sign of Jonah, Denunciation of Pharisees and Lawyers, the Rich Fool and other Parables and Sayings, the Healing of 10 Lepers, the Days of the Son of Man, The Unjust Judge, the Pharisee and Publican.
xix 1-27	Zacchaeus, the Parable of the Pounds.
xix 37-44	Entry into Jerusalem and Lament over the City.
xxi 18, 34-36	Sayings about the End.
xxii 14 to the end of the Gospel, except for such verses as are	derived from Mark, the identification of which is very problematical.

This hypothetical ' gospel ' has incorporated material from Q, and some at least of its other material, according to Streeter and Dr. Taylor, can be ascribed to Luke's activity in Caesarea during Paul's imprisonment there (*c.* 56-57). Its general framework is similar to that of Mark, the Baptism and Temptation prefacing a ministry in Galilee followed by a journey to Jerusalem through Samaria (ix 51-52), Galilee itself (xvii 11), and Jericho (xix 1) ; there is more teaching than in Mark, and although

---

[1] Dr. Taylor's reconstruction, on similar lines, has been published (in English) as *The First Draft of St. Luke's Gospel* (S.P.C.K.).

there appears to be the same distinction as in Mark between Jesus' enigmatic teaching about himself to the multitudes (cf. vii 16-17) and his private teaching to the disciples (esp. x. 21-24), the distinction is sometimes blurred (iii 22, iv 18-21, vii 22, 34, xi 29 ff., etc.). Within the framework the order of many incidents is different (e.g. the Rejection at Nazareth, the Call of Peter, the Anointing), and their details are often hard to reconcile with those of the parallel accounts in Mark. Thus the Last Supper may have been distinguished from the Passover meal (xxii 14-16), there is an additional trial before Herod (xxiii 8-12), and the Resurrection Appearances are all in or near Jerusalem.

The importance of the Proto-Luke theory, if it be accepted, lies in the evidence which it provides for the existence of a tradition about the course of Jesus' ministry, independent of Mark but confirming much of the substance of Mark, and of a date possibly earlier than the writing of Mark. On the other hand, the existence of such an earlier ' gospel ' of Luke is denied by many critics who maintain that, especially in the Passion Narrative, Luke has used Mark as the foundation of his narrative. It is possible to account for Luke's use of Mark largely in separate ' blocks ' as due to his methods of utilising his sources, for he apparently treats Q in the same way, inserting Q material in separate sections which are edited but not conflated with other sources on a large scale.

LUKE'S TREATMENT OF MARK

In using Mark, Luke frequently abbreviates, and he leaves out a number of passages, some because he prefers another account, e.g. the Beelzebub Charge, some for reasons at which we can only guess, e.g. the Seed Growing Secretly, the Cursing of the Fig Tree. His greatest omission is to leave out everything in Mark from Mk. vi 45 to viii 26. It has been thought by some that his copy of Mark did not contain these verses, or that Luke left them out accidentally, but the most probable explanation is that he left them out deliberately. This part of Mark includes the Walking on the Water, Summaries of Healings, Disputes with Pharisees, a second Feeding ; the Healing of the Syro-Phoenician woman (Mk. vii 27) is in sharp contrast to that recorded by Luke in the story of the Centurion's servant (cf. p. 51). The Healing of the Deaf-Mute, involving the touching of the affected parts (Mk. vii 33), and that of the Blind Man of Bethsaida, involving material means of healing (Mk. viii 23) and stages of healing (viii 24-25) were both omitted by Matthew as well.

This explanation fits in with Luke's rather cavalier treatment of Mark as a whole. He treats the general framework of Mark with respect, and preserves, with some significant exceptions, his order, but whether he is fitting Mark into Proto-Luke or not, he does not hesitate to omit Mark's stories and sayings when he has what he considers a better version. Thus he prefers Q's version of the Temptation and the Beelzebub Charge, although he incorporates two Mission charges, one from Mark, and one, in greater detail, partly at least from Q, and two Discourses on the End, one from Q, and one much edited, but partly at least from Mark. He prefers different versions of Peter's Call and the Anointing to those given by Mark, and makes many alterations in Mark's account of the Passion. He omits one of Mark's references to Jesus' promise of a Resurrection Appearance in Galilee (Mk. xiv 28), and completely alters the sense of the other to suit his own account of the Appearances at Jerusalem (cf. Mk. xvi 7 with Lk. xxiv 6).

There is a double significance in this. Luke knew Mark (Col. iv 10, 14), and he could hardly have treated the gospel of Mark as he did if he had known it to be Mark's record of Peter's teaching. Luke's attitude to the second gospel is perhaps the strongest argument against its traditional authorship. On the other hand Luke himself writes with a certain authority. Although he was a Gentile, and does not seem to have spent more than a few weeks at most in Jerusalem (Acts xxi 17 ff.), he stayed some time in Caesarea (Acts xxvii 1) and had met many men who were closely connected with the Christian communities in Palestine, e.g. Mark,

Silas (Acts. xv 40, xvi 10 ff.), Philip (Acts xxi 9-10) Mnason (Acts xxi 16), not to mention his close association with Paul and the possibility of his having been a member of the church at Antioch. It would be too much to claim for his gospel complete accuracy and freedom from exaggerations and mistakes, but the claim of his Preface (Lk. i 1-4) is at least partly justified.

LUKE'S OTHER SOURCES

It is unlikely that Luke, with all these opportunities for gaining information, depended for the bulk of his information, outside what was provided by Mark and Q, on written sources. He may, of course, have kept a diary or have recorded material in notebooks, but there is no way of proving or disproving this. Nor is there any satisfactory means of determining from which of many possible informants he derived any particular incident or parable.

The first two chapters, with their accounts of the birth and childhood of John the Baptist and Jesus, stand apart in the gospel both because of the close connection they assume between John and Jesus and of the Semitic style in which they are written. Luke may be using a written Palestinian source here, but it is quite possible that he has himself recorded the narrative in the style of the Greek LXX version of the Old Testament to suit its general nature and the hymns, which are clearly of Palestinian origin.

In the main non-Marcan section, ix 51-xviii 14, much of the material peculiar to Luke gives the impression of having been fitted by him into a loose and at times artificial narrative, e.g. the grouping of a healing, teaching, and a parable round a meal (xiv 1-24) and a collection of three parables on the Lost Sheep, the Lost Coin, and the Prodigal Son in a context where the Pharisees are murmuring against Jesus for receiving sinners (xv 1-32). The comparatively unsystematic arrangement of this material with matter from Q is consistent with the view that Luke derived most or all of it from oral tradition and not from documents.

The Lucan changes in Mark's Passion Narrative, e.g. in his variant accounts of the Institution of the Eucharist (xxii 15-21), of the Trials (xxii 66-71, xxiii 4-16), and of the details of the Crucifixion (xxiii 34, 39-43, 46), also seem to indicate that, while Luke shared Mark's general view of the course of events, he was able to supplement it and correct it (e.g. by the transference to another context of the Anointing Mk. xiv 3-9) from familiarity with different and fuller versions that circulated orally in communities which he had visited. His account, too, of the Resurrection Appearances in and near Jerusalem would have been influenced by the oral information which Paul (1 Cor. xv 3-8) and many others were able to give; his limitation of these appearances to the neighbourhood of Jerusalem must rest on what he considered to be the best authority, although it must be remembered that he gives only a selection of the appearances known to him (cf. his own variant account in Acts i 1-11) and that he knew of the tradition of appearances in Galilee.

CIRCUMSTANCES OF WRITING

Luke's purpose in writing is sufficiently explained in his preface to Theophilus (i 1-4). It is to give to Theophilus —and other Gentile Christians—in a period when original ' eyewitnesses and ministers of the word ' are no longer available, an accurate narrative to confirm them as to the truth of what they have been taught. Luke refers to predecessors who have taken this task in hand, but writes in the consciousness that he is able to offer a more complete and accurate account.

The tradition that he wrote in Greece need not be doubted and it is probable that the date of the gospel is to be put after the disastrous Jewish revolt against Rome that culminated in the fall of Jerusalem and the destruction of the Temple in A.D. 70 (cf. xix 42-44). This date marks a watershed in the history of the Church; the Christian community at Jerusalem had fled from the city before the siege to the little town of Pella across the Jordan, and from now on the Jewish element in the Church became insignificant and the Jerusalem Church no longer enjoyed the position of being, as it were, the headquarters of Christianity. Most of the original apostles seem to have been already dead, and with them leaders like Paul and Barnabas. The need for preserving in writing what was still remembered of the life and teaching of Jesus had become imperative, and Luke, with his previous special opportunities for acquiring information, set himself to supplement and improve upon the earliest documents.

While his gospel is in some ways the most important historically of the four, it is probable that he wrote under the handicap of being no longer able to check the value of some of his material. With the example of Paul before our eyes we are perhaps inclined to exaggerate the ease with which travel was possible for other Christians; Luke himself, after accompanying Paul from Troas to Philippi (Acts xvi 11-17), is apparently still there six years later (xx 6) when he rejoins Paul for a longer journey. It seems likely that, when he wrote the gospel, he did so on the basis of his own recollections and some written sources, but without a further visit to Palestine or consultation with such of the oldest disciples as were still living, but were not within reach of Luke, living as he did in Greece. This would account for some of the defects of the gospel, as Luke's earlier intercourse with Palestinian Christians accounts for many of its great merits.

6

CHAPTER X

THE GOSPEL OF JOHN

THE PROBLEM PRESENTED BY THE TRADITIONAL ATTRIBUTION TO JOHN, THE SON OF ZEBEDEE

THE tradition that this gospel was written by the apostle John can be traced back to the second century, but has been widely challenged during the last hundred years. Two difficulties in particular stand in the way of the acceptance of the tradition, the slowness and difficulty with which it became established, and the difference between the Synoptic and the Johannine portraits of Jesus.

Justin Martyr (*c.* 150-160), who had visited Ephesus, and who quotes extensively from the three synoptic gospels as from ' the memoirs of the apostles and of those who followed them ', appears to show occasional knowledge of the fourth gospel, but never quotes it directly with such an introductory formula. This is particularly striking in view of Justin's statement that the Apocalypse was written by John ' one of the apostles of Christ '. The first acknowledgement that survives of John's authorship of the gospel is not from orthodox but from heretical writings of the sixties and seventies of the second century; Irenaeus (*c.* A.D. 185) knows of other heretics who reject the gospel. Irenaeus himself, with Theophilus of Antioch (*c.* A.D. 190) and the Muratorian Canon (between A.D. 170 and 200), provides the first orthodox witness to John (' the apostle ' and ' the disciple of the Lord ') as author of the gospel. On the other hand there seem to have been Christians at this period, nicknamed ' Alogi ' (= anti-' Word ' men, also = anti-Reason men) by their opponents, who rejected the Johannine authorship of the gospel and the Apocalypse, but were not generally regarded as heretics.

The terms of their protest show that at that time the gospel was generally attributed to John, although the fact that it could be openly challenged within the Church is hard to reconcile with a long-established belief in the authorship of one of the Twelve. A similar attack on both the gospel and the Apocalypse was made by Gaius, an orthodox presbyter at Rome (c. A.D. 210), whether independently or in connection with that of the ' Alogi ' we do not know.

The difficulties of accounting for this comparatively late and disputed tradition are increased by the confused nature of the earliest traditions about the apostle himself. The tradition which triumphed was that John the apostle came to Asia and died at Ephesus in extreme old age during the reign of Trajan (A.D. 98-117). Against the truth of this tradition is the inexplicable silence of Ignatius (c. A.D. 110) about the apostle John in his letter to the Ephesians, where he does refer to their connection with Paul. A possible solution to many of the problems involved is provided by Papias (c. A.D. 120), who appears to distinguish between John the apostle and ' the elder John . . . a disciple of the Lord ', the latter of whom was resident in Asia round about A.D. 100. Polycarp of Smyrna, who was born in or before A.D. 69, had heard John the disciple of the Lord speak in his youth, and it may well be that this elder John, who is perhaps the author of the Apocalypse (cf. p. 240), was later confused with the son of Zebedee.

According to two late writers Papias stated in his second book that John and James his brother were killed by the Jews, and this tradition has been accepted by many scholars as correct ; but the evidence must be considered as very doubtful, and possibly due to a misunderstanding. If the elder John, however, is really to be distinguished from the apostle, it is probable that the apostle himself never in fact came to Ephesus.

The internal evidence of the gospel also presents complex problems. In xxi 24 he ' who wrote these things ' is identified with ' the disciple whom Jesus loved ', but apparently by another hand, and both the narratives and the discourses of the gospel raise difficulties for those who regard them as the work of the apostle John.

It is not, perhaps, surprising that the gospel should often supplement the synoptic gospels, e.g. in its description of a ministry largely conducted in Judaea and Jerusalem, and occasionally contradict them, as in placing the Cleansing of the Temple towards the beginning of the ministry (iii 15 ff.), and in placing the Last Supper before the Passover (xiii 1 ff.). The very limitations of the synoptic gospels that have been pointed out by modern scholars make it easier to accept many of the Johannine variations as possibly resting on better tradition. There are, however, a number of features in the fourth gospel which can only be accepted as apostolic by an undue depreciation of the historical value of the Marcan framework. Thus Jesus' Messiahship is proclaimed from the beginning by John the Baptist (i 29-30), by Jesus' disciples (i 41), and by Jesus himself (e.g. iii 26) ; this contradicts the whole plan of the Marcan ministry (cf. p. 58). Again it is hard to understand how Mark and the other synoptists could have ignored the story of the raising of Lazarus if it was indeed, as represented in the fourth gospel (xi 46 ff.), an event of such public importance as to lead to the plot of the Chief Priests against Jesus' life. Moreover some of the incidents recorded in the fourth gospel are narrated in a way that suggests, not the eye-witness account of one of the Twelve, but an inferior version to that given in the synoptic gospels. The story of the Nobleman's Son (Jn. iv 46-54), for example, appears to be a heightened version of the Healing of the Centurion's Servant (Mt. viii 5-13 ; Lk. vii 1-10).

There is the same difficulty in reconciling the teaching of Jesus as given in the fourth gospel with that given in the synoptic gospels. The almost complete absence of parables is hard to account for, and while allowance must be made for the tendency of the fourth evangelist to introduce into the discourses of Jesus the fruit of his own reflections and meditations, there is a striking difference between the style in which Jesus speaks in this gospel and that of the short pithy utterances of Jesus in the synoptic gospels. At the same time there is much in the teaching of Jesus in the fourth gospel which all critics would allow to have an authentic ring.

How is this combination of such apparently authentic material and elements of doubtful value to be accounted for? Most critics would agree that it is impossible to regard the gospel in its present form as wholly the work of John, the son of Zebedee, but widely differing views are held about the circumstances in which the gospel was composed. The problem is admitted on all sides to be at once one of the most difficult and one of the most important of the historical problems in the New Testament.

THE UNITY OF COMPOSITION

The gospel shows a remarkable unity of style and language. Many distinctive words, phrases, and constructions occur repeatedly in the gospel and nowhere else in the New Testament except in the Johannine epistles which are probably by the same author (cf. pp. 220-223). This unity extends to the Appendix (xxi) as a whole, although it is disputed in the case of the last two verses (24-25). Only in the story of the Woman taken in Adultery (vii 53-viii 11) are the distinctively 'Johannine' characteristics altogether lacking, and the textual evidence—only one early Greek MS. contains the story—as well as the way in which it breaks the close connection between ch. vii and viii 12, make it clear that this story is a later insertion in the gospel. It has been shown, however, that there are a number of passages in the gospel where the 'Johannine' characteristics of style, although not entirely absent, are relatively scarce.[1] These passages are all narratives of a synoptic type and include the Miracle at Cana (ii 1-11), the Cleansing of the Temple (ii 14-16), the Healing of the Nobleman's Son (iv 46-53), the Anointing at Bethany (xii

[1] E. Schweizer, *Ego Eimi*, 1939 (a German work, not yet translated into English).

1-8) and the Triumphal Entry into Jerusalem (xii 12-15);
it is at least possible that the evangelist was here using
a written source or oral tradition that had become comparatively ' fixed ' in form.

In a number of places the arrangement of the gospel
material is perplexing; thus in chapter v Jesus is represented as being in Jerusalem, but in vi 1 he ' went away
to the other side of the Sea of Galilee '; again in xiv 31 he
finishes a speech with the words, ' Arise, let us go hence ',
but the speech is at once resumed and continues for three
more chapters. If the gospel was originally written, not
on a continuous roll, but—as is now generally admitted to
be possible—in a book with pages, it would be possible to
account for some transposition of passages as due to the
putting together of the pages in the wrong order after some
accident had happened to the book. It is probable, for
example, that such a disarrangement of leaves explains
differences between the Hebrew and Greek texts of Ecclesias-
ticus xxx-xxxvi. On the other hand there is no general agreement on the subject, and many scholars prefer to accept
the disarrangements of the present gospel order as due
to some other cause, i.e. the use of sources, the dictation
of the gospel in a number of stages, or the carelessness of
the author.

Whatever sources have been employed, and whatever
dislocations have disturbed the original order, the gospel
bears upon it the stamp of a single mind, with a distinct
and profound conception of the significance of the Incarnation. In the other gospels the authors have been
primarily compilers of material, and their personal interpretation of the events of Jesus' life and of his teaching play
only a subordinate part in the shaping of their material.
In this gospel the historical facts of Jesus' life serve primarily
to illustrate the author's main themes, and the speeches
put into the mouth of Jesus are made the vehicles for the
author's own interpretations of Jesus' thought. This is not
to deny that there is much both in the narratives and in the
discourses of the gospel which is historically true, but the

element of interpretation is so great that much of the historical value of the gospel depends upon who the author was, and upon his apostolicity or his connection with an apostle. The discourses of Jesus, for example, upon Baptism (iii) and upon the Eucharist (vi) reflect the same fundamental conception of the significance and necessity of these two rites; that this conception was that of the evangelist is plain, e.g. from iii 16-21, where Jesus' words have passed insensibly into the evangelist's reflection upon them; if the evangelist was the son of Zebedee, it would be natural to accept his accounts as substantially correct records of incidents and discourses from Jesus' ministry, but, if he was not, a comparison with the synoptic gospels and with the teaching of Paul and others on the sacraments would suggest doubts as to the historical value of both discourses.

THE AUTHORSHIP OF THE GOSPEL

In three verses in the gospel reference is made to a personal witness of the events described. In i 14 we read—

> And the Word became flesh, and dwelt among us (and we beheld his glory, glory as of the only begotten from the Father), full of grace and truth.

The interpretation of this verse, to which there is a parallel in 1 Jn. i 1-2, is difficult. It is taken by some scholars as an indication that the author of the gospel was himself an eyewitness of the events of Jesus' life, but the use of the plural seems to indicate that the author as in xxi 24 and in many passages in 1 John, is here appealing to the corporate witness of the Church, and not to any recollection of his own.

In xix 35 a description of blood and water coming out of Jesus' side is followed by the assertion—

> And he that hath seen hath borne witness, and his witness is true : and he knoweth that he saith true, that ye also may believe.

' He ' who ' knoweth ' has been interpreted as a reference to Jesus himself (cf. 1 Jn. iii 5, 7, 9) and as a circumlocution for ' I ', the evangelist, but the most natural interpretation is to take it as referring to the same person who has seen. In this case the evangelist is appealing to the witness of a spectator of the crucifixion, presumably the disciple whom Jesus loved (cf. 26-27), who is still alive. There is nothing, however, in the passage that identifies this witness with the evangelist, and the impression that it leaves on the mind is rather of the evangelist recording something to which another, whose testimony is unimpeachable, has borne witness.

In xxi 24, the story of Jesus' appearance at the sea of Tiberias and of his words to Peter and the disciple whom he loved is followed by an identification of this latter disciple—

> This is the disciple which beareth witness of these things, and wrote these things ; and we know that his witness is true.

Three problems obscure the meaning of this verse. Many critics regard it as an addition to the gospel, made, with or without 25, by the Elders of the Church in Ephesus, to vouch for the authorship of the gospel as a whole. ' These things ' can be interpreted either of the whole gospel, or of the story contained in xxi. ' Wrote' is taken by some scholars as meaning ' dictated ' or ' caused to be written ' in an indirect sense. Where so many solutions are possible, and so much hangs on the evidence of a single verse, it is not easy to choose ; but two considerations point to the verse being the work of the author himself and having a special reference to the story of the last chapter, or to a part only of the gospel. A comparison with the other two verses quoted earlier shows a striking similarity of expression between them which is most easily explicable if they come from the same pen ; and while the possibility of interpolation in all three cases must be taken into account, the most reasonable explanation remains that they are the comments of the author himself. There are very great difficulties, as has been pointed out, in the way of accepting the whole of the gospel as the work of an original apostle, but much of the material in the gospel implies knowledge which only an eyewitness can have possessed.

If this view be accepted it carries with it the implication that the evangelist was not himself an apostle, but had available information from an original disciple, perhaps in written form, and that he wrote while this disciple was still alive (xix 35, xxi 24). The disciple is the disciple ' whom Jesus loved ', and there can be little doubt that this phrase is meant to describe the apostle John, the son of Zebedee. John is not mentioned in the gospel, but the beloved disciple has a place next to Jesus at the Last Supper (xiii 23) and is entrusted with the care of Jesus' mother (xix 27) ; he is a fisherman (xxi 2-3), and is closely associated with Peter (xiii 24, xx 2, xxi 20). If any reliance can be placed on the narrative of Mark, the identity of such a disciple with John, the son of Zebedee, can be assumed with some confidence.

The evangelist's name we cannot know. If, as is probable, he wrote the Johannine epistles, he was ' the Elder ' of 2 and 3 John. From the knowledge of Palestine which he displays in the gospel he seems to have been a bi-lingual Palestinian Jew familiar with Jerusalem. We can only guess at the circumstances in which the gospel was composed, but the evidence favours its composition in Asia Minor. The first epistle of John was known to Papias and, almost certainly, to Polycarp, and it is possible that Papias also made use of the gospel.

The date of the gospel until recently was usually placed round about A.D. 100. It is possible, however, that this date should be put back by some years. There has been discovered in Egypt a papyrus fragment of the gospel, which is dated by experts as having been written in the first half of the second century,[1] and many modern critics have abandoned the belief that the author of the fourth gospel used the gospels of Mark and Luke in favour of the view that he drew upon a tradition similar in some respects to that behind these gospels (cf. p. 91).

[1] C. H. Roberts, *An Unpublished Fragment of the Fourth Gospel*, 1935.

We may imagine the future evangelist a member of a Christian community in Palestine, where the apostle John was well-known and some document written by John or inspired by him was in circulation. There is nothing, however, in the gospel to suggest that the evangelist was in any special sense a disciple of John, although he may have heard him speak. Perhaps as a result of the unsettlement and chaos that accompanied the Jewish rebellion against Rome the evangelist left Palestine for Asia, where he later wrote the gospel, while John was still alive in Palestine, partly from recollections of what the apostle had said or written, but largely from his wider knowledge of traditions about Jesus and his teaching, and in the light of his own interpretation of the teaching and of the significance of the facts of Jesus' life. Such a reconstruction of events is of course speculative in the extreme, but would account for some at least of the distinctive features of the gospel, as well as for Papias' statement that he ' inquired about the words of the Elders : what . . . John . . . or any other of the Lord's disciples (had said).'

THE SOURCES OF THE GOSPEL

To distinguish sources in a work whose author writes in such a distinctive and interpretative style is an almost hopeless task. Even to delimit with any accuracy those parts of the gospel where the influence of the apostle John is most likely is extremely difficult. The place in the gospel where such an influence seems most evident is the narrative of the Last Supper, the Trials, Crucifixion, and Resurrection. Here the repeated references to the disciple whom Jesus loved, and the many indications of special knowledge, e.g. xiii 3 ff., 21 ff., xviii 10, 15 ff., 26, 28, xix 25 ff., 34 f., xxi 2, 15 ff., imply a dependence upon an apostolic source. But the evangelist, who may well no longer have had access in Asia to whatever document John wrote, has clearly shaped his material even here, possibly with the help of other traditional material available to him.

It is clear that the evangelist was able to draw upon such traditional material in the narrative parts of his gospel, and it is probable that most of this information he had already learnt in Palestine. He knows for example that John was baptising at Bethany beyond Jordan (i 28) and later at Aenon near to Salim (iii 23), that Andrew and Peter, like Philip, came from Bethsaida (i 44), and he links two healings with the pool of Bethesda (v 2) and the pool of Siloam (ix 7) respectively. It was only in Palestinian tradition that such detailed localisation of events would be of general interest and importance.

Even where his narratives are closely parallel to those in Mark and Luke it is possible to explain the verbal similarities by the dependence on a Palestinian tradition which had become largely stereotyped in form. Thus the phrase in the healing at Bethesda, ' Arise, take up thy bed, and walk ' (v 8) is very close to Mk. ii 9, and the result is described in the next verses in very similar words to those used in Mk. ii 12, but such verbal similarities are to be expected in oral tradition, and can be found in other places where literary dependence is unlikely (cf. Lk. xiv 3-4a with Mk. iii 4).

In two places the parallelism of the fourth gospel with Mark is of special interest and importance. In John vi a series of events is narrated—the Feeding of the Five Thousand, the Journey across the Lake, the Walking on the Water, the Demand for a Sign, and a Controversy with the Jews—in an order and in language reminiscent of that of both Mark's parallel cycles (vi 30-viii 26, cf. pp. 36, 56). It has been argued that the fourth evangelist is indebted to both accounts, which appear to be variants of the same tradition, and that he must therefore have found them already combined in Mark. It seems more probable, however, that he is dependent on another version of the same events, which gives at least one piece of valuable additional information (cf. Jn. vi 15), and that he is here reproducing, perhaps from memory, a tradition which he has learnt in Palestine. The Anointing in Jn. xii 1-8 is also very close verbally to that in Mk. xiv 3-9, and in a lesser degree to that of Lk. vii 36-39. Both John and Mark use the rare phrase 'pistic nard', the meaning of which is uncertain, and agree in giving the value of the ointment at (Mk. more than) 300 pence, and the language of their versions is at times very similar (cf. Jn. xii 7-8 with Mk. xiv 6-8). John also shows remarkable similarities with Luke, e.g. in the anointing of the feet, and the woman wiping Jesus' feet with her hair. Yet to say that in this one place in his gospel the fourth evangelist was careful to compare Mark and Luke and adopt phrases from each, while at the same time making important changes in the story on his own account, is to solve the problem by creating even greater difficulties. It is simpler and perhaps more reasonable to assume that here, too, John is drawing on the oral Palestinian tradition from which both Mark and Luke probably derived their accounts.

There are other passages in the fourth gospel where a similar dependence is visible upon Palestinian tradition also employed by Luke. John knows of Mary and Martha (xi 1, 5, etc.) but what he has to tell of them is very different from Luke's isolated account (Lk. x 38 ff.) ; John and Luke agree in many details of the Passion and Resurrection, e.g. Jn. xiii 2, Lk. xxii 3, John xiii 38, Lk. xxii 34, Jn. xviii 10, Lk. xxii 50, Jn. xix 41, Lk. xxiii 53, Jn. xx 12, Lk. xxiv 4, but they also differ widely in their accounts, as would be natural if they both drew much of their material from the tradition of different communities at different times.

The case for the fourth evangelist's use of other gospels must be considered not proven. One argument, however, remains in its favour. How did the fourth evangelist come to write a 'gospel' which preserves substantially the same shape as that of Mark if he had not himself read Mark. It is possible that he had heard of the existence of Mark's gospel without ever having seen it himself, or that he hit independently on a similar literary form which preserved the structure of some earlier oral form of 'Life of Jesus', but it must be admitted that the problem remains.

If the task of distinguishing the narrative sources of the fourth gospel is beset with difficulties, that of disentangling from the discourses sayings which come from the apostle, sayings which come from tradition, and the evangelist's own meditations, is even more difficult—and often quite impossible.

The gospel does in fact contain a considerable number of sayings which find parallels in the synoptic gospels, and which must rest on good tradition, some of them perhaps on apostolic witness, e.g. v 47 (cf. Lk. xvi 31), xiii 16 and xv 20 (cf. Mt. x 24, Lk. vi 40), xv 14 (cf. Mk. iii 35). To these may be added many of the short aphoristic sayings, which have no close parallel in the other gospels, but are in accord with their general account of Jesus' teaching, e.g. ii 19, iii 3, iv 48, viii 51, ix 41, xiii 35.

If the apostle is ultimately responsible for some of the narrative material concerned with the Passion, it may be that some of the sayings in this part of the gospel come from him, especially those which are connected with the questions of apostles, e.g. xii 23 f., xiv 2-11, 21-23. But the editorial work of the evangelist in xii-xiv is so manifest that little can be built on this.

Some scholars would defend the substantial authenticity of many continuous sections of the discourse, e.g. in the 'rabbinical' arguments vii 15-24, viii 16-19, x 24-38, but for the most part the discourses must be considered as artificially built up around genuine words of Jesus, in an attempt to give what the evangelist considered a right interpretation of some aspect of his teaching as a whole.

THE VALUE OF THE GOSPEL

It is on the value of these interpretations of the evangelist that much of the value of the gospel depends. That the gospel has preserved details of great historical worth in its narrative is certain, and although its framework supplements rather than replaces that of Mark, it makes plain much of what is obscure in Mark and the other gospels. The account of the ministry in Judaea and Jerusalem is particularly valuable here. At the same time the tradition on which the evangelist relies is at times defective, e.g. in his account of John the Baptist, and the placing of the Temple-cleansing at the beginning of the ministry.

The miracles recorded in the gospel follow the same general pattern as in the synoptic gospels, although the tendency of the evangelist to use them as a peg for a controversy or discourse introduces a further artificial element into his gospel. There are parallels in the synoptic gospels to the Healing of the Nobleman's Son (iv 46-54, cf. the Centurion's Servant, Mt. viii 5-10, Lk. vii 1-10), the Feeding of the Five Thousand (vi 4-13, cf. Mk. vi 35-43, viii 1-9 and parallels), and the Healings of the Impotent Man and of the Blind Man (v 2-9, ix 1-7 ; the synoptic parallels are here not so close), and the fourth evangelist appears to be drawing on a tradition similar to that used by Mark and Luke. In all these stories there is probably a sub-stratum of truth, but the pointing of the moral in Jn. v 10-47, vi 26-58, ix 8-41 appears to be the evangelist's own interpretation of the events.

In the story of the Raising of Lazarus the problem becomes even more acute. The miracle itself may come from tradition, as the Turning of the Water into Wine at Cana (ii 1-11) probably does, although neither miracle is recorded in the synoptic gospels. Yet in neither case is it easy to accept the miracle as based on a true happening, and the peculiar significance attached to the Raising of Lazarus in the gospel would seem to be at least in large part built up from the imagination of the evangelist himself.

The conversations with Nicodemus and the Samaritan Woman betray a similar incongruity. Nicodemus is told of the necessity of baptism with the spirit (iii 5) at a time when the spirit was not yet given (vii 39), and Jesus' open declaration of his Messiahship to the Samaritan Woman (iv 26) is in conflict with Mark's account of his refusal to avow himself as the Christ in the early stages of his ministry.

Both these discourses, and possibly their settings, appear to be constructed by the evangelist as a means of giving his interpretation of Jesus' teaching on Rebirth and the Universality of the Religion of the Spirit.

In assessing the value of the evangelist's interpretations of Jesus' teaching it is necessary to take into account three influences which have been united in the evangelist's mind, the sayings of Jesus as he received them, the interpretations of Jesus' relationship to God and of his teaching which were known to the evangelist through apostolic and early Christian tradition, and the influence which was exerted upon his mind by the acquaintance with Jewish, and particularly Hellenistic Jewish thought of the period. It is the fusion of these three elements in his representation of Jesus' life and teaching that makes it a matter of the greatest difficulty to distinguish in any particular discourse between what rests upon a deep understanding of the true meaning of Jesus' actual words and what is read into them in the light both of experience and of preconceived ideas as what the Word of God should fittingly proclaim.

It is possible to say that much of what the gospel says about Jesus' filial consciousness is interpretation built upon a few sayings of Jesus (e.g. Mt. xi 27, Lk. x 22), but Christian tradition from the earliest period has accepted the essential truth of this. In his representation of Jesus' teaching on Eternal Life and on Judgement the fourth evangelist disagrees with much of the teaching of the primitive Church and even with some of the teachings ascribed to Jesus in the synoptic gospels, but that his account is based on a fuller understanding of the real teaching of Jesus seems clear (cf. p. 255). The sacramental teaching of the gospel, on the other hand, while much of it certainly reflects the experience of early Christians, seems, in comparison with the rest of the New Testament evidence, to be only partially based on the teaching of the Jesus of history. The interpretation given of Jesus as the Logos in the Prologue is confessedly interpretation, and interpretation influenced by the intellectual thought of Hellenistic Judaism, but at the same time one justified by the belief of the Church in Jesus' Sonship.

As a historical document the fourth gospel will always be differently assessed by different scholars. As an interpretation of the meaning of the gospel story it will always have a special and inestimable value of its own.

CHAPTER XI

THE LIFE OF JESUS

THE LIMITATIONS OF OUR KNOWLEDGE

FOR the facts of Jesus' life and the words of his teaching we are almost entirely dependent on the four gospels and a few allusions in Acts and the epistles. The references to Jesus in pagan and Jewish writings of the first and second centuries A.D. do little more than confirm that he really lived, was put to death under Pontius Pilate (so Tacitus, *Annales*, xv 44), and was recognised by those who believed in him as the Christ.

This comparative silence of non-Christian writers is easily explained. It took a considerable time for the Christian impact upon pagan civilisation to become seriously felt in literary circles; Tacitus (*c.* A.D. 116) mentioned Jesus only in connection with Nero's attempt to fasten the responsibility of the Fire of Rome in A.D. 64 upon the unpopular Christians, and Josephus, who as a Jew might have been expected to have some knowledge of Jesus, considered the Christian sect of such little importance that his only reference to Jesus comes in a statement that James, who was killed by the Jews *c.* A.D. 63 was ' the brother of Jesus, who was called Christ' (Josephus, *Antiquities*, xx, ix, 1, *c.* A.D. 95).[1] The devastation of Palestine in the Jewish revolts of A.D. 66-73 and 132-135, followed as they were by the imposition of a tight religious censorship by the Pharisaic-Rabbinic school which thereafter dominated Jewish thought, has left little available information about Jesus from Jewish sources, except for a handful of hostile references, mostly of doubtful interpretation.

---

[1] A passage in Josephus, *Ant.* xviii, iii, 3, which mentions Jesus' ministry, his death under Pontius Pilate, and his resurrection, is open to the suspicion of being a Christian interpolation in the original text.

The evidence of Christian writings outside the New Testament is not much more helpful. Fragments have survived of a number of 'apocryphal' gospels, written in the second or succeeding centuries, which purport to record the infancy and childhood of Jesus or to rewrite the gospel story in fuller detail; but a cursory examination of these is sufficient to expose the doctrinal motives or legend-loving piety which have led to the invention of these details. Only in a few sayings which have survived from these gospels, from collections found in Egyptian rubbish-heaps, and from the main stream of Christian tradition, does the authentic ring of Jesus' voice sometimes make itself felt. Perhaps the best known of such sayings occurs in a third century papyrus found at Oxyrhyncus :

> Wheresoever there are two, they are not without God : and where there is one alone I say I am with him. Lift up the stone and there shalt thou find me : cleave the wood, and I am there.

Within the New Testament the occasional references of Paul to the details of Jesus' life and teaching are of great interest and importance, e.g. 1 Cor. vii 10, ix 14, Gal. i 19, iv 4, 1 Thess. iv 15, and above all his allusions to the Last Supper, 1 Cor. xi 23-25, and to the Resurrection Appearances, 1 Cor. xv 3-8. For the teaching of Jesus the epistle of James has a special significance (cf. p. 167), and for the outline of the ministry the speeches in Acts, e.g. x 37-42, have a certain value. The teaching of Acts and the epistles as a whole provides valuable evidence for the spirit of the teaching of Jesus which his followers wished to pass on to new converts. Yet it is to the four gospels that we must turn for the great bulk of our information.

What has already been said in the preceding chapters about the gospels and their sources makes it clear that even their evidence needs careful assessment before it can be used for reconstructing the life of the historical Jesus. In the first place the gospels can no longer be considered as fully apostolic in the traditional sense. Behind them lie sources, some of which may well contain the reminiscences of Matthew, Peter, and John, but these sources have been edited and the gospels given their final form by men of a later generation who had not themselves known Jesus in the flesh. The student who seeks for historical truth must be content to accept the gibe of Monsignor Knox :

> Twelve prophets our unlearn'd forefathers knew.
> We scarce are satisfied with twenty-two—
> They were content Mark, Matthew, Luke and John
> Should bless th' old-fashion'd beds they lay upon :
> But we, for ev'ry one of theirs have two,
> And trust the watchfulness of blessed Q.[1]

In the second place it must be admitted that the gospels, written as they were to confirm and instruct Christian faith by authors who were themselves zealous Christians, show a tendency to distort the facts in the interest of Christian apologetic. The historical motive is inextricably intertwined with that of edification, and it is impossible in many incidents and sayings recorded in the gospels to know how much was said or done by Jesus and how much has been added in the tradition.

The difficulties to which these deficiencies of the gospels give rise are many and serious. For the birth and infancy of Jesus we have only the first two chapters of Matthew and Luke to guide us, for the period of his boyhood and early manhood only a single story in Luke of his visit to the Temple when he was twelve years old (Lk. ii 41-52). For the period of his ministry we have no comprehensive and worked-out scheme, but merely a number of incidents and discourses loosely knit together with a minimum of chronological framework. Only for the last week in Jerusalem have we a day to day account of Jesus' activities, culminating in the detailed descriptions of his trial and crucifixion. Of the resurrection appearances enumerated by Paul some only are described in the gospels.

Not only are the gospel-narratives extremely limited in their extent, but they are often conflicting and some of them

---

[1] R. A. Knox, *Essays in Satire*, p. 87.

artificially constructed. It is impossible satisfactorily to reconcile the birth and infancy narratives of Luke and Matthew, and in both gospels the true story seems to have been overlaid with a considerable amount of legendary material. The ignoring of the Judaean ministry in Mark and the concentration upon this period of the ministry in John serve to show the limited sources available to each evangelist; the plan of the ministry in both gospels is to some extent artificially constructed, that in Mark by the grouping together of controversies, that in John to suit the dramatic purposes of the evangelist. We cannot know how far the divergences between the resurrection-narratives in the different gospels are due to imperfect knowledge and how far to deliberate selection, but it seems clear that developments in the tradition and editorial work have both in part obscured the original experiences of the apostles.

The tendency at work in the resurrection-narratives to demonstrate in ever more striking and external manifestations the divinity of Jesus finds its counterpart within the earthly ministry itself, especially in the accounts of miracles and in the claims put into Jesus' mouth. This is not to deny that Jesus really did work miracles of healing or that he knew himself to be in a unique sense the Son of God, but a comparison of Mark with Matthew and John show a continual tendency in the later gospels to heighten the miraculous and to magnify the evidences of his Godhead. Even in Mark we have reason to believe that this process has gone some distance already and that the nature-miracles, for example, are the invention of early Christians or the distortion into miracles of what originally was not miraculous, e.g. the feeding of the multitude.

Side by side with this eagerness to multiply proofs of Jesus' divinity went the willingness to reinforce his claim to be the Christ by putting into his mouth, or into that of others (cf. Mt. iii 14, Jn. i 36), unequivocal statements of his Sonship. While it is impossible in most cases to speak with certainty, and it cannot reasonably be denied that Jesus did claim to be the Christ, the tendency of the tradition

to multiply his claims must also be admitted. A further
distortion of the facts arose from the reading back into Jesus'
mouth of what had become incorporated in Church teaching
out of ecclesiastical needs, the reading of Jewish apocalypses,
and the meditation of Christians on actual words of Jesus.
Examples of the way in which the practical problems of the
Church altered the gospel-record of Jesus' teaching have
been given above (p. 32 on Divorce, p. 72 on Excommuni-
cation), and the ascription to Jesus, e.g. in Mk. xiii, of much
that is really drawn from Jewish apocalyptic ideas is discussed on pp. 249, 253; that much of the discourse-material
in John represents the reflections of the evangelist upon
Jesus' life and teaching rather than the *ipsissima verba* of
Jesus is manifest, as can be seen, e.g. in the conversation
with Nicodemus, Jn. iii 3-21, where Jesus tells Nicodemus
to be born of water and the Spirit, although ' the Spirit was
not yet given ' (Jn. vii 39) and the last verses of the discourse
are clearly the evangelist's own interpretation of Jesus'
mission on earth.

The defects of the gospels as historical material for the
life and teaching of Jesus are certainly very great. But
criticism of the gospels has positive as well as negative results
to offer. Although the gospels in their present form are not
eye-witness accounts of Jesus, some of the sources on which
they are based are of high historical value. It has been
suggested above (pp. 58-62), that the general plan of Mark
preserves a trustworthy, though incomplete account of the
chief stages of the ministry, such as Peter may well have
narrated, and that much of the historical framework of John
goes back to early Palestinian tradition, some of it at least
possibly to the apostle John himself. Even though it is
impossible fully to disentangle these sources from the surrounding material and from the editorial revisions to which
they have been subjected, we are enabled to reconstruct a
broad outline of Jesus' activity which is intelligible in itself
and has a solid claim to represent what actually happened.
For filling in this outline many of the incidents related in
the gospels, especially in Mark and Luke, may be accepted

as historically reliable, but not inerrant, versions of what took place. For the teaching of Jesus the material of Q and much of the discourse-material of Matthew are of first-class value, with a strong claim to represent in substance what the apostles had recalled of Jesus' words : these sources supplement, and occasionally correct the somewhat scanty teaching material in Mark and help to establish some parts of the discourses in John as representing what Jesus himself had said.

By concentration on what appear to be the best and most nearly apostolic sources behind the gospels we can obtain a firm nucleus of material, consistent in itself and adequate both for giving us a rough sketch of Jesus' ministry and teaching, and for checking the value of the material drawn from other sources. This material in turn can then be used in part for filling out the picture in more detail with occasional aid from the epistles.

It remains true that a life of Jesus in the normal sense can never be written. The earliest Christians were too concerned with the urgency of their message about the risen Christ to set down in writing any detailed record of what Jesus had said and done during his time on earth. What they did hand on in their preaching was all related to their proclamation of his saving power, a confirmation by illustration of what he had taught on particular subjects, his mighty works, his conflicts with authority, and a connected account only of the last days in Jerusalem, his crucifixion, and his resurrection. When at last the gospels came to be written the apostles were no longer available to help the final authors in their historical task. The shape and form of our gospels was conditioned both by the difficulty of finding full material and by the bias that had been acquired by such material as was available.

Given these limitations, however, we can still gain a picture in broad detail of the course of Jesus' ministry and of the main themes of his teaching, which, if not of guaranteed accuracy in every particular, yet preserves a generally truthful likeness of Jesus as he came to men in Palestine nineteen hundred years ago. It is the likeness of a man consistent in his teaching and in his actions, who claimed to be the Christ of God. What we can know of him as he lived on earth agrees with the Christian claim that the Christ of apostolic faith was in truth before his resurrection the Jesus of history.

THE COURSE OF THE MINISTRY

The birth of Jesus is recorded in Matthew and Luke, but with differing detail and a wealth of legend, whose full extent is difficult to determine. Many critics would reject even the placing of the birth at Bethlehem, as a Christian attempt to satisfy the prophecy of Micah v 2, and the tracing of his descent from David as a similar attempt to satisfy Messianic tradition (contrast Jesus' use of Ps. cx 2 in Mk. xii 35-37). Of the first thirty years (Lk. iii 23) of his life we know little more than that he was brought up at Nazareth as a carpenter, the reputed son of Joseph and his wife Mary, with brothers, James, Joses, Judas, Simon, and sisters (Mk. vi 3). It is only with his baptism by John and the beginning of his ministry that it becomes possible to take up the story in any detail.

1 The Chronology and Duration of the Ministry

Luke fixes the beginning of John the Baptist's preaching ' in the fifteenth year of the reign of Tiberius Caesar ', probably to be reckoned as A.D. 28-29 ; in Jn. ii 20 allusion is made to the fact that the Temple has been in course of building for forty-six years, and as we know from Josephus that Herod the Great began to rebuild the Temple in 20-19 B.C., the date given would appear to be A.D. 27 or 28. It would seem therefore not unlikely that the beginning of Jesus' ministry is to be dated from late in A.D. 27 or early in A.D. 28, although allowance must be made for the possible error of a year or two either way. The date given for the crucifixion must largely depend on the view taken of the length of the ministry. Pontius Pilate was procurator of Judaea from A.D. 26-36, and Caiaphas seems to have held the office of high priest from A.D. 18-36. Attempts have been made to discover in which of these years the 14th Nisan, the day before the Passover, when, according to John, Jesus was crucified, fell on a Friday, but none of the calculations which have been made have been generally accepted as decisive.

The duration of the ministry cannot be established with certainty. The ' green grass ' of Mk. vi 39 suggests springtime,[1] and would involve a period of at least a year before the crucifixion, also in the springtime. John's narrative includes references to three successive passovers, ii 13, vi 4, xi 55, but the first of these is linked with the Cleansing of the Temple which Mark with more probability puts in the final week at Jerusalem. The choice seems to lie between a ministry of rather over one year, and one of two or three years; on the whole the balance of probability is in favour of the shorter period. The plan of Mark's gospel may be accepted as generally accurate within its limits, but Mark has passed over a preliminary period of the ministry in Judaea, and has given a very summary account of the period between Jesus' final departure from Galilee and the last days in Jerusalem. It is possible to dovetail into this account most of John's extra material, and some of Luke's, in such a way as to produce a connected narrative covering the main stages of the ministry and occupying some 15-18 months. These stages, and their approximate dates, may be tabulated as follows :

A.D. 27 Winter	Jesus' Baptism and Temptation, and a period of activity in Judaea and Samaria.
A.D. 28 Early Spring	John is arrested, and Jesus begins his Galilean ministry.
Early Summer	The climax of his popular success, and the Feeding of the 5,000.

[1] The plucking of ears of corn, Mk. ii 23, cannot be stressed as affording a clue to the season of the year at the beginning of the ministry. Mark seems here to have collected material, some of which, at least, may originally have had a different context (cf. p. 57).

Summer	Growing Hostility of the Authorities. Herod's suspicions are aroused and Jesus leaves Galilee for the borders of Tyre and Sidon and Decapolis.
Late Summer	Jesus returns to Galilee in secret, and leaves it for the last time.
Autumn	Jesus is in Jerusalem for the Feast of Tabernacles.
Winter	Jesus retires across the Jordan after the Feast of the Dedication, and later removes to a remote district of Judaea.
A.D. 29 Spring	Jesus makes his triumphal entry into Jerusalem, is arrested, tried, and crucified.

Such a reconstruction must inevitably contain speculative elements, but raises fewer difficulties than most alternatives. It is used as the basis for the more detailed account of the ministry below.

2 The Beginning of the Ministry in Judaea

The baptism of Jesus by John and his temptation in the wilderness were the prelude to his own active ministry. Mark has preserved an account of the baptism (Mk. i 9-12) and Q an account of the Temptation (Mt. iv 3-10, Lk. iv 3-12) which contain interpretations of these events such as Jesus may well have himself given to his disciples at a later stage of his ministry, although the actual wording of both accounts has been moulded in Christian tradition. It is significant that the revelation of God at the baptism in Mark's account is to Jesus alone, and that there is no sign of any recognition of Jesus by John as in later accounts, e.g. Mt. iii 14, Jn. i 29. That John recognised Jesus at his baptism as ' he that should come ' appears to be ruled out by his later enquiry from prison (Q, Mt. xi 2-3, Lk. vii 18-19).

John the Baptist had appeared in Judaea prophesying the imminence of divine judgement, and proclaiming himself the unworthy forerunner of one mightier than himself who would have power to save and to destroy. He exhorted men to undergo a baptism of repentance in Jordan, and to bring forth fruits worthy of repentance. His message was a continuation of that of the Old Testament prophets, and his practice of baptism as an initiation into the community of those who would be saved seems to have been derived from such passages as Is. i 16-17, Ezek. ix 4-6, xxxvi 24-26. Josephus (*Ant.* xviii 5, 2) confirms the gospel accounts of the great enthusiasm kindled by John, and tells of his arrest and later execution by Herod as the potential leader of a rebellion, but does not repeat Mark's story of Salome's dance, which is probably only a popular fiction.

Jesus found in John's preaching, imperfect as he saw it to be (Q, Mt. xi 7-11, Lk. vii 24-28) the preparation for himself and his own greater mission, and recognised in John the Elijah redivivus of Mal. iv 5-6 who was his own forerunner (Mk. ix 11-13). He underwent the baptism of John in recognition of this and received in a spiritual experience associated with the baptism a confirmation of his Sonship (Mk. i 10-11). Whether this experience marked a development in Jesus' thought we cannot tell : a variant reading of the voice at the baptism in Luke is, ' Thou art my beloved son ; this day have I begotten thee ', and some scholars hold that this may be the original reading and may even be derived from Q; on the other hand this variant may be due only to assimilation with Ps. ii 7. Jesus seems, at any rate, to have found in his baptism the impulse to begin his own ministry.

His first step was to withdraw into solitude for a period —the ' forty days ' of the gospels are only a conventional figure—in which to prepare himself by physical fasting and the meeting of mental temptation. Although the Q account of the Temptation has been ' materialised ' and cast in the form of a biblical-quotation match, it preserves the substance of the internal conflict which Jesus in his humanity must have faced before he finally committed himself to the supreme task.

For the beginnings of Jesus' active ministry we are

dependent on the early chapters of John, where the evangelist's narrative is confused and highly-coloured. He portrays scenes at Bethany beyond Jordan, without actually mentioning Jesus' baptism, followed by a short visit to Galilee, a visit to Jerusalem, missionary activity by Jesus and his disciples in Judaea, a journey through Samaria to Galilee, another visit to Jerusalem, and a return once more to Galilee and the eastern side of the lake. The account includes elements of doubtful historical worth; thus the cleansing of the Temple is associated with the first visit to Jerusalem, ii 13 ff., and the testimony borne to Jesus both by John and by himself betrays the hand of the author of the gospel. Yet there may well be a nucleus of truth in the description of Jesus' call of some of his disciples for the first time from among those who had come to hear John, and in the description of Jesus and his disciples as active in Judaea for a time before returning to Galilee through Samaria. It is possible, too, that the fourth evangelist is correct in depicting Jesus' disciples as baptising during this stage of the ministry until they found themselves in competition with John and withdrew to Galilee (iii 22-iv 3); such a practice would help to explain their adoption of an altered rite of baptism after the resurrection (Acts ii 38). For Jesus' teaching at this time the fourth evangelist, with his concern to emphasise Jesus' divinity, is not a safe guide; it seems more likely that Jesus began with a message closely akin to John's, such as Mark records he proclaimed in the first days of his Galilean ministry (Mk. i 14-15), and that he did not publish abroad, except in a veiled way, his own Sonship.

3 The First Days of the Galilean Ministry

Mark portrays Jesus as coming into Galilee and beginning his ministry only after John's arrest (Mk. i 14), and it may be that Jesus did in a sense make a fresh start then, after an interval during which the disciples had returned to their homes. This would explain the instant response to his renewed call of Peter and Andrew (Mk. i 16-18).

For a period of some months Jesus went about Galilee, especially in the districts and villages near the sea of Galilee, preaching in the synagogues and in the open air, performing miraculous healings, and gathering about him a little company of close disciples.   The content of his teaching was in some ways similar to that of John, the imminence of the Kingdom of God and the need for men to repent, but there were also significant differences.   He was no less stern than John in his description of the penalties of sin, but his message was fundamentally one of good news and of the rewards that God offers to men.   This note of joy was particularly associated with the position which he assumed himself and which he emphasised in his teaching.   He not only performed healings and exorcisms and spoke with authority (Mk. i 22), but he emphasised his own rôle in calling men to salvation (Mk. ii 17), and even claimed the power to forgive sins (Mk. ii 5).   This assumption of authority, coupled as it was with wonder-working powers and with the disregard of traditional religious customs when they conflicted with the doing of good (e.g. Mk. ii 16, iii 2), impressed the majority of his hearers (Mk. ii 12, iii 7-9) but also aroused the hostility of others, especially the religious leaders (Mk. ii 6, iii 6).   His relatives thought he was ' beside himself ' (Mk. iii 21), scribes from Jerusalem that he was possessed by Beelzebub (Mk. iii 22), and a visit with his disciples to his own village was a comparative failure because of the unwillingness of those who knew him and his family to accept his authority (Mk. vi 1-6).

Mark and the other gospels give us only short glimpses of this phase of Jesus' ministry, and we can reconstruct only a rough pattern of the course of events.   Two incidents, however, stand out as of special importance, the Mission of Jesus' disciples and the Feeding of the Five Thousand.

It is clear that from the beginning Jesus distinguished between the crowds of hearers, drawn by every kind of motive, and an inner band of disciples who had left all and followed him (Mk. x 28).   To the outer circle he presented himself as a healer and as one who spoke with authority, but often in riddles; thus he spoke of himself as ' the Son of Man ' (e.g. Mk. ii 10 ; Q, Mt. xii 39, 40b, Lk. xi 29, 30), a term which could be interpreted either as ' a man ' or in the celestial sense of the ' son of man ' in Dan. vii 13, and he spoke of the Kingdom of God for the most part in parables, which he explained only for his close disciples (Mk. iv 10-12). How far Mk. iv 10-12 correctly interpret Jesus' motives for so teaching is disputed, but it is clear that Jesus, for all the urgency of his message, did not want half-hearted followers (Q, Mt. viii 19-21, Lk. ix 57-60) and sought also, without abating his claim to authority, to avoid the acceptance of men's allegiance to him based on wrong motives. Even to the inner band of disciples he seems to have revealed his message at this stage only in part, training them first for the task of spreading to all the neighbouring region the imminence of the coming of the kingdom and the need for repentance (Mk. vi 7-13 ; Q, Lk. x 3-12).

This mission had a double purpose : it was not only for the training of the disciples, but for challenging with his good news as many people as possible before the growing hostility of the authorities should make Jesus' own public activity difficult and dangerous. The picture which Mark gives of the rising tide of opposition rings true : he mentions first the offence taken by local scribes (ii 6), then the opposition of Pharisees who consult with Herodians (the meaning of this name is obscure, but it implies some sort of connection with Herod Antipas, the ruler of Galilee) how to destroy him (iii 6) ; scribes come down from Jerusalem to investigate (iii 22) and show themselves equally hostile, and later, during the mission of the Twelve, Herod himself hears of Jesus' activity and success (vi 14).

The feeding of the multitude is described twice over by Mark, and once by John, with the added and significant detail of the crowd's attempt to make Jesus king (Jn. vi 15, cf. p. 91). The gospel accounts of the feeding represent it as miraculous, but this is probably the work of Christian tradition, and of many possible interpretations the most

likely is, perhaps, that Jesus in some way anticipated the
ceremony of the Last Supper in a ' sacramental ' meal.   The
effect, however, was to heighten the popular belief in Jesus
as a potential leader with divine authority who might fulfil
traditional hopes of a warrior king.   Jesus managed to
escape from the crowds and to reach the western side of the
lake only to be met with the demand for a sign (Mk. viii
11-13) based on the same misconception of his claims, but
this time from his enemies.   To avoid the inevitable results
of such misguided popular enthusiasm, Jesus left Galilee
with his disciples and abandoned for a time his public
preaching.

4 The Journey in the North and the Later Judaean Ministry

Mark has recorded a journey of Jesus with his disciples
' into the borders of Tyre and Sidon ' during which he
sought to keep himself from public attention (vii 24),
and speaks of him as then coming ' through Sidon unto the
Sea of Galilee, through the midst of the borders of Decapolis '
(vii 31).   There are difficulties in interpreting this last
sentence (cf. p. 60), but it seems probable that Jesus did
in fact travel through the country to the north and east of
Galilee, in his determination to avoid the political enthusiasm of the Galilean crowds and conflict with Herod's
government, and that he devoted himself at this time
especially to further private training of his disciples.

What form this training took we can only guess, but
Mark places here the scene ' in the way ' near Caesarea
Philippi, to the north-east of the Lake of Galilee, where
Jesus asked his disciples who they thought him to be, and
Peter answered, ' Thou art the Christ ' (Mk. viii 27-29, cf.
Jn. vi 66-70).   It seems clear that Jesus had so far made
no claim to this title, and that his teaching about himself
and the kingdom had largely avoided terms liable to misunderstanding in a political sense, especially after the feeding
of the multitude.   The Marcan narrative represents him
as neither accepting nor rejecting the title, but as at once

foretelling his own suffering and resurrection. The historicity of these verses has been attacked by many critics on the ground that Jesus did not yet foresee his death, but thought of the coming of God's kingdom on earth in the immediate future. The rebuke to Peter, however, ' Get thee behind me, Satan : for thou mindest not the things of God, but the things of men ' (viii 33), is couched in terms which can hardly be the product of later Christian tradition, and have every appearance of being in substance derived from Peter himself.

While Peter's confession marks a stage in the disciples' understanding of Jesus, their comprehension remained imperfect. Convinced more than ever of his divine authority they continued to interpret this in terms of their own background of thought; a suffering Messiah was something unheard of and almost impossible for them to believe. That the human Jesus was from God, and, in the light of his claims about himself, the Messiah, they were quite sure, but because of his humanity they apparently thought that he might not himself yet fully understand how he was to achieve God's purpose. It is probable, for example, that Mark has correctly placed late in the ministry the request of James and John for seats on Jesus' right hand and left hand in his ' glory ' (Mk. x 35 ff., cf. ix 33 ff.).

Jesus now entered upon the final Judaean phase of his ministry, passing through Galilee as secretly as possible (Mk. ix 30) and coming ' into the borders of Judaea and beyond Jordan ' (Mk. x 1). Mark has foreshortened this stage in his narrative, and regard Jesus' journey as leading up to his final visit to Jerusalem (x 32, 46, xi 1), but, if we follow John's account, Jesus seems to have visited Jerusalem for the Feast of the Tabernacles in the autumn (vii 2, 14), to have preached publicly, and to have encountered opposition (vii 32, viii 59, x 39) which led him to retire once again beyond Jordan (x 40) and later to a small village, Ephraim (xi 54), some fifteen miles north-west of Jericho.

John pictures Jesus as gathering round him at this period many who ' believed on him ' (x 42), and a period of public preaching during the winter would account for some of the details in the Marcan account of the final entry into Jerusalem from Jericho, which represents Jesus as accompanied by a number of followers (x 46, xi 8), convinced of his Messiahship (x 47, xi 9).

5 The Last Days in Jerusalem

The gospels agree in representing Jesus as entering Jerusalem a few days before the Passover, surrounded by enthusiastic supporters who expected the speedy coming of the Kingdom of God (Mk. xi 10, Lk. xix 38, Jn. xii 13) and recognised Jesus as ' coming in the name of the Lord '. They portray the general interest and excitement (e.g. Mk. xii 35, Jn. xii 18, 20-21), such as the cleansing of the Temple, placed here by Mark, would have stimulated to fever pitch, and the determination of the religious leaders to arrest him as a dangerous impostor (Mk. xiv 1-2; Jn. xi 48, 53). The substance of this is clearly historical. Jesus, by his acceptance of popular support and by his assumption of authority at a time when Jerusalem was packed with pilgrims, had delivered a direct challenge to the chief priests and the scribes.

A quiet arrest, without the risk of a popular tumult (Mk. xiv 2) was achieved by the treachery of Judas, which seems to have consisted in the betrayal of the whereabouts of Jesus on Thursday night. It is at least possible that Jesus' nightly withdrawals from the city (Mk. xi 19) and the signal for finding the room where the last supper was to be held (Mk. xiv 13) were part of a plan to postpone his capture. The arrest achieved, and the disciples dispersed, the authorities hurried on the trials. The details of these are obscure, as there is considerable divergence between the accounts of Mark, Luke, and John, but two points stand out. In the trial before Pilate the charge was that of claiming to be the King of the Jews, in effect a charge of treason. Such an accusation could only have been made on the basis of a claim by Jesus to have Messianic authority, and

Mark, for all the difficulties presented by his narrative of the trial before the high priest, is almost certainly right in making the high priest ask, 'Art thou the Christ, the Son of the Blessed'? and Jesus admit the charge.

The sentence was carried out immediately. After scourging, Jesus was led outside the city and nailed to a cross at nine o'clock in the morning in company with two thieves; by three o'clock in the afternoon he was dead.

6 *The Resurrection*

That Jesus rose from the dead and appeared over a period of time to some of the disciples is the belief of Christians, and was the decisive factor which led to the growth of the Christian Church by giving a new and fuller meaning to the events of his earthly life. Paul in 1 Cor. xv 3 ff. gives a list of resurrection-appearances which he had received from tradition, and says that they began 'on the third day', but gives no description of these appearances other than what is implied by the inclusion of his own sight of Christ in the list. The accounts in the gospels have some strange omissions, e.g. the first appearance to Peter and that to James, and they contain many difficulties. Even among Christians there is no general agreement as to the form of the appearances, and a critical examination of the evidence can do little more than establish certain tendencies within the early Christian tradition about the resurrection.

Matthew's account seems to mirror a late and developed form of Christian belief, where the original experiences have been converted into formalised external manifestations with legendary additions, such as the placing of the guard and the earthquake (xxvii 62-xxviii 4, 11-15). It is possible that even Mark's description of the angelic appearance and the empty tomb (xvi 4-6) represents an earlier stage of such a development, and that Paul's silence about the empty tomb may indicate that this detail was no part of the original Christian belief in Jesus' resurrection. Yet

8

it is by no means certain that Paul's silence is to be thus interpreted, any more than it can be assumed that Paul's silence and the accounts in Acts of his own vision of Christ on the Damascus road rule out the physical nature of the appearances. Mark's hints at a Galilean appearance, Luke's description of appearances in and around Jerusalem only, and John's mention of appearances both in Jerusalem and Galilee, are best reconciled by the supposition that Jesus appeared to disciples in both regions. Each of these gospels clearly gives only a partial picture, in which the details have already undergone change and expansion, but the evidence which they afford, although circumstantial, gives strong support to the reality of the experience undergone by those to whom the risen Jesus appeared.

THE TEACHING OF JESUS

Perhaps the strongest proof of the reality of the resurrection lies in the implications of the teaching of Jesus as we can recover it from the gospels, and the key which only the resurrection can provide for understanding this teaching. The gospel-picture of Jesus, in Mark no less than in John, shows no sign of a development in Jesus' thought but only of a tactical development of plan. Jesus shows human traits in his physique (Mk. xv 21, Jn. iv 6), and in his emotions (Mk. i 41, iii 5, xiv 35-36, Jn. xi 35); there are limitations to his knowledge (Mk. xiii 32) and to his power (Mk. vi 5); yet there is an inner consistency in his claim to reveal God's will that binds his ministry and teaching into one uniform whole. If he reveals his full teaching only little by little, e.g. in the gradual unfolding of his Messiahship, this is represented in the gospel not as a development or change of his original intention, but as a calculated policy.

This consistency has been denied to Jesus by many critics who would attribute it to a deliberate attempt on the part of Christian tradition to idealise the human Jesus in the light of their knowledge of him as the Christ of experience. It is true that such an idealising tendency can be traced in the gospels, not only in John where it has seriously distorted the presentation of events, but, to a lesser degree, in the synoptic gospels also. On the other hand, the Marcan narrative, in its general outline, has a strong claim to preserve a trustworthy record, and this claim receives a tremendous reinforcement in the body of Jesus' teaching which, with due allowance made for tendencies in its transmission, presents just such a picture of Jesus himself as compels belief in a ministry similar in essentials to that described by Mark.

The fact that this teaching has been preserved for the most part in short incidents and sayings, whose original setting is hard or impossible to determine, brings into relief how much ' of a piece ' it is. That Jesus' thought developed before he started his ministry is in the nature of his humanity; it is possible that in certain aspects it developed under the impacts of the events of the ministry itself; but the underlying conception of his Sonship and of the nature of the kingdom of God and its spiritual demands remain constant, varying only in its adaptation to suit the particular needs of each separate situation.

1 The Background to Jesus' Teaching

There are two ways in which especially the form and expression of Jesus' thoughts were moulded by the circumstances of his earthly life, his study from boyhood of the Old Testament and the necessity of proclaiming his message to a small section of the ancient world where a religion based upon the Old Testament had assumed new and bizarre shapes.

Jesus' deep knowledge of the writings of the Old Testament is abundantly shown in his constant use of them in his teaching. He is represented as frequently quoting from the Law and the Prophets in his controversies, e.g. on the Sabbath (Mk. ii 25 f.) and the Resurrection of the dead (Mk. xii 26), and in his discourses; moreover, the whole of his teaching is permeated with phrases, which, if not direct quotations, yet are reminiscent of the Prophets and the Psalms.

How far this knowledge was based on the private reading of the Old Testament we cannot tell. Jesus does not seem to have undergone regular instruction from scribes (Jn. vii 15), but must have attended the weekly synagogue services, where psalms were sung and passages from the Law and the Prophets read aloud, first in Hebrew and then in the Aramaic of contemporary speech. He himself during his ministry often taught in synagogues (Mk. i 21, vi 2), and Luke describes a sermon at Nazareth which followed Jesus' own reading of Is. lxi 1-2.

To these writings Jesus attributed divine authority, and from them he drew many of the ideas which shaped his thought; his teaching has been aptly described as ' the distilled essence of the Old Testament '. Yet he also transformed what he found. He saw in his mission the fulfilment of the Law and the Prophets (Mt. v 17), but his interpretation of the central profundity of the Old Testament revelation enabled him to set on one side what was only for the hardness of men's hearts (e.g. Mk. x 3-6) or of external significance, e.g. in his revision of the old commandments (Mt. v 21, 27, 33, 38, 43). He employed a vocabulary whose important words and phrases were almost all of Old Testament derivation, but gave to this vocabulary a new and sublimer meaning.

If Jesus' knowledge of the Old Testament shaped his interpretation of his own experience, his immediate environment was also responsible both for forming his thought and for forcing upon him certain methods of approach to those whom he taught. Central to the religion of Jews in first-century Palestine were belief in the one true God, the observance of His Law, and—for the overwhelming majority —the veneration of His Temple, but here general agreement ceased. The Sadducees, a small but influential party, who monopolised the office of High-Priest, held nominally conservative but often sceptical views, rejecting belief in a resurrection and refusing to acknowledge as authoritative the oral tradition which had grown up round the interpretation of the Law. The Pharisees, a more numerous

sect, who counted among their members most of the distinguished scribes, endeavoured to make the Law a more
real guide to daily conduct by a series of traditional interpretations; they believed in a resurrection of the dead, and
some, at least, of them hoped for the coming of the Christ.
Politically they had little power, but as teachers of religion
they played the leading rôle among the people.

Their teaching often contained flashes of great religious
insight, and many of Jesus' utterances can be paralleled
by passages in the Rabbinic writings which often go back to
first-century Pharisaic teachers. Thus Jesus' words on the
Two Great Commandments (Mk. xii 29-31), when he joins
Deut. vi 4-5 to Lev. xix 18, find a partial parallel in the saying
attributed to the Pharisee Hillel (60 B.C.-A.D. 20), ' Do not
to another what thou wouldst not that he should do to thee;
this is the whole law, the rest is commentary '. On the other
hand the Pharisees often seem to have substituted correctness
in external observance for sincerity of motive, and the
denunciation of these traits in the gospels (Mt. xxiii 1-31,
Lk. xi 37-44) is all too clearly based on fact. It is probable
that Jesus learnt much from the Pharisees, with some of
whom he seems to have been on friendly personal terms
(cf. e.g. Lk. xiii 31), both positively from their development
of Old Testament theology and ethics, and negatively from
their failure to live up to their professed beliefs.

One failing of the Pharisees in particular was their
spirit of exclusiveness, and their contempt for the ' am ha
'aretz ', ' the people of the land ', who would not or could
not conform to their rigorous rules of ceremonial purity,
Sabbath observance, and payment of tithes. Probably
the great mass of the population, the peasant cultivators,
fishermen, shopkeepers, tax-collectors, and so on, fell into
this category. They owed no formal allegiance to the
Sadducees or Pharisees, and few of them belonged to the
curious ascetic sect of the Essenes, mentioned by Josephus
as living a separated puritanical existence in many places in
Palestine. It was among the ' people of the land ' for the
most part that Jesus seems to have been brought up, and

it was they who formed the mass of his hearers when he began his ministry.

The religious beliefs of such people varied enormously, but it is clear that for many among them a combination of revolutionary nationalism and crude apocalyptic belief aroused the same enthusiasm as had inspired the Maccabaean revolt two hundred years before. Onerous taxation and the subjugation of the land to the Roman yoke fanned the nationalist spirit, and a series of apocalypses, in which a forthcoming divine intervention in history was forecast in lurid terms, had spread abroad an expectation of God establishing by supernatural means a new order upon earth or in heaven. The apocalypses current at this time which have survived differ widely in the descriptions which they give of the coming world-catastrophe, the means of God's intervention, and the nature of the new age (cf. p. 251). It is probable that the enthusiastically religious Galilean had a very confused picture in his mind of how God was to achieve his will, but he had a very vivid hope that God was about to reveal himself in some way.

For our understanding of the teaching of Jesus this fact has a special importance. Jesus himself must have been acquainted with much apocalyptic expectation, and from it he drew, in a transmuted form, some of the ideas and language which figure so prominently in his teaching, and which he used to lead his hearers from a material and imperfect conception of God's actions to a truer and spiritual understanding of the new age which was to come.

2 The Kingdom of God

Jesus is represented by Mark as beginning his ministry with the message,

> ' The time is fulfilled, and the kingdom of God is at hand : repent ye, and believe in the good news.'

It is clear from the repeated occurrence of the phrase ' kingdom of God ' in Mark and Q as well as in our other gospel sources (Matthew prefers ' kingdom of heaven ' as avoiding the use of the divine name) that this theme was indeed central to Jesus' teaching. He spoke of the kingdom in two quite different ways, which are, at first sight, hard to reconcile. The kingdom is near (Mk. ix 1 : Q, Mt. x 7, Lk. x 9), and it is associated with judgement (Mk. ix 47); it is represented in the form of a banquet (Mk. xiv 25 : Q, Mt. viii 11 f., Lk. xiii 28 f.). It is also present in a spiritual sense (Mk. xii 34, Lk. xvii 20-21, although the meaning of these last verses is not altogether clear), and is portrayed in parables as like seed growing secretly (Mk. iv 26-29), like mustard seed or leaven (Q, Mt. xiii 31-33, Lk. xiii 18-20) : it is the possession of the ' poor ' (Mt. v. 3, Lk. vi 20).

To understand Jesus' teaching here contemporary beliefs are important. The actual phrase ' kingdom of God ' does not occur in Jewish literature before the first century A.D., but the idea of a future kingdom of Israel to be set up by God's will occurs over and over again in the Old Testament (e.g. Jer. xxiii 5, Dan. ii 44), and had come to be particularly, although by no means exclusively, associated with the expectation of a Davidic Messiah who would establish his rule over the Gentiles (Psalms of Solomon xvii 23-38). Jesus' teaching on the kingdom of God undoubtedly raised hopes of such a kingdom being established on earth, especially among his close disciples when they came to see in him the Messiah (Mk. x 37, Lk. xxiv 21, Acts i 6).

A number of scholars have thought that Jesus in fact shared this belief, and interpret the urgency of his call to repent as a sign that he expected the coming of such a kingdom to follow hard upon his ministry. It would not have been incompatible with the demand for repentance and spiritual righteousness (cf. Ps. Sol. xvii 28-30, 36). Yet such a view conflicts not only with the passages where Jesus speaks of the kingdom as a present spiritual reality, but with the tenor of his teaching as a whole.

The real purpose of Jesus' teaching on the kingdom seems to have lain in his intention to use the popular phraseology of his time in order, by transforming its meaning to lead men to the spiritual reality that lay beneath their crude and material phrases.   When he taught his disciples to pray

> Our Father . . . Thy kingdom come.   Thy will be done, as in heaven, so on earth.

he was showing them the essentially spiritual nature of the kingdom as it was to be on earth.   His words to his disciples (Mk. iv 11)

> Unto you is given the mystery of the kingdom of God : but unto them that are without, all things are done in parables.

whether or not they were originally spoken to explain the significance of his parabolic teaching, indicate that the true meaning of his teaching on the kingdom could only be understood in the context of his teaching as a whole, and of his revelation of God.   The full realisation of the kingdom of God lies beyond this life in a heavenly kingdom, where only those who repent will gain entrance, but in another sense Jesus claimed to bring the kingdom of God upon earth in his own person.   This can be seen in two passages of the utmost significance that stood in Q.

In Mt. xii 28, Lk. xi 20, Jesus says

> If I by the spirit (Lk. finger) of God cast out devils, then is the kingdom of God come upon you,

and in Mt. xi 11, Lk. xvi 16 he draws a clear distinction between John the Baptist as the culmination of the Law and the Prophets and the kingdom which only now is open to men.   The true meaning which Jesus attached to the kingdom can only be understood in the light of his teaching about himself.

3 Son of Man, Son of God, the Christ

When Jesus gave up his public teaching in Galilee he was regarded by many of his hearers as a prophet or as Elijah, whose coming was expected before God's final intervention in world history (Mk. vi 15, cf. Mal. iv 6). It is noteworthy that these terms are used, and that belief in him as Messiah had not yet taken firm hold of the people as a whole in spite of the abortive attempts to ' make him king ' (p. 109). It is plain that Jesus' teaching about himself had so far been in veiled terms.

The gospels represent him as using about himself from the beginning of his ministry (Mk. ii 10) the mysterious term ' Son of Man '. The contemporary meaning of this title is much disputed, and it seems clear that it could be taken as a mere periphrasis of ' man '; it had, however, been used in this sense by Daniel (vii 13 f.) of one who was to come with the clouds of heaven, and to be given an everlasting kingdom over all peoples, and there is evidence for the use of the term to describe an apocalyptic figure in the pre-Christian ' Similitudes of Enoch '.

When Jesus used it of himself it would, at least at first, have conveyed to his hearers only a slight feeling of mystery ; they could hardly have understood such a phrase used by a man in their midst as implying that he was a celestial figure. It is probable that this was Jesus' purpose ; it was no part of his plan to speak fully and openly of his own relationship to God at the very beginning of his ministry.

Yet he had a further motive in so describing himself. ' Son of Man ' was a term whose full implications would become clear in the end to those who believed in him, although it could be employed without arousing serious misconceptions in his early teaching.

Jesus knew himself to be in a special sense the Son of God (cf. the voice at his baptism and Q, Mt. xi 25-27, Lk. x 21-22, also Mk. xiv 61-62), and the fulfilment, not of this or that passage of the Old Testament only, but of the whole Old Testament revelation. To have proclaimed this Sonship in open terms, however, would have involved also an assertion of his Messiahship. The Old Testament conception of Israel as the son of God (e.g. Ex. iv 22, Hos. xi 1) had led to the growth of a belief that the Messiah was God's son in some special sense, in fulfilment of God's promise to David (2 Sam. vii 14, cf. Ps. ii 7, Ps. lxxxix 20-27) ; that such a belief was current in Jesus' day is shown by the High Priest's question to Jesus (Mk. xiv 61) ' Art thou the Christ, the Son of the Blessed ' ? and is confirmed by the application of this title of Son to the Messiah in 1 Enoch cv 2 and 4 Esdras vii 28 f., xiv 9. Jesus seems therefore to have avoided in the early stages of his ministry open references to his Sonship, although his allusions to ' my father ', sometimes in conjunction with a claim of his own authority (e.g. Q, Mt. x 32), did indirectly assert his close relationship with God. At a later stage of the ministry when the disciples had recognised his Messiahship Jesus seems to have been more explicit ; three passages in Mark from the last days in Jerusalem, if they can be accepted as recording the actual words of Jesus, affirm his claim to be THE Son of God (xii 6, xii 37, xiii 32). At his trial he reaffirmed his Messiahship in conjunction with his claim to be the Son of Man and Son of God (Mk. xiv 61-62).

Jesus' claim to be Messiah has already been discussed in connection with its gradual unveiling in the course of his ministry. While the expectation of the Messiah was not the only form taken by popular hopes of God's intervention, nor the only interpretation possible of Old Testament prophecies, it was certainly the most widespread and the one most attuned to the nationalist desires of the people as a whole : a century later Bar-Cochba was to lead a national revolt and be accepted as the ' Son of the Star ' (cf. Nu. xxiv 17) and as Messiah in his fight against Roman oppression.

The term Messiah (Greek *Christos* = Anointed) had assumed its special sense, or rather senses, from the Old Testament hopes of the restoration of an idealised Davidic monarchy (e.g. Is. ix 6-7, Jer. xxxiii 14-17, Hos. iii 5). These hopes were developed in Pharisaism and in later apocalypses in many different ways. Sometimes the Messiah appears as a merely human being who is to restore righteousness and material prosperity to an earthly Israel : sometimes he is a supernatural being whose kingdom is described with a wealth of apocalyptic imagery, often in close connection with the final judgement of God.

Jesus' own conception of his Messiahship must be understood in the light of his understanding that he was also Son of Man and Son of God, and in his taking up into his own person of the fulfilment of the Old Testament revelation as a whole. He accepted only so much of the traditional expectation as could be reconciled with his purpose as a whole; both his delay and caution in accepting the Messianic title and his teaching on his forthcoming death—the idea of a suffering Messiah seems to have been no part of the tradition in his time—show that he interpreted the title in a new and deeper way.

4 Jesus' Interpretation of his Death

Mark represents Jesus as following Peter's confession of his Messiahship with an immediate reference, for the first time, to his forthcoming rejection, death, and resurrection (viii 31). The warning is repeated again and again (ix 9, 12, 31, x 33, 38, xii 8, xiv 41), sometimes with explicit reference to the fulfilment of Scripture (ix 12, xii 10-11), and Jesus speaks of how he has come 'to give his life a ransom for many' (x 45) and at the Last Supper both foretells his betrayal and distributes bread and wine with words that link this act to the new covenant of his blood 'which is shed for many' (xiv 21-24).

The historicity of Mark's account has been denied by many critics who see in it a later Christian interpretation of this stage of Jesus' ministry and think of Jesus as having hoped almost to the end that the kingdom of God would come without his death. While some of Mark's summaries of Jesus' teaching about his death may well be editorial additions of his own (e.g. ix 9, 12, 31, x 33), and the parable of the Wicked Husbandmen (xii 1-12) seems to have undergone changes in the course of tradition, the accounts of Jesus' words at Caesarea Philippi and at the Last Supper have a strong claim to represent his actual teaching. Two passages in Luke which appear to rest on old tradition independent of Mark put similar forecasts into the mouth of Jesus (xii 49-50, xiii 31-33).

There is a further reason for defending the authenticity of at least some of the passages where Jesus predicts his own coming death. Jesus was well acquainted with the book of Isaiah (e.g. Mk. vii 6-7 : Q, Mt. xi 5, Lk. vii 22 : Lk. iv 18-19), and with the passages in that book which are now commonly called ' The Servant Songs ', and attributed to an unknown religious genius of the Exile, although no direct quotations of Jesus from these ' Songs ' occur in the gospels. In the surrounding contexts of these passages ' my Servant ' is a description of God's chosen people, Israel (e.g. Is. xli 8, xlviii 20), but within the passages themselves He is described as an individual whose sufferings and death are to be on behalf of the transgressions not only of Israel but of the Gentiles as well (Is. xlii 1-4, xlix 1-6, l 4-9, lii 13-liii 12).

Whatever the original intention of the prophet—and there are many views as to this—it is impossible to read these ' Songs ' to-day without being struck continually by the way in which Jesus' life fulfilled the spirit of the prophecy in its deepest sense. His call by God (xlii 1) to ' restore the preserved of Israel ' and to be ' a light to the Gentiles ' (xlix 6); his endurance of shame (l 6, liii 7); his rejection by men (liii 3) and his death ' although he had done no violence, neither was any deceit in his mouth '; the purpose of his death, ' he was wounded for our transgressions, he was bruised for our iniquities . . . and with his stripes we are healed . . . and the Lord hath laid on him the iniquity of us all ' (liii 5-6); his final triumph (liii 10-12, where the text unfortunately is corrupt); all of these were seen by the earliest Christians as fulfilled by Jesus' life, death and resurrection (e.g. Acts iii 13, viii 32-33, 1 Cor. xv 3, 1 Pet. ii 22-24).

That Jesus thought of his mission as involving his own suffering and death, at least from the end of his Galilean ministry, and that he thought of himself and the redeeming

power of his passion in terms of these prophecies, seems the
best explanation of these facts.   At the same time he was
no more bound by this conception than by those of Messiah
and Son of Man, and his own interpretation of his death
seems to have contained elements not present in the ' Servant
Songs '.

The final victory of the Servant is described in obscure
terms which seem to imply a personal survival (Is. liii 10-12),
although the original meaning may only have been the
survival of the chosen community.   Jesus' teaching about
his death was closely associated with affirmations that he
would rise again and survive death to come into his kingdom.
The references to his rising again ' on the third day ' may
be due to Christian tradition, but the repeated emphasis
on his forthcoming entrance into his kingdom must be
accepted as an integral part of his message (e.g. Mk. x. 39-40,
xiv 25) even in the period when he foresaw the near approach of his execution.   The meaning of his death was
in fact bound up with his survival of it.   His departure
from earth was to be the prelude for his eventual return
from heaven to bring the consummation of all things
(Mk. xiv 62, Q : Mt. xxiv 27, Lk. xvii 24).

Jesus also thought of his death as on behalf of ' many '
(cf. Is. liii 11).   He declared that the purpose of his coming
was ' not to be ministered unto, but to minister, and to
give his life a ransom for many ' (Mk. x 45).   ' Ransom '
would be better rendered ' redemption ' here (cf. Is. li 11,
Lk. ii 38), although the idea is not worked out.   At the
Last Supper, where the wine is equated with ' my blood of
the covenant, which is shed for many ', the parellelism with
Exod. xxiv 8 and the covenant of Moses (cf. too Jer. xxxi
31 ff.) shows that Jesus in his thought of his approaching
death, as in his adoption of titles to describe his person, was
interpreting the significance of his own actions in the light
of more than one strand of the Old Testament belief.
Only one who believed himself to fulfil the rôle of God's
' Servant ' and to be a greater than Moses in the sight of
God could have spoken such words.

5 *The Continuing Community*

There is little direct teaching of Jesus in the oldest gospel sources on the continuance of his disciples as a Church after his death and resurrection. This fact has often been pointed to by those who see in Jesus a disappointed human fanatic as proof that he did not look beyond his lifetime for the coming of the apocalyptic kingdom of God, or that at least he expected this kingdom to appear immediately after his death. Yet there is no need for such a solution of the problem, which indeed is no true solution.

In the first place Jesus' teaching about the kingdom of God presents it on two planes of thought, as a future kingdom to come and as a present spiritual reality. Significantly enough it was the latter aspect of the kingdom that figured most largely in Jesus' teaching after the Confession at Caesarea Philippi.[1] The ethical teaching of the early period of the ministry was reinforced by demands upon his disciples which presupposed a lifetime of work in his cause, even if a lifetime which might be cut short by persecution, e.g. Mk. ix 37, x 17-21, 23-31, xi 23-25, xii 28-34. Editorial re-arrangement and alteration may have played a part in the location and adaption of such passages, but the impression remains that Jesus envisaged a continuation of life on earth after his resurrection.

Such an impression is strengthened by Jesus' eschatological teaching (cf. pp. 246-250), once it is realised what a distorted and confused version of his words Christian tradition has produced in the synoptic gospels. Both Jesus' prophecies about the future that Jerusalem and the Temple would be destroyed, and that the Son of Man would return in judgement at a time he did not know (Mk. xiii 32), are consistent with an expectation that earthly life would continue its course for some time (Q, Mt. xxiv 37-39, Lk. xvii 26-27, 30).

The accounts of the Last Supper, too, imply the continuance of a community of Jesus' followers in the world.

[1] Manson, *Teaching of Jesus*, pp. 129 ff.

The Pauline version (1 Cor. xi 23-25) contains a definite command to continue the rite, and even if Mark's version be preferred (Mk. xiv 22-25) the implications of the covenant involve the persistence of a fellowship of believers on the earth.

When Jesus' belief in an interval of time between his resurrection and the final end of the world is grasped, the whole of his teaching gains a new emphasis and importance. The eschatological element becomes the temporal framework within which the spiritual message is contained. Jesus proclaimed the coming of a new relationship of men with God achieved through his own life, death, and resurrection. Although this relationship could only finally be established completely on his return in glory, it had become possible of realisation for all who accepted the fact that with Jesus' appearance God had manifested his power in the world. It now becomes possible to put Jesus' teaching on how men should live into its proper setting.

6 Repentance and the New Life

Jesus' call to men was to turn away from their old life and accept as good news the fact of the coming of God's kingdom. This message was a continuation of what John the Baptist had preached, but also the fulfilment of what John had only anticipated, and acceptance of Jesus' challenge involved not only a belief in the coming judgement and redemption but a trust in the authority of Jesus himself. He was at once the interpreter of the true meaning of the kingdom and the personification of it (Q, Mt. xii 28, Lk. xi 20) and with his appearance a new understanding of God's will was possible for his disciples (Mk. iv 11 : Q, Mt. xiii 17, Lk. x 24).

Although Jesus' teaching was not delivered in any systematic way, and of his preaching only isolated sentences and paragraphs seem to have survived, often in an artificial editorial context, there is a unity about it which enables us to arrange it around the central themes and recognise the consistency of his thought. It is this very consistency of his ethical teaching, for example, at a level which great religious leaders of other faiths have sometimes approached but never sustained, that marks out Jesus as unique among the teachers of mankind.

At the very centre of Jesus' message stood the proclamation of the loving Fatherhood of God and of the sonship of men. It is his good pleasure to give us the kingdom (Lk. xii 34), he loves us and cares for us continually (Q, Mt. vi 26, Lk. xii 24 : Mt. xviii 14), and he rejoices over our repentance (Lk. xv 7). Repentance on man's part involves acknowledgement of his sinfulness (Lk. xviii 13), and a subordination of his will to God's (Q, Mt. v 48, cf. Lk. vi 36). Only thus can he come to know his sonship and to love God, which is the first commandment of all (Mk. xii 29, Lk. x 27-28). This love in turn enables man to accept as his first and supreme obligation the seeking of God's kingdom and His righteousness (Q, Mt. vi 33, Lk. xii 31), and involves necessarily the love of his fellow-men who are also sons of God (Mk. xii 31, Lk. x 27-28).

From this central basis of Jesus' teaching spring his interpretation of the authority of the Law and his practical demands on men. He accepted the divine purpose of the Law (Mt. v 17), but drew a clear line between what was fundamental in it, and what of no permanent validity (Mk. vii 1-23, Mt. v 21-48). He had no hesitation in denouncing the traditional Sabbath regulations when they conflicted with the deeper purposes of God (Mk. ii 23-iii 6), and it was this claim of his to supersede the traditional interpretation of the Law that aroused the hostility of the Pharisees (Mk. ii 24, iii 6), who rightly perceived in it an assumption of authority greater than that of Moses. He distinguished even within the written law itself between the minor ritual regulations and ' the weightier matters of the Law, judgement, and mercy, and faith ' (Mt. xxiii 23), and in fact subordinated the whole of the ceremonial element to the final ethical principles behind the Decalogue. In so doing he in effect substituted for a code of ex-

ternal law the inward law that springs from man's desire to
obey God.

The repentance that Jesus demanded was the prelude to
the growth of this desire.   Only a man conscious of his sinfulness could keep the ' weightier matters of the Law ' in
sincerity and pureness of motive ; thus Jesus distinguishes
between true and false almsgiving and prayer (Mt. vi 1-8),
and makes the efficacy of sacrifice dependent on previous
reconciliation with a brother (Mt. v 23-24).   He makes it
clear, too, that men's actions will in the long run betray
their true motives, and that the tree is known by its fruit
(Q ? Mt. xii 33-35, Lk. vi 43-45).

In this stress on motive Jesus' teaching showed itself as
at once permanent and universal.   The impossibility of
keeping the lofty demands made by Jesus has sometimes
been interpreted as a sign that he regarded his teaching as
an ' *interimsethik* ', to be observed by his disciples until the
kingdom should suddenly appear in the very near future.
But this is nowhere indicated in the gospels, and the nature
of Jesus' teaching proceeds from the nature of God, as he
revealed him, and from principles which, as history has
shown, maintain their validity in all places at all times.

The universality of the teaching, and its appeal to
Gentile as well as to Jew, help us to understand Jesus'
conception of his mission to all men.   The rarity of his
contacts with Gentiles during his time on earth stands out
in the gospels, and these contacts are clearly exceptional
(Q, Mt. viii 10, Lk. vii 9 : Mt. x 5-6, Mk. vii 24-30) ;
Jesus' earthly mission was in the first place to his own people,
the Jews.   Of the few texts which directly envisage the
entrance into the kingdom, some appear to be the creation
of Christian tradition (but cf. e.g. Q, Mt. viii 11, Lk. xiii 29).
Yet once it is accepted that Jesus looked forward to a period
of time between his death and his final coming, the limitation of his sphere of ministry becomes intelligible and the
expansion of the Church to Gentile lands is seen to be in
accord with Jesus' ultimate purpose.

The ethics of Jesus envisage life in a world where his

9

challenge is not yet universally accepted, and the whole fabric of society is subjected to searching criticism. Just as the Scribes and Pharisees are condemned for their social conduct (Q ? Mt. xxiii 25, Lk. xi 39 : Mk. xii 38-40), men in general are envisaged in their ordinary social relationships, whether as stewards (Lk. xvi 1-13), householders (Lk. xi 5-8), kings (Lk. xxii 25), or guests (Lk. xiv 7-14). And always they are given as the supreme guide to conduct the need to put the kingdom of God first even if it means renunciation of wealth (Mk. x 21 ff.), family (Mk. x 29, Mt. x 37) or earthly life itself (Lk. xiv 25-27). The kingdom remains the supreme goal, for the attainment of which any sacrifice is justified.

CHAPTER XII

THE STUDY OF THE ACTS OF THE APOSTLES

ACTS is a beautifully told narrative of great and exciting events in far-off days, and its fascination as a story never fails. It is also our most important historical source for the earliest development of Christianity, and as such of immediate relevance for present-day Christians. The different views, for example, held by Christians as to the right forms of church government and the right meaning to attach to Baptism are ultimately dependent on the interpretation of New Testament texts, among which passages in Acts are of special significance.

Acts is essentially a book to be studied in connection with the epistles, which help to illuminate both the narrative and the teaching which it contains. The problems of Acts are many and of great importance. In the first place the question of its authorship is not a merely academic one, for much hangs on its attribution to Luke the companion of Paul and the eye witness of many of the events which he describes. The difficulties of the early chapters, where Acts is often our sole source of information, have to be faced if we wish to gain a coherent and intelligible picture of the nature of the Church in its very first days. Of particular importance are the questions that arise as to the historical value of the speeches. How far do they enable us to reconstruct the faith of the earlier disciples ?

On all these questions, as on those of the interpretation of particular passages, e.g. the Apostolic Decree (xv 20), Paul's baptism of twelve men at Ephesus (xix 1-7), Acts must be read with continual reference to the epistles. Sometimes it is Acts that throws new light on Paul's movements and preaching, but the comparison of the different documents is essential for gaining a true picture of Paul himself or of the apostolic church.

BOOKS FOR READING

A brief but excellent introductory commentary on Acts is that of A. W. F. BLUNT (Clarendon Bible).   Those of FOAKES JACKSON (Moffatt) and RACKHAM (Westminster) are also useful.   W. L. KNOX, *The Acts of the Apostles* (Cambridge), is a short up-to-date Introduction of great value.   The fullest treatment of Acts is to be found in FOAKES JACKSON and LAKE, *The Beginnings of Christianity* (Macmillan) : Vol. I, on 'The Jewish and Gentile Backgrounds' ; Vol. II, on 'Prolegomena to Acts' ; Vol. IV, 'Commentary and Translation' ; and Vol. V, 'Appended Notes,' are a mine of information, and can be used with profit even by those who know no Greek.   C. H. DODD, *The Apostolic Preaching and its Developments* (Hodder and Stoughton), is of particular value for the study of the speeches in Acts.

For the history and development of the New Testament Church the following books will be found useful :

T. G. JALLAND, *The Origin and Development of the Christian Church* (Hutchinson).

E. F. SCOTT, *The Beginnings of the Church* (Scribner).

J. WEISS, *History of Primitive Christianity* (Macmillan—2 volumes).

H. LIETZMANN, *The Beginnings of the Christian Church* (Nicholson and Watson).

CHAPTER XIII

THE ACTS OF THE APOSTLES

AUTHORSHIP

It is stated in the first verse of Acts that the book is a continuation of our third gospel, and the common authorship of both books is confirmed by innumerable points of detail and the general uniformity of the vocabulary. That Luke, the physician and companion of Paul (Col. iv 14, 2 Tim. iv 11), is the author of both volumes is now generally accepted (cf. pp. 74 f.), although a few critics maintain that the attribution is due to the use by the unknown author of Luke's diary for certain parts of the narrative in Acts. This latter view is largely based on an exaggerated view of the historical difficulties raised by the early chapters of Acts; the great majority of scholars, however, prefer to explain the admitted historical deficiencies of Acts and the differences between the Paul of Acts and the Paul of the epistles as due to Luke's special objects in writing and to the limitations of his sources of information.

THE PURPOSE OF ACTS AND ITS LIMITATIONS

The main purpose of Acts is sufficiently indicated in the preface to the gospel of which Acts is confessedly a continuation (The title 'Acts of the Apostles' was almost certainly prefixed later, when Acts often circulated separately from the gospel). In Luke i 3-4 the author proclaims his intention of writing to Theophilus that ' thou mightest know the certainty concerning the things wherein thou wast instructed '. After describing in the gospel ' all that Jesus began both to do and to teach, until the day in which he was received up ' (Acts i 1) Luke proceeds in his second volume to trace for Theophilus the stages by which the Christian message had spread from Jerusalem in A.D. 29 to a time and place where Theophilus' own knowledge could continue the story. We know nothing of Theophilus, not even whether his name (= friend of God) is the real name of an individual, but, if Luke was writing in Greece *c.* A.D. 80 (cf. p. 80), the narrative of Acts gives a remarkably good account of how Christianity had spread to that region and most Greek Christians would be able from their own knowledge to complete the story as it affected their own church.

This overriding purpose accounts for the general plan of Acts, which does not profess to be in any sense a complete account of the early rise of Christianity. Nothing is said of the expansion of Christianity in other directions, and the early history of the Jerusalem, Palestinian, and Antioch churches is only sketched in sufficient detail to illustrate the successive steps by which the gospel came closer to Theophilus; it is significant that the two main actors in the narrative are Peter and Paul, who played such leading parts in the development of the Gentile mission to Antioch and beyond.

Within this general plan lie other subsidiary ones, indicative of Luke's special interests. Thus Acts has been described as the Gospel of the Holy Spirit, and as an Apology for Christianity to the Roman Imperial authorities, and Luke's narrative has clearly been influenced by his desire to bring out the working of the Spirit in Christian history and his anxiety to present the movement as law-abiding, but it may be questioned how far the story has been consciously shaped along these lines. It does, however, seem probable that Luke has to some extent glozed over the asperity of the controversies within the Church, notably the opposition to Paul and his views as described by Paul himself in Galatians and 2 Corinthians, in his attempt to emphasise the fundamental unity of the early Church.

More serious are the limitations imposed upon Luke by the comparative scantiness of the material available to him,

and by the nature of much of this material.   Whether he
was able to use written sources is discussed below, but such
sources, if he did use them, seem to have been of only small
extent.   Luke appears to have been a pioneer in writing
an extended narrative of the Church's growth, and for the
most part he probably relied on his own recollections of
events long past.   It is unlikely that there would have
been many Christians in Greece *c.* A.D. 80 who could have
given him much information of value about the earliest
Palestinian church, and it would have been difficult, if
not impossible, to fill up the lacunae of his notebooks and
memory.   There is nothing surprising, therefore, in the
variations between Paul's clearly accurate record of his visits
to Jerusalem (in Gal. i and ii) and Luke's version of Paul's
movements; they are reasonably to be ascribed, at least in
large part, to Luke's failure to remember the exact sequence
of events and their significance.   It is noteworthy that the
later chapters of Acts, in which Luke himself was closely
concerned, are generally agreed to preserve a high standard
of accuracy, while most of the difficulties of Acts i-xv are
connected with events which happened at Jerusalem, a
place where Luke does not seem to have spent more than a
few weeks.

THE SOURCES OF ACTS

This difference in the value of the two halves of Acts
as history is linked with the nature of the sources available
to Luke.   For the later journeys of Paul he was able to
depend not only on his own acquaintance with Paul, but on
what he had learnt from many of Paul's other companions,
amongst these Silas (Acts xvi 16-19), Timothy, Gaius, and
Aristarchus (Acts xx 4; Col. i 1, iv 10, 14).   For the early
period, too, Luke had a number of acquaintances from whom
he must have learnt much, e.g. Philip, during his time in
Caesarea (Acts xx 8-10, xxvii 1), John Mark (Col. iv 10),
Silas, and Paul himself.   But it remains doubtful whether
Luke had yet formed his plan of writing Acts when he was

in contact with these men, and in his narrative in the early part of Acts he seems to be stringing together, as best he may, a number of different stories and narratives, some of which appear, by the time they reached him, to have been seriously distorted in the telling.   A number of historical problems confront the reader.   How is the story of Judas' death in Acts i to be reconciled with that in Mt. xxvii ?   How far is the account of Pentecost, as it stands, of historical value ? Was Peter really imprisoned three times, and miraculously released twice ?   Did Paul's call to the Gentiles really ante-date Peter's reception of Cornelius ?

Many attempts have been made to show that Luke is dependent in the first half of Acts on one or more written sources, and some scholars think it possible that an Aramaic document of early date underlies at least i 1-v 16, ix 31-xi 18. Others think it more likely that Luke relied throughout on material which he had collected from oral tradition.   It may be doubted whether these controversies are in the last resort of great importance.   Luke must have been de-pendent on sources, whether oral or written, and as his informants included such men as Philip, Silas, Mark, and Paul, some of his material at least came to him upon good authority.   It is, however, clear from the difficulties of the early chapters of Acts, that, even if he had written sources available to him, they must have been of limited extent and not altogether free from confusions and errors.

THE SPEECHES IN ACTS

The narrative of Acts is interlarded with a number of ' skeleton ' speeches, mostly put into the mouth of Peter or Paul.   While the insertion of such speeches, to enliven the action, was a recognised convention of ancient historians, and their contents often bore little relation to what had actually been said on the occasion, there are good grounds for regarding the speeches in Acts as providing precious evidence for the way in which the Christian message was proclaimed by the apostles.   This is especially true of the speeches of Peter, some of which may perhaps be drawn by Luke from an early Palestinian source. They contain what appear to be primitive titles of Jesus, e.g. ' Servant ' of God (Acts iii 13, 26), and avoid the title ' Son of God ', nor do they explicitly connect forgiveness, as Paul does, with the death of Jesus. It is possible, moreover, to trace a common pattern of preaching in these speeches, which recurs in Paul's speech at Pisidian Antioch (xiii 17-41), and can be occasionally glimpsed in Paul's epistles side by side with Paul's own more developed message.

This pattern consists of a number of connected statements about Jesus and a call to conversion :

> Jesus of Nazareth did mighty works and wonders, was crucified by God's will, and raised up by God. God has now exalted him, and he is both Lord and Christ, and will come again to judge the world. All this has been foretold by the prophets, and the apostles are witnesses to his resurrection. Men must therefore repent and be baptised to obtain forgiveness of their sins and the gift of the Holy Spirit.

There are good grounds for thinking that such a pattern represents the main lines of the apostolic preaching from early times, although there must have been many individual variations and a continual process of development, such as finds later expression in 1 Peter and in the Pauline epistles. The speeches in the first half of Acts may therefore be regarded not as a resumé of the actual words spoken on various occasions, but as a series of brief summaries which give a generally accurate picture of the main points of the apostolic preaching at an early stage ; these summaries have been suitably varied by an editorial hand, whether Luke himself or the original compiler of a source used by Luke, to fit in with the particular situation in which they are placed.

The importance of this view of the speeches in the first half of Acts lies in the fact that with such evidence for the pre-Pauline preaching of the Church a juster estimate is possible of the process of development that took place in the

Church's message between the early days of the Jerusalem church and the close of the first century.

The speeches put into the mouth of Paul in the second half of Acts are also of considerable importance. At first sight they are strangely different from the teaching of Paul in the epistles; the Paul of Acts has little to say about the great ' Pauline ' doctrines of Faith and Works and of Union with Christ which are so prominent in the epistles (yet cf. Acts xiii 39, xx 21, 24), and he uses many expressions which do not recur in the epistles (e.g. Acts xx 28, xxvi 23). This divergence indeed has furnished one of the grounds on which a few scholars have refused to accept the Lucan authorship of Acts. It must be remembered, however, that Paul's epistles were written to Christians who accepted his main teaching, and that Paul's theological instruction is for the most part to deal with difficulties of interpretation that have arisen or to develop the deeper implications of his teaching. In Acts, on the other hand, Luke seems concerned to give summaries of Paul's speeches to illustrate his variety of approach to different audiences, and those for the most part composed of men who were hearing Paul, or even the Christian message itself, for the first time.

THE TEXT OF ACTS

The problem of the original text of Acts is of great interest and some importance. The text has survived in two main forms, which show such considerable variations from each other as to suggest that there once existed two different editions of the book, and raise the question, ' Which of these two editions is the original one ?'

The English Authorised and Revised Versions for the most part follow the text which from the fourth century A.D. onwards has the support of the great majority of the best manuscripts. On the other hand there is enough manuscript evidence to prove the existence as early as the second century A.D. of a type of text which contains a great number of variations, additions, and omissions. This latter text is often called the Western text, although it was known very early in the East as well, and sometimes from the name of the manuscript which is one of the chief witnesses to its existence, Codex Bezae (now in the University Library at Cambridge), the Bezan text.

The variants of this text often have a specially graphic interest; thus Peter, escaping from prison, ' went down the seven steps ' (xii 10), Paul lectured in the school of Tyrannus ' from the fifth to the tenth hour ', i.e. from 11 to 4 (xix 9), and Mnason's house is described as being not in Jerusalem, but in ' a certain village ' (xxi 16). While most of the variants are only changes of minor interest and significance, two are of considerable importance. In xi 28 the Bezan text reads ' and when we were assembled together ', introducing Luke into the narrative at Antioch before the first missionary journey, whereas in the usual text he does not appear until Paul reaches Troas on the second missionary journey; in xv 20, 29 the Decree of the Council of Jerusalem, as given in the Bezan text, omits ' and from what is strangled ' thus making it possible to interpret the decision of the Council as a series of injunctions to avoid murder, idolatry, and fornication in place of the ' ritual ' demands of the usual text, abstinence from ' pollutions of idols, and from fornication and from what is strangled, and from blood '.

Scholars are not agreed as to how these variations arose. Various theories have been put forward to explain one type of text as a later revision of the other, and it has even been suggested that Luke himself wrote two drafts of Acts. This is improbable, however, and it is perhaps best to accept the Bezan text as an early revision of the original text, which was more akin to that followed in most English translations, or to assume that both types of text are in fact revisions, each of which has preserved original readings. There is good reason for thinking that in the first century or so of its existence the text of Acts was treated by the scribes who copied it with some freedom, especially as Acts seems to have circulated for the most part separately from the Gospel of Luke.

CHAPTER XIV

THE GROWTH OF THE CHURCH

THE SCANTINESS OF OUR INFORMATION

WE know too little of the history of the Christian Church for the first century of its existence to enable us to reconstruct the details of its growth with any completeness. It is just this lack of knowledge, and our dependence on isolated fragments of information, not always consistent with each other, which have led to so many different interpretations of the available evidence and to such varying estimates of the development of primitive Christian doctrine and organisation.

From pagan writers of the early second century A.D. it can be gleaned that Christianity had spread from Judaea to Rome, possibly before A.D. 50,[1] and that Nero had put the blame for the great fire of Rome in A.D. 64 upon the followers of 'this detestable superstition'.[2] Pliny, the governor of Bithyria, asked and received advice from the Emperor Trajan, c. A.D. 112, as to how he was to deal with numerous Christians who had practised their religion there for some time : he had heard that they met before daylight and offered hymns to Christ as a God, that they bound themselves with an oath not to steal or commit adultery, not to break their word or deny a deposit when demanded, and that they had also been in the habit of taking common meals until he had issued an edict forbidding the existence of clubs. Some of these Christians he had put to death : others had denied their faith, recited a prayer to the gods, and offered incense and libation to Trajan's statue ; some of the persons interrogated had stated that they had already

---

[1] Suetonius, in his *Life of Claudius*, says that Claudius expelled the Jews from Rome for continual rioting ' at the instigation of Chrestus ', a phrase which has been variously interpreted, but may refer to trouble between Jews and Christians. [2] Tacitus, *Annales*, xv, 44.

given up their Christian faith many years before.[1] These few passages exhaust the evidence of value that pagan literature affords for the early growth of Christianity.

Jewish writings are not much more informative. Josephus,[2] in a text whose authenticity has been questioned by some scholars, tells of the stoning at Jerusalem in A.D. 62 of James ' the brother of Jesus who was called Christ ' and some others ' as breakers of the Law ', an act that aroused the displeasure of the more fair-minded of the Jews. The evidence of the Rabbinical literature, which is mostly of late date and uniformly hostile to Christianity, adds little of historical worth, but confirms that Jews who became Christians formed a community to some extent separate from other Jews, and by the end of the first century at least were regarded as heretics.

The Christian documents of the second and later centuries which contained information about the Apostolic age handed down by tradition, must also be regarded as providing a very limited help for the reconstruction of the history of the earliest period. A certain number of facts have been preserved in the work of the fourth-century historian Eusebius who drew on earlier sources not now available to us. He tells of the withdrawal of the Jerusalem Christians from the city before the siege of A.D. 70 to the little town of Pella beyond Jordan, and of the appointment of Symeon, son of Clopas, a cousin of the Lord, to succeed the murdered James. He has also handed down, on the authority of Papias (cf. p. 54), some information about the early days of Christianity in Asia Minor. But it is the meagreness of the knowledge available even in his time which is most striking.

While Eusebius can be regarded as a serious, though by no means always an accurate historian, the numerous Christian Acts of various apostles, none of them earlier than the middle of the second century, are for the most part fictional romances, full of pious legend, but of little or no

[1] Pliny's Letters, x, xcvi and xcvii.
[2] *Antiquities*, xx, 9, 1.

use as history.   Only occasionally does some piece of personal description raise our hopes that it may conceivably be based on a true reminiscence, e.g. that Justus Barsabas (cf. Acts i 23) was flatfooted, and that Paul was ' a man short of stature, thin-haired upon the head, crooked in the legs, well-built, with eyebrows joining, and nose somewhat hooked, full of grace ' (Acts of Paul).

For the early history of the Church, as for the life and teaching of Jesus, the books of the New Testament are virtually our sole important sources.   Only one of these books, the Acts of the Apostles, is in any sense a history of the Church, and that to only a limited degree and for certain phases only of its development (cf. p. 136).   The epistles of Paul contain passages of great value historically, and the incidental allusions of the other epistles and of Revelation add a little to our knowledge, but the total sum of our information is very small, and we shall never know, for example, how Christianity spread to Egypt, or what became of the majority of the apostles.

It is possible, however, to exaggerate the effects of this lack of material.   The evidence of Luke and Paul, although sometimes in need of reconciliation, indicates the main lines of Christian development towards the north-west.   Much of the detail is obscure, but certain stages of progress can be traced with a fair degree of certainty.   And it was the ' Pauline ' branch of the infant shrub that was to develop into the main trunk of the full-grown tree when the early Jerusalem ' leader ' had atrophied into a withered twig after the calamities that swept over Palestine in A.D. 70 and 135.

THE GEOGRAPHICAL SPREAD

The extension of the Church from its beginnings as a single small fellowship at Jerusalem (with possibly sister-fellowships in Galilee) to a chain of communities extending from Babylonia to Rome was accomplished within a single generation, while many of the apostles were still alive.

This period of the Church's development can be divided into three main stages. (1) For the first few years the Church grew primarily among Jews and within Palestine; the Jerusalem community was both the seat of apostolic authority and the scene of most intensive missionary effort. (2) Following a wave of persecution a number of Christian missionaries then carried the gospel farther afield, notably to Phoenicia, Cyprus, and Antioch (Acts xi 19); at Antioch, the capital of Syria and a city which ranked with Alexandria as second only to Rome in size and importance, Gentiles were for the first time admitted into the Church in large numbers, apparently without becoming Jewish proselytes in any full sense. Jerusalem remained the headquarters of the Church as a whole, and the authority of its leaders seems to have been accepted without question by the new churches which had been established outside Palestine. Barnabas, who had been sent down from Jerusalem to inspect the new community at Antioch, brought Paul from Tarsus to help with the work which prospered exceedingly (Acts xi 22-26). It must be considered likely that Christianity was spreading simultaneously in other directions outside Palestine, e.g. to Egypt and Babylonia, although perhaps success was not so outstanding and the approach was still confined to Jews; the evidence for such developments, however, is lacking.

It is difficult to give precise dates for these two stages. Paul's conversion is usually dated before A.D. 36, and by that time Christianity seems to have been well-established at Damascus. Probably the Church at Antioch had already become a vigorous and important community by A.D. 40. (3) At Antioch the Gentile Christians were numerous but the Church contained also a fair number of Jewish Christians, among them many of the Church leaders (Acts xiii 1, Gal. ii 13). The churches which were set up by Paul and his companions on a series of lengthy journeys from Antioch, and which extended the range of Christianity throughout southern Asia Minor and Greece, were to be, some of them from their foundation, predominantly Gentile. In a period of some ten years, from *c.* A.D. 47 to *c.* 56, the Gentile wing of Christianity became, in all probability, numerically stronger than the Jewish wing. Acts and the Pauline epistles focus our attention on the individual part played in this development by Paul, but, outstanding as he was, the spread of Christianity in a Gentile environment did not depend on his work alone. Many of the Pauline churches were to become the centres of further missionary effort and expansion (cf. the foundation of the Church at Colossae, p. 200), and Paul's companions in travel seem to have continued his work when he himself was isolated by imprisonment at Caesarea and Rome. The opening verse of 1 Peter bears witness to the establishment within this period by unknown missionaries of Christian churches in many parts of Asia Minor that Paul had left untouched (p. 172), and it cannot be doubted that similar expansion was proceeding in other regions too. Even in Palestine the expansion of the Church seems to have gone on with considerable success among the Jews during the period covered by Acts (Acts xxi 20).

Acts closes with Paul in prison in Rome *c.* A.D. 60. Christian tradition for centuries affirmed that both Paul and Peter perished in the Neronian persecution of A.D. 64, and, though this tradition may well be incorrect (cf. p. 171), there are reasonable grounds for assuming that both were dead before A.D. 70. James, too, had suffered martyrdom in A.D. 62, and death must have begun to take its toll among the rest of the apostles by the time that the Jewish revolt and the final capture of Jerusalem in A.D. 70 by the Romans had disorganised the life of Palestine for a generation.

The events of A.D. 60-70 must inevitably have transformed the Christian Church. With the great leaders of the first generation for the most part dead or in extreme old age, and Jerusalem in ruins, the Judaean church ceased to occupy the centre of the stage, and the new and by now overwhelmingly Gentile churches entered upon a period of consolidation and further expansion in which guidance and authority had to be sought elsewhere. Unfortunately, for the next half-century it is only through occasional glimpses given us by the later books of the New Testament and a few other Christian writings that we can conjecture the processes of development.

The Earliest Days

That Jerusalem was the effective centre of the earliest Christian Church is certain. Even if Luke has selected his material in portraying the early days, as he has suppressed the Marcan hint of resurrection appearances in Galilee (cf. p. 78), the Galilean communities appear to have played little part in the development of the Church, and the apostles and brethren of Jesus seem either to have remained in the neighbourhood of Jerusalem from the time of the crucifixion or to have taken up residence there within a comparatively short time. Nor is there any adequate reason for doubting that Luke's account of the descent of the Spirit at Pentecost, confused as it is, describes the decisive moment in the history of the Church, which first started it on its work of proclaiming the faith which it had learned to others.

The nature of the earliest community stands out clearly in the narrative of Acts. Bound together in fellowship by their common possession of the Spirit (Acts ii 38) and their common belief in the Messiahship of Jesus (Acts ii 36), they came naturally to worship and to 'break bread' as a united body (Acts ii 42), and 'had all things common' (Acts iv 32). They continued to live as pious Jews, to frequent the Temple and to keep the Law, but knew themselves to be also set apart as true believers. Entrance to the community was by a rite of baptism, probably modelled on John's baptism but with the additional invocation of Jesus' name, whose saving power was shown by its efficacy in healing (Acts iii 6). The leaders of the community were the apostles whom Jesus himself had chosen, and who had known both the Jesus of the earthly ministry and the Jesus who had appeared to them after his resurrection (Acts i 21-22). They showed themselves eager to make converts, though, living as they did in a predominantly Jewish environment, it was to their fellow-Jews that they first proclaimed the Messiahship of Jesus, the coming judgement (Acts iii 23), and the teaching that Jesus had given on how men should live.

In the course of time the community was naturally subject to development. The Church grew in numbers, and new problems were created by this growth. Not all the converts maintained their first enthusiasm, and there were cases of deceit (Acts v 1-11) and of grumbling (Acts vi 1). The apostles, busy as they were with the ' ministry of the word ' (Acts vi 4), had to delegate some of their functions to seven deacons. Persecution hampered the work and led to the death of Stephen and the dispersion of many Christians through Palestine, where they found new opportunities of evangelism among both Jews and Samaritans (viii 1).

This latter mission marked an important step, as the Samaritans held the Law of Moses as a sacred book but were bitter enemies of the Jewish nation : the Christians in admitting them to the Church were already on the way to acceptance of Gentiles. It is possible that in isolated cases Gentiles had already been accepted in special circumstances. Some scholars hold that the Hellenist Christians of Acts vi 1 were Gentiles, and not, as has been generally assumed, Greek-speaking Jews ; neither the Ethiopian eunuch (Acts viii 26 ff.) nor Cornelius, the centurion of Caesarea (Acts x 1 ff.) were proselytes to Judaism, though both were clearly sympathetic to its teachings.

In considering the acceptance of these ' outsiders ', it is essential to remember the part played in the Christian community by the Spirit (cf. p. 251 for the place of prophets in the Church). The authority of the apostles was real, but the guidance of the Spirit was unhesitatingly accepted by them as by other Christians. In this matter the teaching of Jesus, as we have seen (p. 129), gave support to the teaching of the Spirit, and the problems about the terms on which Gentiles could be admitted had yet to become acute.

The Conversion of Paul and the Church of Antioch

The conversion of Paul on the Damascus road was, as we know, an event of tremendous significance for the future of Christianity, but at the time it probably made little more than a fleeting impression upon the Church, which had many converts from among the Pharisees (Acts xv 5) and the priests (Acts vi 7). It was only when he emerged as a leader of the Church at Antioch that he began to exert an important influence upon the Church as a whole.

The formation in the great pagan city of Antioch of a Christian community to which Gentiles were admitted in large numbers, was in itself an important development in the history of the Church. It was inevitable that the conditions on which Gentiles were to be admitted would eventually have to be settled, once the number of Gentile converts became considerable. The occasion for a dispute to arise was a superficial one, a matter of whether Jewish and Gentile Christians could eat together without the Jews incurring defilement (Gal. ii 11-16), but Paul at once raised the real and profound question whether the Law had not been superseded by the new and universal gospel that men can be saved by faith in Jesus Christ.

The question was remitted to the Council of Jerusalem (*c*. A.D. 49), where Peter, convinced by Paul's attack upon his conduct at Antioch, took Paul's side (Gal. ii 14, Acts xv 7-11). The text of the final decree of the Council is uncertain (cf. p. 141), but permission was given for Gentiles to become Christians without becoming Jewish proselytes as well, and subject only to certain ritual or moral conditions. The decision was a vital one which was to lead in time to the complete severance of the Christian Church from the Jews. Its immediate effect was to leave Paul and those who shared his view free to continue the Gentile mission with the support of the leaders of the Jerusalem church, but with an interpretation of Jesus' life and teaching different in some important respects from their own (cf. p. 139).

Paul's Later Journeys

Paul had already established a number of churches in Galatia (p. 183) on a journey with Barnabas; he now proceeded on an extended journey with Silas which took him across Asia Minor to Greece. The missionary methods which he employed on this and on his third journey which covered much of the same ground were to determine the main lines of Christian development that followed his imprisonment and death, and through the later circulation of his epistles to have a permanent influence upon the form of Christian organisation and belief.

In the first place he effected a virtually complete separation of the Christian Church from the Jewish synagogue. Although he made use of any available synagogue, as he had done on his first journey, for preaching to the local Jews and such Gentiles as ' feared God ' (Acts xiii 16) and were allowed to attend, Acts makes it clear that Paul's words always led to an early breach with the majority of the Jews and the setting up by Paul of a separate Christian Church (e.g. Acts xix 8-9). Some Jews might be converted, but the majority of church members would be Gentiles, and with the passage of time and the expansion of the community the Gentile part of the community tended more and more to predominate.

Upon these Gentile Christian churches Paul impressed the mark of his own strong personality. By his insistence on his apostleship (Gal. i 1, 2 Cor. xi 5) and the authority of his gospel (Gal. i 11) he established a pattern of belief and conduct for Christians that could be changed, as it was in many respects, when he was no longer alive to reinforce it by his presence, but which for a vital fifteen years, at the close of which Judaistic Christianity was overwhelmed with troubles of its own, could be maintained against any attempt to bring it into closer conformity with the legalistic views of other Christian missionaries (2 Cor. xi 2-4).

When Paul returned from his third missionary journey to pay his last visit to Jerusalem he still retained the confidence of James and the Jerusalem elders (Acts xxi 18-20), but the smouldering dislike of many of the church members for his teaching is apparent (Acts xxi 21). His arrest and trial were to mark the beginning of yet another conflict for Christians with the power of the State.

As long as Christianity remained recognised by the State as a sect of Judaism (cf. Acts xviii 14), the Church had only to fear mob violence and the limited powers of Jewish religious authorities. The separation so largely brought about by Paul was to result in Gentile Christians becoming subject to the drastic Roman laws against 'illegal super-stitions', often in abeyance, but always liable to be put into effect. It seems probable that Nero's implication of the Christians in the fire of Rome was the first occasion on which such an imperial edict was specifically applied to Christians; once issued, the edict, put into force only sporadically and in particular regions during the next century, was to menace Christians with persecution when-ever they grew strong or incurred the enmity of pagan or Jewish neighbours.

The Post-Apostolic Age, A.D. 70-100

We know from the subsequent history of the Church that this period too must have been one of great and sustained advance, but only occasionally can we glimpse the details of this advance. The seven churches of the Apocalypses, like the Asia Minor churches to which Ignatius writes early in the second century, and the missionary journeys of 3 John, are examples of the way in which the Church was growing, but for the most part the growth is hidden from us.

With growth went persecution and a new emphasis on discipline. For the most part the persecution seems to have taken the form of the enmity of the surrounding population finding vent in isolated cases of violence. Such would appear to be the persecutions referred to in 1 Peter and the Epistle to the Hebrews, and possibly even 'Antipas, my witness' of Revel. ii 13, but the allusions are guarded and only guesswork is possible. It is certain, however, that the

Church found it necessary to strengthen its organisation and its discipline to meet such attacks whether from the populace or the State authorities.   The problem of authority was bound in any event to arise in a period when the Jerusalem Church had ceased to be an effective force and the apostles had passed away; the development of a stable form of church government had become a matter of urgency, and in settled churches where the first enthusiasm had often become lukewarm (Revel. iii 15) the temptation to re-inforce the authority of the Spirit by a code of Law was often irresistible.   There is at least a hint of this in Matthew's arrangement of his gospel, and in some of its contents, e.g. Mt. xviii 15-17, and the Pastoral epistles illustrate the way in which Paul's successors attempted to deal with some of their problems in such a ' legal ' way, e.g. 1 Tim. v 1-25.

THE DEVELOPMENT OF ORGANISATION AND WORSHIP

Jerusalem

The acknowledged leaders of the first Christian community at Jerusalem were the eleven apostles : they added Matthias to their number from among those who had been disciples of Jesus during his ministry and witnesses of his resurrection (Acts i 21-26).   The brethren of the Lord seem to have ranked as leaders with the apostles (1 Cor. ix 5, Gal. i 19), and one of them, James, became the first man of the Church within a few years of the resurrection (Gal. ii 9, Acts xv 13 ff.).   Luke significantly only twice extends the title to Paul and Barnabas (Acts xiv 4, 14), and seems to regard James and the twelve apostles as the holders of supreme authority in the Church; Peter and John, for example, are sent by the apostles to lay hands on the Samaritans that they may receive the Spirit (Acts viii 14 f.), and Paul is ' brought to the apostles ' by Barnabas (Acts ix 27).

At Jerusalem itself the continued presence of the majority of the apostles simplified the question of authority, because they seem to have acted on all important questions as a body which sought and obtained the consent of the Church as a whole (Acts vi 12-16, xv 22) under the joint guidance of the Spirit (Acts xv 28, cf. vi 3). As the Jerusalem community grew, special deacons (Greek *Diakonos* = servant) were appointed for the day to day work of charity, and elders (= Greek *Presbyteroi*) are mentioned (Acts xi 30, xv 2) who probably corresponded to the elders of the normal Jewish synagogue (cf. Lk. vii 3). The deacons had hands laid on them by the apostles (Acts vi 6), and it is probable that the elders were similarly appointed by the apostles with the consent of the Christian community as a whole; their functions included the control of finance (Acts xi 30) and must also have involved the arrangement of worship.

Christian worship at Jerusalem centred round the Temple (Acts ii 46, iii 1, xxi 20-24), but Christians also shared a separate communal worship of their own in each other's homes. Any twelve Jews were allowed to form a synagogue, and, although many Christians may have continued at least for a time as members of normal Jewish synagogues (Acts vi 9, ix 29), they probably established house-synagogues of their own as well; to the usual scripture-reading and interpretation, followed by prayer and praise to God, they brought a new and special unity of purpose.

Two features, in particular, marked the Christian assembly for prayer. ' They continued stedfastly . . . in the breaking of bread and prayers ' (Acts ii 42, 46). Whether this means that they celebrated the eucharist as a fulfilment of Jesus' command (1 Cor. xi 24-25), or only that they continued Jesus' practice of a fellowship-meal with his disciples, is much disputed, but the testimony of Paul (1 Cor. xi 23), taken in conjunction with the firm tradition that Jesus had given to bread and wine a new significance at the Last Supper, support the view that from the very earliest days Christians repeated the substance of that rite. The second mark of a Christian assembly was the open manifestation of the Spirit in the utterances of those who spoke. ' Prophets ' appear in the narrative of Acts ' from Jerusalem ' (xi 27, cf. xxi 8) and the nature of such prophecy can be estimated from the messages of Agabus (Acts xi 28, xxi 11) and from Paul's discussion of prophecy and speaking with tongues (1 Cor. xiv 1-19). The ecstatic utterance of sounds nonsensical to those who heard them but full of meaning to those who spoke them and to those who had the gift of interpretation (1 Cor. xii 10) was probably a constantly recurring phenomenon in Christian worship from Pentecost to the time when 1 Corinthians was written, but more important was the intelligible prophecy in which the understanding of the speaker contrived to interpret the purport of his experience and to ' edify the church ' (1 Cor. xiv 4. For the effect of prophecy on the apocalyptic distortion of Jesus' teaching cf. p. 251).

The Multiplication of Churches

As new communities were started, the need for organisation both to connect Christian churches together and to meet internal problems came slowly to the front, but the methods of organisation adopted were highly flexible and did not conform to a single pattern.

All churches were linked with the mother-church of Jerusalem by a feeling of gratitude, which showed itself in the voluntary contribution of alms (e.g. Acts xi 29-30, Rom. xv 26-27), and by a recognition of the authority attaching to the original community which contained the acknowledged leaders of the Church (Gal. ii 2, Acts xv 2). Letters (e.g. the Epistle of James, cf. Acts xv 23 ff.) and visits by delegates of the Jerusalem church to the newer communities helped to reinforce both the bond of unity (Acts xv 31-33) and the acceptance of that authority (Acts viii 14 ff., Gal. ii 11-12) ; it is noteworthy that Paul, in spite of his insistence upon his own independence of man (Gal. i 11-12), continued to pay periodical visits to Jerusalem and to consult with James and others about his plans (Gal. i 19, ii 2, Acts xxi 19, 22 ff.). As the expansion of the Church created new Gentile communities at a great distance from Palestine the difficulties of communication increased, but the journeys of Silas (cf. pp. 170-172) and the possible presence at Corinth of ' unofficial ' representatives of the Jerusalem church (cf. p. 193) indicate that attempts were made to keep in touch with new developments as far as possible.

For a time the new Christian churches were started within the Jewish synagogues and contained a large proportion of Jews; the form of organisation adopted for each community seems to have followed, within limits, the Jerusalem pattern. The missionaries for the most part seem to have worked in groups and to have formed around them a nucleus of new believers, amongst whom some would be appointed, probably with the consent of the whole body of believers, as elders (Acts xiv 23, Ja. v 14), while some would display the gifts of prophecy or teaching (Acts xiii 1). The laying on of hands to confer the gift of the Spirit after baptism or as the prelude to the undertaking of some special task had at Jerusalem been apparently the prerogative of the apostles (Acts vi 6, viii 17), but this power had now been extended to others (Acts xiii 3). In the early years of any community the personal influence of its founders must have been very great and their authority, if available, decisive in matters of discipline.

New problems were created as the Gentile element in the churches increased, notably because of their defective sense of morality and their lack of previous religious discipline; 1 Corinthians throws a lurid light on the low standards of Christians who had not been brought up to keep the Law and attend the synagogue (cf. pp. 190 f.). Yet there are few traces of any changes in the existing simple methods of organisation while Paul and Peter were still active. Elders seem to have been appointed and to be in charge of churches in the absence of their founders (e.g. 1 Thess. v 12, Acts xx 17, 28 ff., 1 Pet. v 1); deacons (Phil. i 1) and a deaconess (Rom. xvi 1) are also mentioned. Entrance to the Church was by baptism (1 Cor. i 13-16), and the laying on of hands for the conferment of the Spirit is referred to in connection with baptism (Acts xix 5-6).

Prophets were active (1 Cor. xii 28, xiv 29) and speaking with tongues continued (1 Cor. xiv 2 ff.); here Paul attempted to lay down regulations (1 Cor. xiv 26-33).

Later Developments

With the deaths of Paul and Peter and the engulfing of the Jerusalem church in the Jewish War, never to re-emerge as the headquarters of Gentile Christianity, a new situation arose. In the absence of any recognised central authority the leaders of the local churches were faced with greater responsibilities. Here and there an 'apostolic man', one of the followers of Paul like Timothy or Titus, or the unknown elder who wrote the epistles of 'John' exerted a personal influence over a number of communities, but we know from 3 John (p. 223) that their authority was sometimes challenged. It is not surprising that for the next fifty years great variations in forms of church-government and of worship are encountered. The evidence of the New Testament books themselves can now be supplemented by that of other Christian writings which are dated from the end of the first and the beginning of the second century, notably by the so-called 'Teaching of the Twelve Apostles', possibly written in Syria before A.D. 100, 'The First Epistle of Clement', written from Rome c. A.D. 96, and the epistles of Ignatius, bishop of Antioch, written c. A.D. 112.

In general the presbyterate seems to have established itself firmly as a method of government within the community. It is perhaps symptomatic that Paul towards the close of his life twice calls the elders 'episkopoi' (Acts xx 28, Phil. i 1); the Greek word means 'overseers', but its interpretation was eventually to be 'bishops'. From this committee-rule emerged by the beginning of the second century in some churches government by one bishop, supported by a number of elders and deacons. In other churches the joint rule of several presbyters seems to have persisted for a while longer. The prophets began to decline in importance; the Revelation provides evidence for the continuation of prophecy as an effective force in the life of the Church in Asia, but the ' Teaching of the Twelve Apostles ', while treating genuine prophets with respect, applies rules to their conduct which suggest that in Syria by the end of the first century prophecy was on the wane. This development of ecclesiastical organisation was accompanied by a new stress on conduct and on the holding of right doctrine ; the rise of heresy in a period when apostolic guidance was no longer readily available was probably one of the main causes for this tightening up of discipline.

The independence of the individual community, which is a feature of this period, was not to endure. Signs are not lacking that the larger churches were already strongly influencing their neighbours ; the First Epistle of Clement is in effect a demand by the church of Rome that the church of Corinth should restore to office presbyters who had been wrongly deposed.

For the details of Christian worship as it developed in these years there is little information available. Ignatius' epistles show that the Eucharist was the central rite of Christian worship at the beginning of the second century. It is significant that for him as for the author of the ' Teaching of the Twelve Apostles ' its celebration was now an ecclesiastical prerogative. There is some evidence that by the end of the first century the Eucharist was celebrated on ' the Lord's day ', and that Gentile Christians did not observe the Sabbath. Yet Jewish influence upon Christian worship was still very great. We hear of fast-days on the Jewish model, but on different days, and the adoption by the Church of the Old Testament as a sacred book played a large part in forming the prayers as well as the instruction of Christians.

PART IV

THE EPISTLES AND THE TEACHING OF THE CHURCH

CHAPTER XV

THE STUDY OF THE EPISTLES

WE read the epistles for the teaching which they give, and for their interpretation of the meaning to be placed upon the life, death, and resurrection of Jesus Christ. Their authority is in one sense inherent in their message; even if Bishop Barnes were right and 1 Cor. xiii was not originally from Paul himself,[1] this great chapter on Christian Love would still have an authority of its own. Yet in another sense there is a special authority attaching to writings which we know to come from the apostles themselves and from men who claimed, like Paul, to have gained their approval for their individual interpretations of the gospel.

The apostolicity of some at least of the epistles is therefore an important issue. It is true that both the gospels and the speeches of Peter and Paul in Acts give important testimony as to what the apostles taught about the Christian life and proclaimed about the meaning of Jesus' own life, death, and resurrection; yet both the gospels and Acts were written, not by apostles, but by later disciples, and their evidence on particular points stands in need of confirmation, if possible, from the apostles themselves.

Of our epistles seven are ascribed by tradition to original apostles or to brethren of Jesus, James, 1 and 2 Peter, 1, 2 and 3 John, and Jude. The Petrine authorship of 2 Peter is almost universally rejected, and the epistles of John are held by the great majority of scholars not to be by the apostle John, the son of Zebedee. The authorship of James, 1 Peter, and Jude, are matters of dispute; the establishment or rejection of their traditional authorship is of more than academic importance.

The Pauline epistles raise further important questions. Few, even of those who reject the apostolic authorship of

[1] *The Rise of Christianity,* p. 230.

James, 1 Peter, and Jude, would deny that Paul had met the leaders of the Church and submitted to them the gospel which he preached (Gal. ii 2 ff.). But Paul's epistles show that some elements of his thought, at least, were highly individual, and that his 'development' of the apostolic gospel was not a static one, but changing in some aspects over the years. A comparative study of the other epistles, including the 'apostolic' ones, shows that developments of various kinds continued through the first century, and that, within a wide unity, there was much variety of expression and interpretation.

In studying the epistles the reader should set before him four aims. First, he should make up his mind, in the light of the evidence, on the problems of authorship taking into consideration the value of the speeches in Acts. By this means he will be enabled to reach a reasoned view of how the earliest Christians proclaimed their faith. Second, he should study the epistles of Paul, in their chronological order to understand both how Paul was a great pioneer in his preaching, and how his thought developed as he grew older. Third, he should study the later developments of doctrine as they manifest themselves in Ephesians, Hebrews, 1 John, etc. It is only then that he will be able satisfactorily to pursue his fourth aim, that of understanding the growth of Christian theology and teaching in New Testament times.

BOOKS FOR READING

A translation in modern English is of great value for understanding the sometimes involved and complicated thought of the epistles. Paraphrases are also useful : a good one is J. W. C. WAND, *New Testament Letters* (*Oxford*).

Commentaries (those marked with a star are particularly helpful).

ROMANS : C. H. DODD * (Moffatt), K. E. KIRK (Clarendon Bible).
1 AND 2 CORINTHIANS : E. EVANS (Clarendon Bible).
1 CORINTHIANS : MOFFATT (Moffatt).

2 CORINTHIANS: R. H. STRACHAN (Moffatt).
GALATIANS: G. S. DUNCAN (Moffatt), A. W. F. BLUNT (Clarendon Bible).
EPHESIANS, COLOSSIANS, PHILEMON: E. F. SCOTT * (Moffatt).
PHILIPPIANS: M. JONES (Westminster).
1 AND 2 THESSALONIANS: BICKNELL (Westminster).
PASTORALS: B. S. EASTON (S.C.M.), E. F. SCOTT (Moffatt).
HEBREWS: T. H. ROBINSON (Moffatt), F. D. V. NARBOROUGH (Clarendon), NAIRNE (Cambridge Bible).
JAMES: KNOWLING (Westminster).
JAMES, PETER, JUDE: MOFFATT (Moffatt).
JOHANNINE EPISTLES: C. H. DODD * (Moffatt).

The Life and Teaching of Paul, etc.

C. H. DODD, *The Meaning of St. Paul for To-day* (Swarthmore Press).
A. D. NOCK, *St. Paul* (Home University Library). An excellent short life.
A. H. McNEILE, *St. Paul* (Cambridge). A good exposition of Paul's thought.
A. H. McNEILE, *New Testament Teaching in the Light of St. Paul* (Cambridge).
C. A. ANDERSON SCOTT, *Christianity according to St. Paul* (Cambridge).
E. F. SCOTT, *Varieties of New Testament Religion* (Scribner).
H. A. A. KENNEDY, *The Theology of the Epistles* (Duckworth).
A. SCHWEITZER, *The Mysticism of Paul the Apostle* (Black). For advanced study.
K. LAKE, *The Earlier Epistles of St. Paul* (Rivington). For advanced study.
W. L. KNOX, *St. Paul and the Church of Jerusalem* (Cambridge). For advanced study.
W. L. KNOX, *St. Paul and the Church of the Gentiles* (Cambridge). For advanced study.

CHAPTER XVI

THE EPISTLE OF JAMES

AUTHORSHIP OF THE EPISTLE

THE writer of this epistle names himself ' James, a servant of God and of the Lord Jesus Christ ' (i 1), and tradition has generally identified him with the brother of Jesus, who appears from Gal. ii 9 and Acts xv to have been the leader of the Jerusalem church.

The traditional view has been challenged on a number of grounds, of which the most important are the language of the epistle, which is in good Greek, the absence of references to the life, death, and resurrection of Jesus, and the slowness with which the epistle was received as canonical.

The argument from the language of the epistle is a weak one. Whether James could speak and write Greek or not, the epistle is addressed to ' the twelve tribes which are of the Dispersion (i.e. outside Palestine), and Greek would be the language which they would most easily understand, especially if, as appears likely, the term is meant to include not only Jewish Christians but Gentile converts as well. There were in Jerusalem Christians fully capable of translating James' words into fluent Greek, as can be seen from the procedure followed in composing a letter to the Gentile Christians of Syria and Cilicia after the Council of Jerusalem in A.D. 49 (Acts xv).

The lack of any appeal to the life, death, and resurrection of Jesus, whose name is mentioned only twice in the epistle (i 1, ii 1), is at first sight hard to reconcile with the authorship of James, the Lord's brother, and has led to speculation as to the possibility of the first verse being a later addition based on an erroneous conjecture as to its authorship.[1]

---

[1] Streeter, *The Primitive Church*, p. 191.

On the other hand the very absence of theological interpretation of the life, death and resurrection of Jesus tells
against any theory that the epistle is the work of a later
anonymous Christian, and it is better to take the silence
of James, like that of Jude, as an indication of the way in
which the brethren of Jesus proclaimed their faith. The
epistle of James is primarily one of teaching on conduct,
and the teaching is often couched in words so reminiscent of
the words of Jesus, yet in a form which tells against use
of the later gospels, that the simplest explanation remains
authorship by one whose knowledge of the Lord's teaching
was first-hand.

The comparative slowness of the epistle in acquiring
canonical recognition also requires some explanation. It
was possibly known to Clement (c. A.D. 96) and to Hermas
(c. A.D. 145) at Rome, but it is not included in the Muratorian
Canon, a Roman list of the end of the second century A.D.
In the east, both Clement of Alexandria (c. A.D. 200) and
Origen quote from it as an apostolic writing, but a century
later Eusebius, although he himself accepts it, says that
others do not, and that not many of the ancients mentioned
it. Even after his time some of the Antiochian fathers did
not include it among the books which they regarded as
canonical.

The reasons for such hesitation in its acceptance must
be sought in the limited circulation which it enjoyed in the
early period, and in the untheological nature of the epistle
which led many later Christian teachers to regard it as inadequate. The original prestige of James, so potent in the
earliest days of the church, soon waned when the church of
Jerusalem lost its position of leadership, and James became
a shadowy figure, known only from a few references in the
Pauline epistles, from the Acts of the Apostles, a work which
for a considerable time seems to have had limited currency,
and from the legends of later Jewish Christians, notably in
the Gospel according to the Hebrews, Hegesippus, and the
Clementine Recognitions. The very simplicity of the
epistle, and its lack of historical data, helped to diminish its

importance. It was only with the passing of time and the rise of a general tendency to extend canonicity to such minor works as Jude and 2 and 3 John that James also came into its own. While the cumulative force of the objections against the traditional authorship must be admitted as considerable, they cannot be regarded as decisive, and it remains probable that we have in this epistle the teaching of the acknowledged head of the early Jerusalem church.

THE TEACHING OF THE EPISTLE
AND THE CIRCUMSTANCES OF ITS WRITING

The message of the epistle is a practical one of encouragement in the face of temptations, and of moral exhortation. The basis of this exhortation is that we are all sinners and therefore worthy of death (i 14-15), but that God of his own will has given us a hope of salvation (i 18, 21), and that the end is near, ' behold the judge standeth before the doors ' (v 9). So far James goes with Paul, but he interprets the means of salvation in terms of keeping ' the perfect law, the law of liberty ' (i 25), and his conception of faith is radically different from Paul's. For James faith can exist without works (ii 18-24), and can indicate only a belief in God insufficient to change a man's actions (ii 19 ' the devils also believe, and shudder '), although at times he uses the word in a much deeper sense (i 6, v 15).

It has been thought by some scholars that James, in part of his epistle (ii 14-26), is attacking the Pauline doctrine of ' justification by faith ', or a perverted interpretation of Paul's teaching, but it is far more likely that his target is not a theological doctrine, but the reluctance of Christians in general to live up to their responsibilities. The emphasis is throughout on Christian conduct, as involving both action (e.g. i 27, iii 13, iv 17) and abstinence from sin (e.g. ii 9-11, iv 11, v 12), and the references even to prayer are practical ones (v 14-18).

The absence of theological interest is in striking contrast to the other epistles, with the significant exception of Jude.

There are two references to Jesus as ' the Lord Jesus Christ '
(i 1) and ' our Lord Jesus Christ of glory ' (ii 1), with a
possible allusion to his death at the hands of the rich
(v 6), but James says nothing of his redeeming power or of
his relationship to the Father.

On the other hand the language of the epistle reminds us
continually of the teaching of Jesus as it is recorded in
Matthew's Sermon on the Mount especially, but also in Luke
and John.   Among the most striking examples are the contrast between living and doing (i 22-23 cf. Mt. vii 21, Lk. vi
46), the command against judging (iv 11 cf. Mt. vii 1), and
that against swearing (v 12 cf. Mt. v 34 ff.), but it has been
estimated that nearly half the verses in James find a parallel
of sorts in the gospels.   The form of the resemblances is
such as to suggest not a literary relationship, but that James
was well acquainted with the teaching of Jesus as it was
remembered in the earliest days of the church.

The date of the epistle and the readers to whom it was
addressed are much disputed.   On the whole it seems best
to accept an early date, c. A.D. 45, and to assume that the
epistle is a general one destined for Christians outside
Palestine, who at this time would be for the most part Jews,
or Gentiles who had come under the influence of Judaism (cf.
the reference to ' your synagogue ' ii 2).   This would account
for the absence of any reference to the controversies connected with the admission of Gentiles into the church,
which seem to have come to a head a few years later, and
seems to suit the ' non-theological ' teaching of the epistle
better than the assumption that it dates from a much later
period.

THE IMPORTANCE OF THE EPISTLE

The authorship and early date of the epistle are matters
of probability and not of certainty.   Yet if James, the
brother of Jesus, is accepted as the author of the epistle,
it becomes our best witness to the beliefs of the earliest
Jerusalem church.   While it is unwise to build too much

on the negative evidence of one short letter, there are striking differences between the presentation of the Christian gospel here and in the other great epistles. Some of these differences may well be attributed to James' personality; there are some striking affinities between the epistle and Luke's account of James' speech at the Council of Jerusalem (Acts xv 13-21). Yet we cannot ignore the fact that James was apparently the unchallenged leader of the early Jerusalem church, and no theory of the teaching of the 'apostolic' church can fail to take into account James' interpretation of the gospel as being at least one of the ways in which the earliest Christians passed on their faith.

CHAPTER XVII

THE FIRST EPISTLE OF PETER

AUTHORSHIP

THE epistle is written in Peter's name to the elect who are sojourners of the dispersion in Pontus, Galatia, Cappadocia, Asia, and Bithynia (i 1) from Babylon (v 13) by the hand of Silvanus (v 12). It was quoted by Polycarp and Papias in Asia Minor in the early years of the second century, and its authenticity was undisputed in the early church, although Babylon was generally understood as a cryptic reference to Rome.

The attribution to Peter has been widely challenged in modern times on a number of grounds. We know that at least three writings were in circulation in the second century which were falsely attributed to Peter, the epistle which is included in the New Testament as the Second Epistle of Peter, an Apocalypse of Peter, and a Gospel of Peter. Some features of this epistle too have led critics to regard it as also being a forgery, dating from the end of the first century or the very beginning of the second century.

The epistle is written in fluent and idiomatic Greek, much better than that of Paul, and the Biblical quotations show an intimate knowledge of the Septuagint; this is hard to understand if the epistle is really the work of an Aramaic speaking and illiterate fisherman (Mt. xxvi 73, Acts iv 13). There are numerous echoes of both the language and ideas of the Pauline epistles, notably of Romans, and some critics have interpreted the general theological tone of the epistle as reflecting a ' central ' churchmanship more compatible with a post-apostolic stage of development, when Paul's epistles were more widely known, than with an earlier period. The references to persecution, especially the possibility of suffering ' as a Christian ' (iv 16), are sometimes taken to imply a date in the time of Trajan (A.D. 98-117) whose letters to Pliny (A.D. 112) furnish the first certain evidence that Christianity was regarded as of itself a crime against the state. It has been suggested, in pursuance of these arguments, that the main part of the epistle (i 3-iv 11) consists of a sermon to newly-baptised converts; this has been incorporated in a letter written to meet a crisis of persecution by a Christian who introduced Peter's name in an endeavour to give his words of exhortation an official and apostolic authority.

The weight of this attack on the Petrine authorship cannot be denied, but the ascription can still be defended with some confidence, especially if the Silvanus of the epistle is, as there is no reason to doubt, Silas, the companion of Paul on his second missionary journey. The case for Peter's authorisation of the epistle, paradoxical as it may seem, is strengthened by the probability that he did not himself have a ready command of the Greek language. It is expressly stated at the close of the epistle that Peter has written ' by the hand of Silvanus '. If Peter could not himself speak Greek and wished to send a letter to Greek-speaking Gentiles in Asia Minor, he could either have dictated a letter in Aramaic for subsequent translation into Greek or have had a Greek letter composed for him by someone he could trust. There is nothing improbable in his adopting the latter course, and there are two curious pieces of evidence in its favour. Silvanus is called ' our faithful brother, as I account him ' (v 12), a description which gains special point if he had actually drafted the letter for Peter in a language which Peter only imperfectly understood. We know, too, from Acts that, when the decree of the Council of Jerusalem was sent to Antioch, the apostles and elders wrote ' by the hand of ' Judas and Silas, a phrase which suggests that Silas had a part in the drafting of the pastoral letter in which the decree was incorporated (Acts xv 23).

This explanation of the composition of the epistle fully meets the difficulties both of language and of ' Paulinism '.

Silas' selection as one of the delegates from the Council of Jerusalem to Antioch was probably due in part to the fact that he spoke Greek well and could explain the decrees to the Gentile Christians there (Acts xv 32), and his intimate connection with Paul on the second missionary journey would account for the affinities of language and thought between this epistle and those of Paul. Nor is it necessary to assume that the 'fiery trial' (iv 12) and the possibility of suffering 'as a Christian' (iv 16) imply a persecution essentially different in kind from that which Paul and Silas had undergone in their travels.

The part played by Silvanus in the writing of the epistle helps us also to understand the circumstances in which it was written. The identification of 'Babylon' with Rome fits in with the general later tradition of Peter's presence at Rome, and although many scholars dispute the historical value of this tradition which they hold to be ultimately derived from the misinterpretation of this very verse in I Peter, a Roman origin for the epistle cannot be ruled completely out of court. Yet there is a real difficulty in accepting the identification. Quite apart from the absence of any intelligible reason for Peter using such a cryptic term for Rome in an epistle in which he bids his readers honour the Emperor (ii 17), no convincing evidence has so far been adduced for Rome being called Babylon before the Jewish War of A.D. 70 had fanned the flames of Jewish hatred.

There is nothing inherently improbable, on the other hand, in Peter having worked in Babylon and its neighbourhood, where we know from Josephus (Ant. xv 2, 2) there were large communities of Jews. The absence of any tradition connecting Peter with Babylon is explicable by the great break between the Christian communities of East and West that followed upon the disasters of A.D. 70 and the subsequent misfortunes of Christianity in Palestine and elsewhere. We know next to nothing of the early spread of Christianity in directions other than that North-West mission whose progress Luke has so faithfully recorded. We know next to nothing of the coming of Christianity to the provinces of Asia Minor named in the epistle other than Galatia and Asia, but it is not rash to see in the evangelisation of Northern Asia Minor the results of the same impetus that led Paul through Southern Asia Minor. Whether Silas himself had played a part in this further spread of the Gospel, or whether his rôle is to be envisaged as that of liaison between the apostles and the actual missionaries, we can never know. He is last mentioned in Acts as being summoned by Paul to come to him at Athens (Acts xvii 15), and Paul mentions him with Timothy as a joint author of his epistles to the Thessalonians in A.D. 49, probably at Corinth (cf. 2 Cor. i 19). It seems reasonable to assume that he continued to be interested in, possibly to share in, missionary journeys to parts of Asia Minor in the years that followed, and that the first epistle of Peter is a message of instruction and encouragement from the apostle through Silvanus to some of the new and predominantly Gentile (cf. iv 3-4) churches which had been founded. The encyclical nature of the epistle and the lack of greetings to individuals suggest that Peter had not himself visited these areas, and that the epistle may in fact have been a kind of official recognition of the churches in a new mission-field, possibly to be carried round by Silvanus on a tour of inspection and confirmation.

The date of the epistle can only be conjectured. If the tradition of Peter's martyrdom at Rome under Nero is accepted, it cannot be later than the early sixties. A dozen years may sound a short time for churches to have sprung up over so wide an area, but the rapidity with which Paul established churches on his missionary journeys indicates that such a swift expansion elsewhere was not impossible.

THE TEACHING OF THE EPISTLE

The epistle falls roughly into three sections, i 1-ii 10 the nature of the Christian calling and privileges, ii 11-iv 11 instruction in the principles and duties of Christian life, iv 12-v 14 special exhortation and consolation for the dangers and difficulties of the present situation. The thought, however, is fluid and spontaneous rather than systematic, and these divisions are in no way watertight; ideas spill over from one to the other.

The most striking feature of the theological allusions and of the instruction on conduct is their ' centrality '. The pattern of doctrinal teaching, which can be traced in its simplest form in the speeches in Acts, and which represents the fundamental core which Paul has overlaid with the results of his own speculations and experience, recurs substantially in i Peter.   As Dr. Selwyn has pointed out in a comparison of the doctrinal teaching of this epistle with that of the speeches of Peter in Acts i-x, ' there is the same emphasis on the priority of the divine counsel, and on God's initiative in the call of the Church and His impartiality in judgement ; the same conception of Jesus as the " suffering servant " portrayed in Is. liii, a conception not found in St. Paul : the same idea of the Church as the Messianic community.' [1]   There are, as might be expected, differences of emphasis and additions.   Thus there is comparatively little stress in the epistle on the work of the Holy Spirit. God's love for men is never mentioned, and man's attitude to God is written of as one of awe (i 17, ii 17) rather than of love, while in place of the simple reference of Peter at Pentecost to the fact that Christ was not ' left in Hades, nor did his flesh see corruption ' (Acts ii 31) the epistle develops the conception of Christ's preaching to the dead (iii 19 f., iv 6).

The epistle is not, however, primarily theological, and the theological allusions are those of a practical man rather than a speculative thinker.   The main body of the epistle consists rather of instruction on the nature of the Christian life and the duties of Christian living.   Here, too, the first impression is one of ' centrality ', and of the following of a common pattern of teaching such as can be discerned in the other, and notably the Pauline, epistles.   The form

[1] *The First Epistle of St. Peter*, p. 75.

of this pattern, which is further discussed in connection with 1 and 2 Thessalonians (p. 186), includes teaching on the holiness of the Christian calling as the new Israel and people of God (i 15, ii 9), the repudiation of pagan vices (i 14, ii 1, iv 3), the law of charity and social obligation (*passim*), the nearness of the end and the need for soberness and watchfulness (iv 7, v 8-10), emphasis on church order (v 1-6), and possibly the duty of obedience to the state (ii 13), for which Romans (xiii 1) and the epistle to Titus (iii 1) offer parallels.

Particular points are stressed, e.g. the privilege of suffering (ii 19), the subjection of wives to their husbands (iii 1-6), and the deference due from the young to the old (v 5), and the epistle bears the marks of being written by one who expected obedience to his authority. After calling himself an apostle in the first verse Peter begins his final admonitions as a fellow-elder, and a witness of the sufferings of Christ (v 1); these allusions, natural in an apostle, are at once in character with the real Peter, whose authority was universally accepted, and too modest and reticent for a forger not to have embroidered (cf. the claims of the author of 2 Pet. i 14-18).

THE SIGNIFICANCE OF THE EPISTLE

While the epistle remains a work of great spiritual power and lasting value, whoever was the author, its especial historical significance is bound up with the connection with Peter. Considered as a pseudonymous writing of the end of the first century, the epistle would furnish additional evidence for the spreading influence of a diluted Paulinism, and a few clues as to the problems of Christian life in Asia Minor in the sub-apostolic age. Taken as written by Peter, or even as composed by Silvanus and approved by Peter, it becomes at once an invaluable piece of evidence for the apostolic approval and support of the main lines of Paul's teaching. Although we have Paul's own word for this (Gal.

ii 9) it has often been challenged. The Petrine authorship of this epistle carries with it the acknowledgement that Peter, after disagreement (Gal. ii 14) and conversion (Acts xv 9-11) on one major issue at least, shared the same fundamental views as Paul, though without many of Paul's individual interpretations and developments.

CHAPTER XVIII

PAUL AND HIS EPISTLES

THE IMPORTANCE OF PAUL

OUR knowledge of Paul is severely limited, and is virtually all drawn from a dozen or so letters written by Paul himself over a period of less than fifteen years and from what Luke has to say about his career and teaching in the Acts of the Apostles. We do not know, for example, the exact year of his conversion, nor how far his thought developed between his conversion and the date of his first surviving letter, at least fourteen years later, nor can we do more than guess at what happened to him after his two years imprisonment in Rome.

Yet the limitations to our knowledge, though tantalising, need not be unduly lamented. We know far more both of Paul's career and teaching than we do of any other Christian of the first generation, and it is not too much to say that the career and teaching of Paul have been of more influence in the growth and development of the Christian church than the work of any other man. There were many Christian missionaries in the first age of the church, and Christianity spread in many directions, but the evidence of the second century makes it clear that the decisive rôle in the formation of Christian doctrine and order was played by those churches which Paul himself had founded, or in which his influence had been at work, e.g. Antioch, Ephesus and the churches of Asia Minor, Corinth, and Rome.

It can therefore be counted as providential that we should know both the main outlines of Paul's missionary work in the spread of the gospel from Antioch to Rome, and the essence of his mature teaching. If the Acts and the Pauline epistles had not survived, the history of later Christianity would have been very different and that of the primitive church impossible to write. Thanks to their preservation we are enabled, admittedly in the face of many lacunae and unsolved problems, to reconstruct an intelligible picture of the way in which ' the faith which was once for all delivered to the saints ' (Jude 3) was transmitted and developed until it became the theological system of the later church.

PAUL, THE MAN AND THEOLOGIAN

The facts of Paul's life, as we know them, can be briefly summarised. He was born of Jewish parents at Tarsus, in Cilicia, and was a pupil of Gamaliel at Jerusalem (Acts xxii 3), where he had family connections (the son of a sister of Paul is mentioned in Acts xxiii 16 as living at Jerusalem in A.D. 56), and where he seems to have continued to live himself. He had been brought up as a Pharisee (Acts xxiii 6), with a strict regard for the traditions which clustered about the written Law, and showed a peculiar zeal for these traditions (Gal. i 14). As a young man he was present at the stoning of Stephen (Acts vii 58), and ' was consenting unto his death ' (viii 1) ; later he took a leading part in the persecution of the Christians, arresting men and women (viii 3), and finally being sent at his own request to Damascus with letters from the high priest to the synagogues there on a similar mission (ix 1-2). He was miraculously converted on the way and after his sight had been restored by Ananias and he had been baptised (ix 18) he preached his new faith in Damascus until his life was in danger and he had to escape by night, being let down through a window in the wall in a basket (2 Cor. xi 33). He returned again to Damascus, and after three years went to Jerusalem where Barnabas vouched for his conversion and he met Peter. After becoming involved in further controversies, this time with Jews from the dispersion, the church got him away to Tarsus, from where Barnabas brought him to Antioch. Fourteen (or possibly eleven) years later he came to Jerusalem again with Barnabas on a deputation from the church of Antioch, and took the opportunity of discussing the gospel which he preached with the leaders of the Jerusalem church, James,

Peter, and John, who gave their general approval and agreed that Paul and Barnabas should go to the Gentiles while they continued their mission among the Jews.   Paul and Barnabas carried out a missionary journey in Cyprus and Southern Asia Minor, and after a dispute at Antioch, which seems to have spread to Galatia, over the terms on which Gentiles should be admitted to the Church, Peter was won over to Paul's view and championed it at the Council of Jerusalem in A.D. 49.   After the council and Paul's return to Antioch he went with Silas on a missionary journey through Asia Minor and Greece, which included a two year stay at Corinth and seems to have lasted some years.   A third missionary journey through Asia Minor and Greece followed, Paul staying some two years at Ephesus, and finally going up to Jerusalem in A.D. 56.   After a few days' stay he was arrested following a riot, and removed, for fear of assassination, first to Caesarea for two years, and then on his appeal to Caesar to Rome.   Here Luke tells us he was kept in confinement to his own hired dwelling for two more years (Acts xxviii 30)—and we know no more.

Of the influences which shaped the thought of Paul, as it finds expression in the letters of his later life—and it is a few of these only which we possess—three can be distinguished as especially important, his upbringing, the experiences of his conversion and later visions, and the teaching of the apostles and of his fellow-Christians.

' After the straitest sect of our religion I lived, a Pharisee' (Acts xxvi 5), in these words Paul describes his religion before his conversion.   They imply that he had been trained not only to regard the keeping of the Mosaic Law, interpreted in the light of numerous oral traditions, as the sole way for a man to be justified before God, but that he had accepted also the hope of a resurrection from the dead (Acts xxiii 6) and the coming of God's Messiah.   Even before his conversion Paul had known the sinfulness of his life and waited for God to intervene and redeem Israel.   It is in this consciousness of his own failure to keep the whole Law, sharpened perhaps by the words of Stephen on Christ's

replacement of Law and Temple, that, even while perse-
cuting, Paul may have been led to doubt some of his own
cherished beliefs and prepared for his conversion.

Whether his conversion came after such searchings of
himself or not, it did not wipe out all the results of his
early training. All Paul's epistles bear traces of the influence
of his Jewish training, a stress on the importance of the Law,
even although it has been superseded by the work of Christ,
a conception of salvation in terms carried over from his
past, the use of Old Testament texts according to a Pharisaic
type of exegesis. Nor did Paul's conversion bring him at
once to a final system of belief. It convinced him indeed
that Jesus was the Son of God, and that he was called to his
service; but Paul's life was from now on to be filled with
experiences and visions which were to shape his beliefs and
guide his actions continually (e.g. Acts xvi 6, 7, 9, xxiii 11,
xxvii 23, 2 Cor xii 2 ff., Gal. ii 2). Thus it seems that his
call to the Gentiles was the result of more than one vision
(Acts ix 15 and Acts xxii 17 ff.).

The third main factor in the development of Paul's
thought was the influence exerted upon him of the general
Christian teaching of his time. From time to time he
stressed in controversy that the gospel which he preached
he had not received from man, ' nor was I taught it, but it
came to me through the revelation of Jesus Christ ' (Gal.
i 12, cf. 1 Cor. ii 10 ff.); it is clear too, that Paul did not
shrink from opposing a majority view in the church when he
saw it to be not according to the truth of the gospel (Gal. ii
14). Yet elsewhere he states explicitly that James, Peter,
and John had given him and Barnabas the right hands of
fellowship after listening to his exposition of the gospel which
he preached (Gal. ii 2-9), and both Barnabas and Silas, men
of standing in the Jerusalem community, found themselves
able to work with him on missionary journeys. While
Paul clearly worked out his beliefs as the Spirit led him, and
some of his teaching bears the stamp of his own personal
experience and of original formulation, much of what he
taught was in fact the common teaching of Christian

missionaries which Paul had more or less unconsciously absorbed from contact with his predecessors and companions.

The conjunction of these three influences, a Pharisaic training and cast of thought, profound spiritual experiences, and conformity with the main lines of primitive Christian preaching, makes Paul's epistles at times difficult for the modern man to understand without the aid of paraphrases and commentaries. At the same time this combination of gifts gives to Paul's teaching a special value, in that he was enabled to clothe his experience in language which has played a decisive part in the classical formulations of Christian doctrine, and has in all centuries led men on to similar spiritual experiences and helped them also to understand them.

THE PAULINE EPISTLES, THEIR GENUINENESS, REVISION, AND ORDER

Not all of the fourteen epistles ascribed to Paul in our Bible can be accepted as his. The epistle to the Hebrews is Pauline neither in its language nor its theology (cf. p. 210 *infra*), and even in antiquity translation by Luke or Clement of Rome and authorship by Barnabas were suggested to solve the difficulty. The tradition of Pauline authorship seems to have been fostered largely in order to secure the inclusion of such a valuable work in the Canon, but modern critical scholars are unanimous in rejecting it. Serious difficulties are also caused by the style and theology of Ephesians and the Pastoral Epistles to Timothy and Titus; the critics are here more divided in their judgements, and it is impossible to speak with certainty, but it is maintained in the discussions of these epistles below (pp. 204-208) in accordance with the views of many scholars, that Ephesians is written by an admirer of Paul, who had a good knowledge and understanding of many of his epistles, and that the Pastoral Epistles, while containing fragments of genuine Pauline letters, are the work of a later age. The doubts which have been expressed about others of the Pauline epistles, notably 2 Thessalonians, are not so generally felt.

While there is no reason to doubt the Pauline authorship of such ' key ' epistles as Romans and 1 and 2 Corinthians, there are signs that both Romans and 2 Corinthians may once have circulated in a different form. The evidence for this—textual in the case of Romans, and derived from the different tone of the beginning and end in the case of 2 Corinthians—is discussed in the treatment of these epistles (pp. 191-196 *infra*) but the conclusions there adopted may be mentioned here, that chapter xvi of Romans, except for the doxology (25-27) probably originally formed part of a letter of Paul's to Ephesus, and that the last four chapters of 2 Corinthians (x-xiii) may come from an earlier letter of Paul to Corinth and have been combined with 2 Cor. i-ix by a later editor, but that the balance of probabilities is against such a theory. In both these cases the patching, if patching there was, seems to have been done with a minimum of alteration to Paul's words, and without any doctrinal motive other than a desire to put as much as possible of Paul's letters into presentable form.

The arranging of Paul's epistles in chronological order raises only two problems of any magnitude, the date of Galatians and the place of imprisonment from which Colossians, Philippians, and Philemon were written. The early date for Galatians, A.D. 49, is accepted in the discussion of this epistle below, and the theory of an Ephesian imprisonment is rejected in favour of a Roman origin for the ' captivity epistles '. The order and date of our epistles can then be approximately given as follows [1]—

		A.D.
1. Galatians (written from Antioch shortly before the Council of Jerusalem) . . .		early in 49
2. 1 Thessalonians (from Corinth) . . .		50
3. 2 Thessalonians (a few months later) . .		50
4. 1 Corinthians (from the neighbourhood of Ephesus)		early in 55
5. 2. Corinthians (from Macedonia) . .		later in 55

[1] The difficulties of New Testament chronology are considerable, but the dates given, if this order is in fact the right one, are not likely to be more than a year or two out.

		A.D.
6. Romans (from Corinth)	.	early in 56
7, 8. Colossians and Philemon (from Rome)	.	late in 59
9. Philippians (from Rome)	. .	60

If A.D. 29 be accepted as the probable date of the cruci-fixion, and Paul's conversion be placed somewhere between A.D. 32 and 35 (cf. Gal. i 18, ii 1), it will be seen that the letters of Paul which we possess all date from a comparatively late period in his ministry. It is well therefore to be careful in speaking of development in his thought at this stage, especially as many of the variations in the teaching of his different epistles illustrate his own maxim, that 'I am become all things to all men, that I may by all means save some'. There is nothing surprising in the similarity of the teaching of Galatians to that of Romans, written some six years later; here Paul is giving once again the very heart of his gospel, worked out long before.

Yet development there is, especially in the later epistles when Paul is in expectation of death, and the earlier hope of the imminent end of the world is replaced by a deeper and even more spiritual interpretation of the life to come. While the epistles do not show a steady change of emphasis in Paul's teaching over a period of ten years or so, there is a marked move away from the framework of Jewish modes of thought to a wider and more universal conception of religion.

THE EPISTLES IN DETAIL
Galatians

CIRCUMSTANCES OF WRITING

Who were the Galatians? This is one of the classical controversies of New Testament criticism. Two answers are possible. The first, given by Bishop Lightfoot, is that they were the inhabitants of North Galatia, who Paul may have visited in the course of his second missionary journey; this would involve a date for the epistle after the Council of Jerusalem, and raises serious problems as to why Paul has so little to say about the Council that agrees with Luke's version of what happened. The second answer, more generally accepted by recent critics, is that the ' Galatians ' were not Galatians by race (i.e. Gauls, who had migrated into the middle of Asia Minor in the third century B.C. and settled there), but Christians of those towns in the southern part of the Roman province of Galatia which Paul and Barnabas had visited on their first missionary journey. If this latter view is accepted, and the epistle is taken as written before the Council of Jerusalem, it becomes easier to reconcile Paul's account of his visits to Jerusalem with those described in Acts ix 26 ff. and xi 30, although even then there are some important variations between the two accounts. It becomes easier, too, to understand the circumstances in which Paul wrote.

The Galatian Christians have been seduced from their newly gained faith by Jewish, and probably Jewish Christian, missionaries who have told them that the keeping of the Jewish Law is essential to their salvation. It was just this controversy within the Christian church that was to be settled by the authority of the Council of Jerusalem, and that had been raised at Antioch itself (Gal. ii 14). Paul accordingly writes to them in the heat of controversy, possibly only a few weeks before leaving Antioch for the Council in A.D. 49.

TEACHING OF THE EPISTLE

The two main issues dealt with in the epistle are the authority of Paul, which had been attacked, and the place of the Jewish Law in the scheme of salvation.

In the first section of the epistle (i 1-ii 14) Paul asserts the divine origin of the gospel which he preaches, which came to him ' through revelation of Jesus Christ ' (i 13), and demonstrates from a short account of his own life that while he has consulted with the Jerusalem leaders of the church and obtained their approval for what he preaches, he has also resisted pressure from these leaders and their representatives (' certain from James ' ii 12) when they were in error. The keynote of this section is the aside in ii 8, 'for he that wrought for Peter unto the apostleship of the circumcision wrought for me also unto the Gentiles '.

From his own part in establishing at Antioch the claim of Gentile Christians to full table-fellowship with Jewish Christians, he passes on in ii 15 to the arguments with which he supports the truth that has been revealed to him, that ' we believed on Jesus Christ, that we might be justified by faith in Christ, and not by works of the Law; because by the works of the law shall no flesh be justified ' (ii 16).[1]

These arguments include a brief appeal to their own experience of the Spirit through faith and not through works of the law (iii 1-5), and the use of Old Testament texts by a Pharisaic type of exegesis to show that Abraham was justified by faith (iii 6. James uses the same text Genesis xv 6 to show that Abraham was justified by works, James iii 21-23), that the promise which Abraham received by faith was not annulled by the law, which came later, and that it was to his seed (i.e. Christ) and not to his seeds (i.e. his descendants in general); through baptism into Christ all, whether Jews or Gentiles, put on Christ, and ' if ye are Christ's, then are ye Abraham's seed, heirs according to promise ' (iii 29). He goes on to develop the inferiority of the law to the full redemption of Christ, again employing Old Testament texts and the story of Sarah and Hagar to prove his point by an ingenious, but to our minds over-subtle use of allegorical interpretation (iv). Then he reminds the Galatians that observance of the law will lose them their freedom, and from this thought is led to remind them that freedom is not an occasion to the flesh (v 13), but for love in the Spirit. With a final attack on the pride and insincerity of the Judaisers he brings them back to the cross of Christ as the centre of his and their hopes (v. 11-18).

---

[1] These words probably formed part of what Paul said to Peter at Antioch : ' We ' are clearly Jews. It is interesting, in the light of this, to read the similar words put into the mouth of Peter at the Council of Jerusalem by Luke (Acts xv 10-11), the most ' Pauline ' speech in Acts.

1 Thessalonians

CIRCUMSTANCES OF WRITING

This epistle was written from Corinth on the second missionary journey in A.D. 50 when Timothy had just returned (iii 6) from a visit at Paul's request to confirm the work that Paul had begun with Timothy and Silas in his three weeks' stay in Thessalonica (Acts xvii 2). Its peculiar interest and value for us lie in the fact that Paul is here largely reminding the new converts of the teaching which he has given them, so that we have in summary form a partial recapitulation of the way in which Paul preached the gospel at the founding of a new Christian church containing both Jews and—in large numbers—Gentiles (Acts xvii 4).

TEACHING

1 Thessalonians is a partial, not a complete recapitulation of Paul's teaching at Thessalonica. We know, for example, from Acts xvii 2-3 that Paul had on three successive sabbaths reasoned in the synagogue with the Jews from the scriptures, ' opening and alleging that it behoved the Christ to suffer, and to rise again from the dead, and that this Jesus, whom, said he, I proclaim unto you, is the Christ '. His converts had accepted the Lordship of Jesus, and had experienced the power and joy of the Holy Spirit (1 Thess. i 5-6) ; their faith (1-8) and their patience in persecution (iii 4-6, 2 Thess. i 4) were outstanding, their love of the brethren (1 Thess. iv 9) such that ' ye have no need that one write unto you ; for ye yourselves are taught of God '.

Paul, therefore, makes only short references to most of the great Christian theological doctrines that he had expounded, the repudiation of idolatry and the service of the one true God (i 9), who had raised his Son from the dead to heaven, whence he was to come again to deliver the faithful from the wrath to come and be ever with them (i 10, iv 17). On one point only does he find it necessary to supplement his former teaching, to reassure them about the destiny of those who have died before the coming of the

Lord (iv 13-18). This passage, taken with others in 2 Thessalonians, makes it clear that Paul expected, and had proclaimed to the Thessalonians, the coming of the end of the world at a time unknown but near (v 2), in largely material terms borrowed from contemporary Jewish Apocalyptic. (This conception, which he shared with other Christian teachers of the first generation, and which involved a corresponding destruction of the wicked (v 9, 2 Thess. i 8) is discussed later (pp. 251-252) and its relation to the teaching of Jesus himself examined.)

This eschatological expectation in turn gives a special importance and urgency to the ethical instruction of which Paul continually reminds the Thessalonians. Sanctification, and abstinence from fornication (iv 3), soberness (v 6), working with their own hands (iv 11), ' knowing them that labour among you and are over you in the Lord ' (v 12), mutual encouragement and long-suffering toward all (v 14) —all these, for which Paul quotes the example of his own behaviour (ii 1-12), are the signs that God has indeed ' appointed us not unto wrath, but unto the obtaining of salvation through our Lord Jesus Christ '.

Such a pattern of ethical instruction, recurs in somewhat similar form in many of the epistles, and not only in Paul's. For our understanding of early Christian preaching it is important to remember that the call to belief in Jesus as the Christ was accompanied by instruction in the way of life which could be recognised as the fruit of Spirit. The teaching referred to and reinforced in 1 Thessalonians can be taken as typical of such a presentation of the gospel to new converts in a predominantly Gentile church.

2 Thessalonians

AUTHENTICITY AND CIRCUMSTANCES OF WRITING

The Pauline authorship of 2 Thessalonians has been attacked on a number of grounds. The vocabulary contains a relatively high proportion of words not found in the genuine epistles, and the style is stereotyped and at times curiously formal; the apocalyptic details of ii 1-12, which form the core of the epistle, are for the most part absent from 1 Thessalonians, and some critics have held the signs before the end to be inconsistent with its sudden coming predicted in 1 Thess. v 2.

Apart from the difficulties raised by any alternative theory of the origin of the epistle, these arguments have not been found convincing by most present-day critics. The epistle is not one of Paul's greatest, and the language and style may well reflect the practical mood in which it was written, if they are not to be attributed, at least in part, to his amanuensis (iii 17). The differences between the apocalyptic expectations of the two epistles are not as great as they are sometimes made to appear, and some reasons for these differences are suggested below.

If the Pauline authorship be accepted, the epistle was written not long after 1 Thessalonians (ii 15). Paul seems to have received further information about the progress of Thessalonians, and to have heard of two problems in the life of the young community, perhaps connected with each other. The teaching is being spread abroad that the day of the Lord is already present (ii 2), and some of the brethren ' work not at all, but are busybodies ' (iii 11). Paul, conscious, perhaps, that some of his own teaching has been misinterpreted (ii 2), writes to inform them more accurately about the coming of the End and the necessity of working and keeping good order.

THE TEACHING OF THE EPISTLE

The most notable feature of the epistle is the section (ii 1-12) on the delay in the coming of the end. This delay is not mentioned in 1 Thessalonians, because in that epistle he mentions the end only in connection with the need for Christian living and with his solution of the problem raised by the death of Christians before the end. He had, however, as he reminds his readers (2 Thess. ii 5) told them, while he was with them, of a power that restrains the already working mystery of lawlessness (ii 7), which will be taken out of the way when the lawless one is to be revealed.   This revelation of the ' man of sin ' (ii 3) who sets himself forth as God, is to usher in a conflict with the Lord Jesus, and the coming of the Lord Jesus will bring him to nought, together with those who follow him and ' received not the love of the truth, that they might be saved '.

The meaning of this obscure passage is discussed later (p. 252) ; here it is sufficient to say that Paul's words reflect the development in early Christianity of apocalyptic views based on the teaching of Jewish Apocalyptic and influenced by Christian prophecy (cf. 1 Thess. v 20).   The apparent inconsistency between the coming of the day of the Lord ' as a thief in the night ' (1 Thess. v. 2) and the war between the man of sin and the Lord Jesus can be accepted as an inconsistency between two different conceptions simultaneously held by Paul (cf. the muddled thought of Mk. xiii in its present form), or it can be resolved by the assumption that ' the day of the Lord ' covers the whole period from the revelation of ' the man of sin ', a period when further evangelism would be impossible and men must stand or fall by the character of their lives hitherto.

Besides reminding them of what he has taught on the End, Paul writes with a new note of stern authority on those who have misconceived ' the day of the Lord ' as a period already begun and those—perhaps the same men—who have abandoned work altogether.   Speaking ' in the name of our Lord Jesus Christ ' (iii 6), and appealing to the teaching they had received by word and ' by epistle of ours ' (ii 15), he commands them to ensure the keeping of ' the tradition ' (ii 15, iii 6) by separation from disorderly and disobedient brethren, ' and yet count him not as an enemy, but admonish him as a brother (iii 16).

1 Corinthians

CIRCUMSTANCES OF WRITING

The authenticity of this epistle has not seriously been challenged, nor have the attempts of such scholars as Dr. Barnes to reject the Pauline authorship of the great passages

on Faith, Hope, and Love (xiii) and on the Resurrection
(xv) commended themselves to the great majority of present-
day critics.   The epistle is indeed perhaps the best attested
of all Paul's epistles in early tradition, and there is general
agreement that it was written from the neighbourhood of
Ephesus, during Paul's stay there on his third missionary
journey (c. A.D. 53-55).

Paul had founded the church at Corinth on his second
missionary journey in A.D. 50 (Acts xviii 1-18), and now
found himself obliged to intervene in the disputes which
disturbed the new and disorderly Christian community.
He had already written at least one letter, which has not
survived, in which he warned them to have no company
with fornicators (1 Cor. v 9), and he now writes again in
answer to a letter requesting guidance (vii 1) and in the light
of information about the church's life supplied to him by
members of the household of Chloe (i 11), probably early
in A.D. 55.

The Corinthian church seems to have been overwhelmingly, but not entirely, Gentile in composition, and to have
included many slaves as well as freemen (xii 13).   Its troubles
were typically Greek, factiousness, lack of stability and order,
and immorality, all of them reflecting the pagan background
of the majority of the new converts.

TEACHING OF THE EPISTLE

Paul finds much to reprove, and has much advice to give,
so that, while the epistle falls into six main sections, Factions
(i 1-iv 21), Sexual Problems (v 1-vii 40), Idolmeats and
Idolatry (viii 1-xi 1), Worship and Spiritual Gifts (xi 2-
xiv 40), the Resurrection (xv) the Collection and Personal
Messages (xvi), other topics keep on intruding and recurring
in these divisions.

The factions which split the church arose from the
championship of different leaders.   Some claimed to be of
Paul, others of Apollos (who had been instructed by Priscilla
and Aquila at Ephesus and had done valuable work at
Corinth in Paul's absence, Acts xviii 24-28), others of Peter,

and others of Christ (if these words in i, 12 are not an interjection of Paul's—'but I of Christ'). Paul reproves the pride that had led to such a state of affairs, and emphasises the supremacy of the Spirit and the subordination of all Christian leaders to God's purpose (iii 7, iv 5). He cannot, however, leave the subject without reminding the Corinthians that he is their father in Christ Jesus (iv 14), and that he will come shortly to deal with those that are puffed up (iv 18-21).

Paul proceeds to deal with sexual problems that have arisen. A reported case of incest is denounced, and instructions given 'to deliver such a one unto Satan for the destruction of the flesh, that the spirit may be saved in the day of the Lord Jesus' (v 5). Every Christian known to be 'a fornicator, or covetous, or an idolator, or a reviler, or a drunkard, or an extortioner' (v 11) is to be shunned completely. Even lawsuits before pagans are not permitted (vi 4). After this digression he returns to the particular sinfulness of fornication (vi 15 ff.), and then, in reply to a question in the letter which he has received, lays it down that no married Christian has a right to refuse normal marital relations except temporarily, or to leave their partner, although, if an unbelieving partner insists on a separation, they are to be let go. In an obscure passage, which seems to imply that some of the Corinthian Christians were living in a 'spiritual' and unconsummated marriage, Paul then gives on his own account wise and tolerant advice.

Another problem about which the Corinthians seem to have enquired was the propriety of eating meat which had been offered to idols (at this time most meat which was offered for sale had formally been so offered). Paul, in his answer, uses his own foregoing of the privileges which he might claim as an apostle to stress the need for charity and regard for the conscience of weaker brethren, and takes the opportunity of warning his readers against participation in any form of idolatry.

He goes on to deal with irregularities in Christian worship, especially the active participation of women in

services and unworthy participation in the Eucharist. The
Corinthians had apparently as yet no church officers of
unquestioned authority, and besides the scandals of behaviour at the Eucharist (xi 21), and the divisions when
they came together in congregation (xi 18), the disorderly
use of spiritual gifts, especially of speaking with tongues and
prophesying, had led to unseemly scenes. Paul urges some
sensible regulations, based on his own experience (xiv 12-33),
and shows them the more excellent way of love as more to be
desired than even the greater spiritual gifts (xii 31-xiv 1).

He concludes the main part of the epistle by reminding
them of ' the gospel which I preached unto you ' (xv 1),
the assurance of the Resurrection and of the change by
which those who are not to die will put on immortality
(xv 53). Instructions for the collection of alms on behalf
of the Jerusalem church and personal messages close the
letter.

2 Corinthians

INTEGRITY OF THE EPISTLE AND CIRCUMSTANCES OF WRITING

Paul refers in 2 Cor. ii 4, vii 8 and 12 to a previous
letter of his on a wrong done at Corinth which had made
them sorry, though it was written rather that they should
know his love toward them. This description does not seem
to fit 1 Corinthians very well, in spite of his fierce words on
the case of reported incest (1 Cor. v 1 ff.) ; on the other hand,
in 2 Corinthians itself the gentle tone of chapters i-ix gives
place in the last four chapters to an indignant vindication
of his authority against some who are challenging it, and
many scholars consider that these last four chapters were
originally part of this earlier ' severe ' letter.

There are at least possible parallels for the incorporation
of fragments of Paul's letters out of their true context in
other letters ; Romans xvi and parts of 2 Timothy and the
epistle to Titus are probable instances of such editorial
work, and some critics have seen another example in 2
Cor. vi 14-vii 1, which interrupt the general thought of

the surrounding passage.   There are, however, a number
of difficulties in the way of this view of 2 Cor. x-xiii,
notably the parallel references in chapters viii and xii to the
sending of Titus and ' the brother' to Corinth, and it seems
better on the whole to accept the epistle as one letter, and
to suppose that the ' severe' letter has not survived, or, less
probably, that 1 Corinthians was so interpreted by the
church at Corinth.   The change of time in chapter x must
then be attributed to a change in Paul's mood, and a determination matched in many others of his letters,[1] not to close
without a vindication of his personal authority against
his opponents.

On this view of the epistle 2 Corinthians was written
within a year of 1 Corinthians (cf. 2 Cor. viii 10 with 1 Cor.
xvi 1 ff.) from Macedonia, as Paul was on his way from
Ephesus to Corinth late in A.D. 55 before his final journey
to Jerusalem (Acts xx 1 ff.).   Since writing 1 Corinthians
Paul had visited Corinth (2 Cor. xiii 2), a visit not recorded
in Acts.   The visit seems to have been marred by opposition
to his authority (x 10 ff. ?) and to have been followed by
the ' severe' letter, the success of which in stirring the church
to repentance was reported to Paul in Macedonia by Titus
(vii 7 ff.).   Paul now seeks by a further letter to express his
joy at the renewal of harmony between himself and the
Corinthians and to reassert in plain terms his authority
which has been disputed.

TEACHING OF THE EPISTLE

2 Corinthians is the most personal of Paul's epistles,
and its main concern is not so much instruction in Christian
doctrine and living as the expression of Paul's tangled
emotions on hearing Titus' account of the general revulsion
of feeling at Corinth towards the acceptance of his authority.
It is the letter of a tried man who has been weighed down for
some time by continual exposure to danger (1 Cor. xv 32,
2 Cor. i 8, xi 23-26), by physical weakness (xii 7-8) and

---

[1] E.g. 1 Cor. iv 14-21, Gal. vi 12-17, 2 Thess. iii 6-15, 2 Tim. iv 14-18.

mental depression (ii 4, 13, vii 5), and above all by ' that which presseth upon one daily, anxiety for all the churches ' (xi 28), but who has never permitted himself to despair (iv 8), and who sees even in his sufferings the working of the power of God (i 4-5, iv 7, 11). Now that events have taken a happier turn he writes to the Corinthians, first to express his thanks for the comfort he has received, and to explain his past actions, and then to appeal to their liberality for the collection that he has been making (viii-ix). He finds himself unable to finish his letter, however, without once more vindicating himself and his authority against those who have opposed him at Corinth (x-xiii).

Of the themes treated in the epistle two are of special significance. In chapters iii-v, Paul treats of his ministry and sufferings in such a way as to indicate that the experiences of the last few months had left a permanent mark upon his thought. From now on there is to be little in his epistles of the coming of a cosmic catastrophe and judgement in his lifetime, and his expectation of the End is rather to be centred on the idea that death is the gateway to life. This deepening and spiritualising of his view, for which generations of Christians have had reason to be grateful, is apparent especially in iii 18, and in the great passage iv 16-v 10, with its emphasis on the temporary and imperfect nature of mortal life, and the earnest of the Spirit as a pledge of our final transformation into the full glory of presence with the Lord.

In the last four chapters Paul treats of his ministry and sufferings again, but in a very different context. We can only guess at who his opponents were who disparaged his bodily presence and speech (x 10) and were in turn attacked as ' false apostles ' (xi 13). They seem to have been Jews (xi 22), and their attitude to Paul suggests that they claimed for their version of the gospel a higher authority, that of the teaching of one or more of ' the chiefest apostles ' (xi 5), possibly even of Peter (cf. 1 Cor. i 12). Paul had met the challenge of the rival teachers of the Galatians with an affirmation of the direct divine revelation of his gospel, and of his independence of human authority, even of Peter's. Here he reaffirms the divine origin of his authority (x 8, cf. iii 5-6) and cites as evidence of his divine calling the dangers he has endured (xi 23-28), his visions and revelations of the Lord (xii 1), and the signs of an apostle that ' were brought among you in all patience, by signs and wonders and mighty works ' (xii 12). The essence of Paul's appeal lay here, as always, in his ability, conscious as he was of his own possession of the Spirit, to ask of other men ' know ye not as to your own selves, that Jesus Christ is in you ' ? (xiii 5).

Romans

INTEGRITY OF THE EPISTLE

The heretic Marcion seems to have used an edition of this epistle that included only the first fourteen chapters. As we know that Marcion often omitted passages in the epistles which emphasised the unity of the God proclaimed by Jesus with the God of the Old Testament, and as there is reason for thinking that even the chapters which Marcion accepted he edited to bring the teaching into closer accord with his own views, there is nothing very surprising in this, except the size of the omission. The description of Christ, for example, in xv 8 as ' a minister of the circumcision for the truth of God ' would have been an embarrassment to him, like the stress on the collection for ' the saints that are at Jerusalem ' (xv 26-27), and the five quotations from the Old Testament in xv 1-13.

The circulation of this shortened Marcionite version has left its mark in the MS. tradition, some MSS. of the Vulgate bearing traces of having originally contained only fourteen chapters, and the final doxology of xvi 25-27 occurring in a large number of MSS. after xiv 23. It is possible that the curious omission of ' in Rome ' by i 7 and 15 by Origen and the MS. G is due to the circulation of such a short form of the epistle, which has no reference apart from these to its historical situation.

A more serious problem is presented by the placing of the

doxology after xv 33 in our oldest surviving MS. (papyrus 46, of the third century, from Egypt), taken in conjunction with the difficulties caused by the acceptance of chapter xvi as part of the original epistle.

Both chapters xv and xvi are clearly Pauline in thought and style, but they do not seem to belong together. Chapter xv implies a Roman destination for the epistle (cf. 24, 28) and closes (33) with a typically Pauline blessing, parallel to those which close other epistles, e.g. Galatians, 1 and 2 Thessalonians. In chapter xvi, on the other hand, after a commendation of Phoebe and salutations to 26 persons by name —a surprising number if Paul had never visited the church— there follow a sharp denunciation of those who are causing divisions, written in a tone which suggests that Paul is writing to a community known to him, and acknowledging his authority, another final blessing (20), the greetings of his fellow-workers, and the doxology 25-27.

Certain features of chapter xvi suggest that it is in fact part of a letter to Ephesus and not Rome. The number of individual greetings include Epaenetus ‘ the firstfruits of Asia unto Christ ’ (5) and Prisca and Aquila, first mentioned at Corinth in Acts xviii 2 as lately come from Rome, and subsequently settled in Ephesus (Acts xviii 18, 26). Moreover vv. 17-20 would come naturally in a letter to the church at Ephesus, which Paul had founded and to which he could speak with authority. Two of the fellow-workers, whose greetings are given, Timothy and Erastus are mentioned in Acts xix 22 as sent on from Ephesus to Macedonia by Paul in preparation for his journey to Jerusalem, and, if this chapter is indeed part of a letter to Ephesus, the date for it would seem to be before or shortly after Paul’s start from Corinth in A.D. 56.

Those who defend chapter xvi as part of the original epistle to Rome point to the lack of direct evidence for the ending of the epistle at xv 33, and explain the long list of names, most of which can be paralleled from Roman inscriptions, as a deliberate attempt on Paul’s part to establish as many personal contacts as possible before his arrival. On the other hand the presence of Prisca and Aquila at Ephesus as late as A.D. 55 (1 Cor. xvi 19) makes their presence at Rome early in 56 improbable, and the balance of arguments would seem to favour the view that chapter xvi was written to Ephesus.

The normal explanation of the attachment of chapter xvi to the epistle to the Romans is that it is another example of the later editorial patchwork suggested in 2 Corinthians and, more convincingly, in 2 Timothy.   Another explanation is possible, that Paul sent a copy of his epistle to the Romans, which contained so much of his mature thought, to Ephesus by the hand of Phoebe with a short note of commendation and greeting.   This latter explanation would furnish reasons for the existence of two recensions of the epistle, of which one originally ended at xv 33, and possibly also for the omission of ' in Rome ' in i 7, 15.[1]   It would seem, at any rate, that the letter to Rome and the note to Ephesus were both written at about the same time (cf. Rom. xv 25-26) and probably both from Corinth.

CIRCUMSTANCES OF WRITING

The epistle can be confidently dated *c.* A.D. 56, when Paul was looking forward to visiting new fields in the western part of the Empire after his journey with alms to the church of Jerusalem.   He names Spain as his ultimate objective (xv 24, 28), and appears to visualise breaking his journey at Rome (cf. Acts. xix 21) to acquaint himself with the situation there ' to impart unto you some spiritual gift, to the end that ye may be established ' (Rom. i 11), and to be ' satisfied with your company ' (xv 24).   He does not seem to have known much about the Christian community at Rome, but assumes that it was composed of both Jews and Gentiles, and sets down for their benefit a carefully composed statement of his own general doctrinal position.   He does not, of course, cover the whole field of Christian doctrine, but concentrates

---

[1] If Marcion edited a copy of Romans that contained only chapters i-xv his omission of the last chapter becomes more easily explicable.

on the fundamental doctrines of Justification and Sanctification (i-viii), with an explanation of the rejection of Israel (ix-xi) and a final section of practical exhortation (xii-xv).

TEACHING OF THE EPISTLE

It is impossible in a short summary to do justice to the teaching of this epistle which above all others rewards close and continued study with a commentary.[1]   The first eight chapters especially contain the most profound working out of the way in which the redeeming work of Christ has bridged over for the believer the chasm between man and God caused by man's sin and God's righteousness, which cannot ignore sin.   Paul's arguments are often involved and difficult to follow, especially when he is applying to the Old Testament Pharisaic methods of exegesis in his treatment of the Jewish Law (e.g. in ch. iv), but the reality of the experience which he is translating into theological terms natural for a Jew of the first century A.D. has made his exposition an abiding source of inspiration to Christians of every age.

Paul is concerned with three stages of his own experience, his feeling of sinfulness in the sight of God before his conversion, the release from the power and penalty of his sins and the reception of the gift of the spirit that followed his conversion and baptism, and the continuing struggle with sin in his life that still went on.

In the light of these personal experiences he expounds the place of Christ's redeeming work in God's plan.   The Jewish Law he knows to be given of God, in spite of its failure to enable men to conquer sin ; its purpose he now sees to have been the focusing of men's minds on the nature of sin and on the penalty of death as the consequence of sin (v 13, 20, vii 7-14).

At his conversion to faith in Christ Paul was baptised (Acts ix 18), a sequence that he assumes as normal for other Christians (Acts xvi 30-33, 1 Cor. i 13), and his interpretation of the consequences of faith is linked with a mystical

---

[1] Those of C. H. Dodd (Moffatt Commentary), K. E. Kirk (Clarendon Bible) and (for those with a knowledge of Greek) Sanday and Headlam (I.C.C.) may be mentioned as of particular value.

conception of the meaning of baptism. Christ's death has achieved what the law could not do (viii 3), our justification (iii 24-25) or acquittal in spite of our guilt. Paul thinks of death as the inevitable consequence of sin (v 12) and, as it were, wiping out sin (vi 7). Christ's obedience to God, culminating in his death on the cross (vi 8-19), has been the means of redeeming us from the curse of Adam. This is achieved or symbolised by baptism, in which the descent into the water and coming out again, together with the bestowal of the Spirit by the laying on of hands represent a mystical death of the believer with Christ (v 13), and the rising of the 'new man' (vi 4) strengthened with the life-giving Spirit (viii 9) and freed by his 'death' from the penalty attaching to the sinfulness of the 'old man' (vii 6).

Paul's own experience has shown him that while he has been justified with God there is still a battle within him against sin (vii 15-23), and that we must struggle, though now with the Spirit's help (viii 9), to attain to sanctification (vi 19). Yet we have the assurance of Christ's resurrection that God will finally quieten also your mortal bodies through his Spirit that dwelleth in you (viii 11), and the Spirit gives confidence to our hope of final glory in spite of all the sufferings of this present time (viii 18-39).

In chapters ix-xi Paul turns aside to a problem that lay very near to his own heart, the rejection of Israel, and shows that it has been both foretold by God in the Old Testament and abundantly justified, but that it is neither complete nor final. Its ultimate purpose indeed is the salvation of all men through God's mercy (xii 25-32).

In these first eleven chapters, although they have become in the course of time determinate for the formulation of Christian theology, Paul is largely working out his own interpretation of the meaning of God's revelation in Christ. He started from the same assumptions as the other Christian preachers of the first generation (cf. i 1-6), and developed from them in the light of his personal experience of Christ and of his Pharisaic training a system of thought to justify his belief that the gospel 'is the power of God unto salvation to everyone that believeth; to the Jew first, and also to the Greek' (i 16). We can only guess how far Paul's interpretation was influenced by that of other Christian teachers and how far Paul's teaching in turn has influenced e.g. the teaching of 1 Peter, but it is clear that much of what is most profound in Paul's conception of the union of the believer with Christ is drawn from his own direct experience.

In his final section, chapters xii-xv, Paul sketches the great principles of Christian ethics that arise naturally from the contemplation of God's mercy, and he closes with a brief reference to his own past work and future plans.

Colossians and Philemon

AUTHENTICITY

The genuineness of Colossians has been attacked on the grounds of differences in style and vocabulary between this epistle and the other undoubted Pauline letters, and because it has been thought that the heresy attacked was a form of Gnosticism more likely to occur in the second than in the first century. But the style and vocabulary, though in some ways remarkable, are judged by the great majority of critics as fully within Paul's compass, and to be accounted for by the late date of the epistle and its special subject. There is a general consensus of opinion, too, that the teaching attacked is of a kind fully compatible with first century developments. To clinch the genuineness is the almost universal recognition of the authenticity of the epistle to Philemon, with its manifest close relationship to Colossians.

CIRCUMSTANCES OF WRITING

The two epistles seem to have been written at the same time to judge by the names mentioned in them, and Philemon was himself probably a member of the church at Colossae (cf. Col. iv 17 with Philem. 2). Paul was in prison at the time (Col. iv 18, Philem. 1), and the epistle is generally dated early in his imprisonment at Rome, *c.* A.D. 59.

An alternative view, which has gained considerable support, is that the epistles were written from Ephesus. Acts does not mention an imprisonment there, but Acts is by no means exhaustive in its accounts of Paul's sufferings, as can be seen from 2 Cor. xi 23-26, especially 23 'in prisons more abundantly', and references in 1 Cor. xv 32, 2 Cor. i 8-10, and elsewhere have been taken to imply that Paul had in fact been in prison and in danger of his life at Ephesus on his third missionary journey. In a Latin prologue to the epistle, possibly of Marcionite origin, it is stated that 'the apostle wrote to them in bonds in Ephesus'. The proximity of Ephesus to Colossae (less than a hundred miles to the south east) is held to make more likely the presence of Onesimus, the runaway slave, with Paul, and Paul's hope of visiting Colossae (Philem. 22).

There is much in this that must be accounted speculative, and a Roman provenance and later date would better account for some of the changes in Paul's thought and style, and for his reference to himself as Paul 'the aged' (Philem. 9). Rome was notorious as a haven for runaway slaves, and Paul may well have hoped in the early days of his imprisonment at Rome for a quick acquittal and a return to some of the fields of his earlier mission-work.

THE CIRCUMSTANCES OF WRITING AND THE COLOSSIAN HERESY

Paul has not himself visited Colossae (ii 1), and the occasion of the epistle lay in what he had learned from Ephesus (Col. ii 7, Philem. 23) and probably from the fugitive Onesimus. He seems to have taken advantage of the return of Tychicus from Rome to his native Asia (Acts xx 4, of 2 Tim. iv 12) to entrust him with the return of Onesimus to his master (Col. iv 7-9) and with general letters to the churches of Colossae and Laodicea, which were to be interchanged (iv 16).

In the second chapter of Colossians Paul warns his readers against a type of teaching which seems to have

combined the observance of Jewish customs such as the
observance of sabbaths and new moons, and the keeping
of food laws (ii 16, cf. ii 11), with the cult of angels as a
humble form of worship (ii 18), and asceticism (ii 23).   We
have only short allusions to these, and it is dangerous to be
too dogmatic about the type of teaching referred to, but, in
view of the known syncretistic nature of much religion in
Asia Minor at this period, the danger may well have lain
in an attempt by some of the Colossians to graft on to their
Christian faith elements of their former pagan beliefs.
Such an explanation would fit the parallelism of Paul's
warning against ' the rudiments of the world ' (ii 8) with
his reminder to the Galatians that before the coming of
Christ we ' were in bondage under the rudiments of the
world ' (Gal. iv 3).

THE TEACHING OF THE EPISTLES

The note to Philemon needs little comment.   It is at
once tactful and truly Christian in its intercession for one
who might legally be punished with the most extreme
severity.

In Colossians Paul, writing to a church that he has not
himself visited, attunes his teaching to what he thinks to be
their special needs.   In the first place he stresses the
uniqueness, completeness and eternity of Christ (i 15-17,
ii 9) against the danger of regarding him only as the partial instrument of revelation, and proclaims Christ as the
mystery of God now at last revealed (ii 2, cf. i 26-27 and
Rom. xvi 25).   We are united with Christ in our baptism
(ii 12), and Christ is the Head from whom all the body
increases with the increase of God (ii 19).

This leads Paul on to reinforce his moral teaching
(iii 1-iv 6) with the reminder that now ' your life is hid with
Christ in God ' (iii 3) and that the Christian virtues are those
of the body in which we are called to the peace of Christ
(iii 15).   Personal messages and greetings (iv 7-18) close
the letter.

Philippians

CIRCUMSTANCES OF WRITING

This letter, too, was written from prison (i 7, 13, 17). Ephesus has been suggested as the place of writing, as in the case of Colossians, and inscriptions from Ephesus have established the presence there of Praetorians (i 13) and of members of Caesar's household (iv 22). There are also a number of close affinities in language with the epistle to the Romans, although this argument loses much of its force if the early date of Galatians, with its resemblances to Romans, is accepted. A Roman provenance, however, and a date towards the end of Paul's imprisonment *c.* A.D. 60, seem more likely on the whole. Paul seems to look back in his old age over a long period (i 5, 23, iv 10, 15), Timothy is with him (cf. Col. i 1), the Praetorians and those of Caesar's household are most natural of all in Rome. Time must have elapsed for the Philippians to have heard of his presence there, for Epaphroditus to have arrived, and to have recovered from his illness (ii 25-28), so that a date towards the end of Paul's imprisonment is probable.

The occasion of the letter is the homesickness of Epaphroditus (ii 25-26), whose return to Philippi Paul accompanies with a letter of thanks for the gift he has received (iv 10-19) and of exhortation to the Church.

TEACHING OF THE EPISTLE

Paul is writing to a church without serious dissensions (iv 2), and one with which his relations seems to have been universally cordial (iv 15-16). For the most part the epistle is concerned with Paul's thanks and his own experiences and plans (i 3-23, iii 4-14, iv 10-23), and with his concern for the Philippians to live worthily of the gospel of Christ (i 24-ii 4, ii 12-22, iii 17-iv 9). Two features of the epistle, however, call for special comment.

In ii 5-11 Paul illustrates the mind that Christians should seek to have by the example of Christ Jesus, self-emptying and humility. It has been noted that 6-11 possesses a certain rhythm, and that a number of the expressions used are without parallel in Paul, some of them indeed without parallel in the New Testament. It has accordingly been conjectured by some scholars that Paul is here quoting from an early Christian hymn, and there is much to be said for such a view, although most of the distinctive christological ideas occur elsewhere in Paul's epistles; with the 'self-emptying' of Christ (7), may be compared 2 Cor. v 21, viii 9, with 'being made in the likeness of man' (7) Rom. viii 3, with 'obedient even unto death' (8) the thought of Rom. v 18-19, vi 10, with the exaltation of Jesus over the whole universe (10) Col. ii 15, cf. 1 Cor. ii 7-8; on the other hand the application of 'servant' to Christ (7) is not in accord with Paul's usage.

In iii 1 Paul is apparently about to close his letter (cf. 'Finally') when the tone suddenly changes to a denunciation of either Jews or Judaisers. Some critics have assumed that here a fragment of another letter has been inserted, but such changes of plan and tone have already been noted as not untypical of Paul, and the connection of thought here is perhaps supplied by the later reference to his experiences at Thessalonica (iv 16), where Paul on his arrival from Philippi during his second missionary journey had experienced the hostility of the Jews and twice received gifts from the Philippians in the midst of his troubles.

THE INFLUENCE OF PAUL: EPHESIANS, AND THE PASTORAL EPISTLES

The wide circulation and influence of Paul's epistles in the later years of the first century and the beginning of the second century are sufficiently witnessed by the quotations that occur in Christian writers of this period and by the early collection of a number of his letters.

It is to the working of this influence that we probably owe the composition in Paul's name of the Epistle to the Ephesians and the Pastoral Epistles to Timothy and Titus. The genuineness of these epistles, especially Ephesians, is still maintained by many scholars, but detailed study of their language and teaching has convinced the majority of modern critics that they are not from Paul's own hand, except for fragments of Pauline letters incorporated in 2 Timothy and Titus.   Ephesians has come to be widely regarded as the work of an unknown religious genius who understood and appreciated Paul's thought so well that the teaching of his epistle can still be justly termed ' the crown ' of Paul's teaching ; the reasons for his assumption of Paul's name are discussed in connection with the date of the epistle below. The Pastoral Epistles do not show the same understanding of Paul's theology, although clearly written by a devoted follower of Paul, who sought to support his views on the doctrine and church organisation by using Paul's name and incorporating fragments of genuine Pauline letters.

Ephesians

NON-PAULINE ELEMENTS IN THE LANGUAGE

The arguments against the Pauline authorship of Ephesians are drawn mainly from the style and vocabulary of the epistle, and from its doctrine.   The relationship with Colossians is so close, and there are so many echoes of phrases from other Pauline epistles, that the choice of authorship must lie between Paul and someone steeped in his teaching.   The style in Ephesians is far more involved than in the genuine letters of Paul, with sentences of great length, e.g. i 3-14, the piling up of synonyms, e.g. i 19, and the repetition of phrases, notably the five times repeated ' in the heavenly places ' which is never used elsewhere by Paul.   The vocabulary, too, contains more than forty words which occur in the New Testament, but not in Paul, and nearly forty words which occur nowhere else at all in the New Testament, a high proportion when the close relationship to Colossians is considered.   A comparison with Colossians shows the use of some of the key-words of that epistle in a different sense, e.g. body, mystery ; the wealth of abstract expressions in Ephesians finds some parallel in Colossians, but, whereas in Colossians these expressions are integral to the argument, in Ephesians they appear to be used without real cause, and to envelop comparatively simple doctrines in mystical language.

The theology of the epistle is of course steeped in Paul's thought, but there are developments and applications which suggest the work of another mind. The first three chapters form in effect a great prayer of thanksgiving in which the mystery of God's will (i 9, iii 4-11) now revealed by Him to men, and proclaimed by Paul (iii 1-3), is declared to have been achieved by the raising of Christ from the dead and his exaltation (i 17-22). The effect of this has been to unite Jew and Gentile (ii 11-18) in the church which is the body of Christ (i 23), and shares his exaltation (ii 6), so that it is the means of God's revelation not only to men but to ' the principalities and powers in the heavenly places ' (iii 9-11). The author's speculation is here influenced by Colossians (especially Col. i 15-20), but the conception of the cosmic function of the church is a new development of his own.

In chapters iv-vi follows exhortation to work out the purpose of God in the new common life (iv 1-6). The influence of Colossians is again manifest, but there are new features, such as the stress on the unity of the Church (iv 4-6) and the parallel drawn between marriage and the relationship of Christ to the Church (v 22-32).

These developments of Pauline thought are of great value and importance, but seem to be the building of another thinker on Pauline foundations rather than Paul's continuation of his own work. This impression is confirmed by the nature of the epistle itself which does not address itself to a particular situation, as all of Paul's genuine epistles do, but is more of a treatise than a letter. The personal references (iii 1, iv 1, vi 21-22) appear to be selected from Colossians, and the reference to ' holy ' apostles (iii 5) sounds strange from Paul's pen, although natural to a writer of the next generation.

CIRCUMSTANCES OF WRITING

The best MSS. of the epistle omit ' at Ephesus ' in the first verse. It is possible, therefore, that the address was originally a general one ' to the saints who are also faithful in Christ Jesus ', although alternative suggestions have been made that the epistle was originally addressed to another church, whose name has disappeared, or that it was a circular letter ' to the saints who are . . .', the place being filled in differently when Tychicus read it in different churches.   These last explanations carry most weight when the Pauline authorship is accepted ; Marcion, for example, styled it ' the epistle to the Laodiceans ' (cf. Col. iv 16), and it is difficult to imagine Paul writing to the Ephesians without conveying numerous personal greetings.

If the Pauline authorship, however, is rejected, the form of a general epistle becomes easily understandable, especially if the theory is accepted that Ephesians was written by an admirer of Paul, who collected his epistles and provided them with a general introduction in this letter, to which he gave Paul's name.   Such a theory, however, is highly speculative, and all that can safely be said is that the epistle must have been written within a generation of Paul's death (it is quoted by Christian writers soon after the beginning of the second century), probably in Asia Minor. Its incorporation in the collection of Paul's epistles made a title inevitable, and the choice of Ephesus seems to have been dictated by the desire of Ephesian Christians to claim one of Paul's letters as written to them (cf. 2 Tim. iv 12).

The Pastoral Epistles

NON-PAULINE ELEMENTS IN THE LANGUAGE AND TEACHING OF THE
    EPISTLES

If the author of Ephesians shows a deep knowledge and understanding of Paul's thought and a devotion towards him, the author of 1 and 2 Timothy and the epistle to Titus shares both his knowledge and devotion but lacks such a profound understanding.   It is clear that, quite apart from the passages in these epistles that are probably fragments of genuine letters of Paul himself, the influence of Paul's teaching and language is everywhere present.   Yet the marks of another hand are evident.

The proportion of words not found elsewhere in Paul's epistles is significantly higher than in any of the nine epistles generally accepted as genuine, and many Pauline words are used in new senses. The difference in the use of particles from the normal use of Paul is particularly marked. The style, too, is smoother and more correct, and lacks the close-knit fervour of Paul. The cumulative force of these arguments is reinforced by the author's treatment of his opponents; he is content to denounce without employing the dialectic of Paul (e.g. 1 Tim. vi 3-5), and he lays down general directions on ecclesiastical organisation in a manner quite different from Paul's more particular instructions.

In matters of doctrine Paul's influence is clear, but there are significant differences (cf. 1 Tim. ii 5 with Gal. iii 20), and instead of Paul's stress on his 'gospel' (Rom. ii 16) we find an insistence on 'the teaching' (1 Tim. vi, Tit. ii 10) as a generally received 'faith' (1 Tim. iv 1, v 8).

The evidence of teaching as of style and vocabulary is strongly against Paul's authorship, nor are these arguments seriously weakened by any supposition that the epistles were written late in Paul's lifetime and to meet a new type of situation. The three epistles show such a unity of thought and expression that they must be the work of one man, but for the author we must look rather to one of Paul's admirers than to Paul himself.

CIRCUMSTANCES OF WRITING AND USE OF GENUINE LETTERS OF PAUL

The key to the understanding of how these epistles came to be written lies in the probable use of at least two short letters, or fragments of letters, written by Paul himself. There are many widely differing views as to the extent of this genuine Pauline matter and its original form, and there is never likely to be general agreement on the subject. Perhaps the simplest explanation of the writing of the epistles is to assume that the unknown author knew or had in his possession short letters written by Paul to Timothy and Titus, and that he used these as frameworks on which to compose 2 Timothy and Titus. Later, encouraged perhaps by the success of his experiment, he wrote 1 Timothy entirely by himself; the affinities of the longer 1 Timothy with Titus suggest that he would hardly have composed Titus if 1 Timothy had been already written.

The separation of the genuine Pauline fragments into their original settings is fraught with difficulties. The letter to Titus *may* have been only a short note, which can perhaps be reconstructed from Titus i 1a, 4, iii 12-15, written from Macedonia in the autumn of A.D. 55 on his third missionary journey and urging Titus to prepare to join Paul at Nicopolis. The Pauline portions of 2 Timothy are more extensive, and seem to include at least the personal references in (2 Tim. i 1-2, 16-18, iv 9-22), as well as other possible fragments (e.g. iv 5-8). If these fragments all come from one letter, they imply that Paul returned to Asia Minor (iv 20) after being released from his imprisonment at Rome (i 17); it is perhaps more probable that fragments from more than one letter have been included.

As 1 and 2 Timothy are both quoted by Polycarp early in the second century, an early date for the pastoral epistles is certain. There is nothing inherently improbable in the problems of ecclesiastical organisation and of ' gnostic ' heresies having become urgent within a few years of Paul's death, and these letters may well have been composed as early as A.D. 70-80, perhaps in the neighbourhood of Ephesus (2 Tim. iv 19).

TEACHING OF THE EPISTLES

The term ' Pastoral Epistles ', first applied to all three in the eighteenth century, hardly fits the exhortation of 2 Timothy, where the author employs his Pauline material to reinforce his general appeal for loyalty to the Pauline ' pattern of good words ' (i 13, cf. iii 10), the avoidance of ' strife about words to no profit ' (ii 14), and perseverance in the face of suffering (iii 12) and false teaching (iii 1 ff., iv 3-4). The epistle to Titus is concerned with the qualifi-cations needed in ' bishops ' (i 7), who appear in fact to be as yet ' elders ' (i 5) and not in sole authority, and with the teaching to be given to older men, women, younger men, and slaves (ii 1-10) ; this leads on to the divine purposes of God and their requirements of Christian conduct (ii 11-iii 8), and to a warning against tolerance of heretics (iii 9-11).

1 Timothy covers much the same ground as the epistle of Titus, but in more detail, e.g. the qualifications of deacons and their wives (iii 8-13), and with instruction on the conduct of public prayer (ii 1-2, 8-9) and on the unity of God, Christ's mediation (iii 5), and the purpose of his death (iii 6). Timothy is given advice on his own teaching and conduct in terms which apply, and were meant to apply by the author, to all young Christian leaders (iv 6-v 2).

CHAPTER XIX

THE EPISTLE TO THE HEBREWS

AUTHORSHIP

THE attribution of this treatise—for such it is rather than a letter—to Paul in our Bible is based on a Church tradition which can be traced back to the end of the second century, although it did not finally triumph in the west until the fourth century. Even in antiquity the differences in language and style between this work and the Pauline epistles led Christian scholars to make such suggestions as that an Aramaic epistle of Paul had been translated and edited by Luke, that reminiscences of Paul's teaching had been embodied in an epistle by a different hand, or that the true author was Barnabas or Clement of Rome. None of these suggestions have met with much support in modern times, although modern critics have confirmed that the epistle cannot be attributed to Paul and have for the most part agreed with Origen's judgement, ' But as to who wrote the epistle, God knows the truth '.

The Greek of the epistle is very different from that of Paul, the author writing in a careful and elaborate style and employing a quite distinctive vocabulary. His treatment, too, of the Jewish Law, of the Holy Spirit, and of Faith, is on such different lines from Paul's as to make it unlikely that he was a disciple of Paul, although in a wider sense he shows his sympathy with the Pauline conceptions of the universalism of the gospel and the free working of God's grace.

CIRCUMSTANCES OF WRITING

Many guesses have been made as to the authorship of the epistle in modern times, but they are either unverifiable, e.g. Apollos (first suggested by Luther) or Prisca, or ruled out on grounds of style, etc., e.g. Peter. It can, however, be dated confidently within the first century, and the last few verses of the epistle itself tell of the release of Timothy (xiii 23) and convey greetings from those ' of Italy ' (24). This last phrase may also be translated ' those who come from Italy salute you ', and it may well be that the epistle was originally sent to Christians at Rome, perhaps from Asia Minor, in preparation for a visit of the author with Timothy (xiii 23) ; it is certainly quoted by Clement of Rome (c. A.D. 95).

The reference to Timothy's imprisonment suggests a date subsequent to the last of Paul's epistle, and, if the epistle is meant for Roman Christians, the persecution of Nero in A.D. 64 appears to be referred to as past (x 32-34) ; some leading Christians of the community are already dead (xiii 7). On the other hand a strict interpretation of viii 4 may imply that the temple at Jerusalem has not yet been destroyed, if the reference is to the temple and not, as has been suggested by some critics, to ' the tabernacle of the written law '. A date about A.D. 66 is perhaps most probable, but the epistle may be as late as A.D. 80.

The title ' to the Hebrews ' could hardly have been the original title of an epistle sent to a specific community, and probably arose from a later misunderstanding of its pre-occupation with the Old Testament. The interest displayed by the author in interpreting the Old Testament, while suggesting that he was himself born a Hellenistic Jew, is no proof of this ; the epistles of ' Barnabas ' and of Clement show that such an interest was widespread in the post-apostolic age among Christians as a whole. This fact also tells against the theories that the epistle was written to a group, possibly of Hebrew Christians, within a larger community.

The curious form of the epistle, beginning as a tract or sermon, and ending as a letter, is best explained, not by supposing that the final verses were added by a later editor to pass it off as Paul's, but by assuming that it was written primarily for reading to a church, and that the lack of an opening formula of address and salutation were to be made good by the person who carried the letter.

THE TEACHING OF THE EPISTLE COMPARED WITH THAT OF PAUL

The epistle is one of consolation, written to stave off apathy and apostasy (ii 1, iv 1, v 11 ff., x 39) by giving a better understanding of the supreme excellence of the new covenant mediated through Christ (viii 6). The author starts, like Paul, from the assurance that ' Christ died for our sins according to the scriptures ' (1 Cor. xv 3), and that the old covenant has been superseded, but he develops his interpretation of these facts in his own way. Paul worked out his theology under the dominating influence of his own spiritual consciousness of Christ's immediate presence in his own life (Rom. viii 9, Gal. ii 20) : in the light of his experience and of the revelation that the gospel was for the Gentiles also (Col. i 25-27) he went on to interpret the incarnation in the terms of universal history, and especially of Jewish history. His judgement on the Jewish Law as impossible to keep (Rom. iii 20), but as having been our tutor to bring us unto Christ ' (Gal. iii 24), illustrates the way in which personal experience and its rationalisation play their part in Paul's thought. His interpretation of the Old Testament is often special pleading by the ingenious use of selected texts to support beliefs really founded upon experience.

The author of Hebrews does not reveal the same intensity of experience or emotion as Paul, but writes more as a mystic and philosopher. The contrast between the two men can be seen in their use of ' faith ' ; for Paul faith is essentially the confident acceptance of Christ which alone gives new life and righteousness (e.g. Rom. iv 5), while for the author of Hebrews it is more a subjective attitude of assurance and expectation (cf. Hebr. xi 1 in the American Revised Standard Version ' Now faith is the assurance of things hoped for, the conviction of things not seen ').

The central theme of the epistle is the supremacy of Christ as Son of God, over the universe (i 2), the angels (i 4-ii 10), and Moses (iii 1-19), and his heavenly and eternal High-Priesthood (iv 14-x 18). In unfolding it the author has made use of conceptions found in first century Alexandrian Judaism, notably in Philo, but whose influence seems to have been much wider. Thus he describes the creation of the worlds through the Son (i 2-3) in terms reminiscent of the Alexandrian doctrine of creation through the Logos (Word), and draws the same distinction between the ideal heavenly universe and its transitory shadow here below which Alexandrian Judaism had borrowed ultimately from Plato. His elaborate allegorical exegesis of the Old Testament (whose authority he accepts without question) to draw even from its silence, e.g. on Melchizedek's father (vii 3), a spiritual interpretation is in line with that of Philo. It is in the light of this background to his thought that his doctrinal exposition must be read.

The supremacy of Christ is shown to be in his Sonship, and his incarnation and death to be not stumbling blocks to faith, but a necessary act of will to enable him, having undergone human temptations (ii 18) and sufferings (xii 2), to act eternally in the glory of heaven (ii 9-10) as a high-priest on our behalf, ' one that hath been in all points tempted like as we are, but without sin ' (ii 17, iv 15). The offering of Christ's body (x 10) was and continues to be the perfect sacrifice, because he ' through his own blood entered in once for all the holy place, having obtained eternal redemption ' (ix 12). And this holy place is not one ' made with hands, like in pattern to the true ; but . . . heaven itself ' (ix 24).

This antithesis between the perfect and abiding sacrifice of Christ (x 10-14), and of the old system of Jewish sacrifices which ' can never make perfect them that draw nigh ' (x 1) fills a great part of the epistle and has a double purpose. First, it offers an explanation of the paradox that the Christians accepted the divine authority of the Old Testament, but not its sacrificial requirements ; here the author of the Hebrews reminds us of Paul in his rejection of the present validity of the Law. More important even than this is the fitting of the historical facts and the religious value of Jesus' life and death by the use of metaphor and analogy into a philosophy that what is true is eternal; here the author of Hebrews shares the perception of the fourth evangelist.

CHAPTER XX

THE EPISTLE OF JUDE

AUTHORSHIP

THE epistle claims to be written by Judas ' a servant of Jesus Christ, and brother of James '. The only pair of brothers James and Judas known to us from the New Testament are the brethren of Jesus (Mk. vi, 3) and there is no reason for doubting that this Jude is intended. A story of Hegesippus (c. A.D. 180) tells of the arraignment before Domitian of two grandsons of Jude, who worked a small farm, and after their release ' ruled the churches, as being both martyrs and of the Lord's family ' (Eus. H.E. III 20). While Jude does not seem to have succeeded James as head of the Church in Jerusalem, he seems to have held a leading place in the early Church, as a brother of the Lord, and to have been supported by the Christian community (1 Cor. ix 5). There would accordingly be nothing strange in his writing an epistle of warning against those who were corrupting the Church.

Two main arguments have been advanced against Jude's authorship, the difficulty of reconciling the conception of ' the faith ' which was once and for all delivered unto the saints (3) and the reference in 17 to ' the words which have been spoken before by the apostles of our Lord Jesus Christ ' with authorship by a brother of Jesus, and the type of error attacked. If, however, a period late in Jude's lifetime be assumed, both these arguments lose much of their force. In the conception of ' the faith ' as something established from the beginning Gal. i 23 and Eph. iv 5 offer instructive parallels, and a general reference to words spoken before by the apostles could well look back on the early days when the apostles as a body shared a common teaching in and around Jerusalem without implying that they were now all dead. The type of error attacked—an antinomian rejection of authority, coupled with immorality, heresy, and insincere respect of persons—has been compared with some justice to the type of error especially condemned by Paul in 1 Corinthians, and could be expected to arise in any Christian community after the first flush of enthusiasm had passed.

The similarities between Jude and 2 Peter are so striking (compare especially Jude 1-19 with 2 Pet. ii 1-18, iii 1-2) that there must be a literary relationship between the two epistles.   Besides the improbability of an author making up such a short epistle from a part only of 2 Peter, there is an added reason for supposing the priority of Jude in the fact that occasionally the meaning of the author of 2 Peter can only properly be understood from a reading of the parallel passage in Jude (compare 2 Pet. ii 10-11 with Jude 9). Moreover there are signs that, unlike 2 Peter, Jude from a very early period enjoyed a wide circulation. It was probably known to the author of ' The Teaching of the Twelve Apostles ', which may be as early as the end of the first century A.D., and by the beginning of the third century it was included in the list of accepted books at Rome given by the Muratorian Canon, quoted by Tertullian in Africa, and commented upon by Clement of Alexandria.   In view of the shortness of the epistle this widespread use and acceptance as authoritative is remarkable, although there seems also to have been a certain hesitation in later times to accept it, possibly because of its references to apocryphal books.

THE TEACHING OF THE EPISTLE

The clear evidence afforded by the epistle of Jude's knowledge of Enoch,[1] and his use of the story of Michael's dispute with the devil over the body of Moses (9), which was probably narrated in another apocryphal book, throw an interesting light on influences at work on early Palestinian

[1] Apart from the loose quotation in 14 from Enoch 1, 9, Chase has collected an instructive series of parallels in Hastings' *Dictionary of the Bible*.

Christianity.   Occasional traces of such influence in passages in the Gospels, in 2 Thessalonians, and above all in the Book of Revelation (cf. p. 241) suggest that from the very earliest days the literature of Jewish Apocalyptic exerted a considerable influence upon Christian teaching, and the epistle of Jude gives us a valuable glimpse at the ways in which such influence affected the presentation of the Christian gospel.

Jude's own message is simple.   While preparing a letter on 'our common salvation' (3) he was constrained—perhaps as the result of receiving some special news about the situation in a community or communities unknown to us—to write instead against the growth of troublesome and heretical errors. The weight of the epistle lies in its authorship. Jude writes as one whose authority is unquestioned, and as one who can himself remember and vouch for the original content of the gospel, departure from which is fatal. A particular situation is envisaged, but, while we can safely assume that the epistle was written from somewhere in Palestine between A.D. 60 and A.D. 80, we have no means of knowing to whom Jude was writing.

CHAPTER XXI

THE SECOND EPISTLE OF PETER

THE EPISTLE NOT BY PETER

THE epistle claims to be a second epistle (iii 1) written by
Simon Peter 'a servant and apostle of Jesus Christ' (i 1)
and an eyewitness of his majesty at the Transfiguration
(i 16-18). The arguments against the acceptance of such
an ascription are, however, overwhelming. In the first
place there is no clear evidence of the use of the epistle before
the third century A.D. Origen, Eusebius, and Jerome all
refer to doubts as to its genuineness, and it gained its place in
the Canon only slowly and with difficulty. The internal
evidence confirms these doubts. Although the author
knew 1 Peter and borrowed some of its vocabulary, the
style of the second epistle is very different from that of the
first; the author seems also to have incorporated virtually
the whole of the epistle of Jude in his work (cf. p. 216),
and refers to Paul's epistles as already collected and widely
known (iii 16). It is hard to avoid the conclusion that this
epistle is yet another of a series of works which appeared in
the second century falsely claiming the authority of the
prince of apostles, of which we possess fragments of a Gospel
of Peter, of an Acts of Peter, and of an Apocalypse of Peter.

THE TEACHING OF THE EPISTLE

This impression is borne out both by the type of teaching
given and errors attached. There is an almost complete
absence of appeal to the example of the life of Jesus Christ,
the redemption through his suffering, the power of his
resurrection, and the work of the Spirit, which furnished
the first generation of Christian missionaries with primary
authority, and all of which are referred to in the first
epistle of Peter. The authority to which the author of
this epistle appeals above all is that of the prophets and

apostles (i 19-21, iii 2), and the vehicle of this authority is
largely the Old Testament and apostolic writings (iii 16 cf.
the use of Jude and 1 Peter).   In giving his main message,
that the day of the Lord will surely come, deferred though
it has been through God's wish that all should come to
repentance (iii 9-10), the writer adapts earlier Christian
teaching to the conceptions of a later time.   Thus he lays
a particular stress on attaining to the knowledge of God and
of Jesus Christ as the means of living a godly life and entering
the Kingdom (i 2-3, ii 18, iii 18), and he introduces the
idea of a final dissolution of the elements in fire (iii 7, 10)
which does not occur elsewhere in the New Testament.

A large part of the epistle is taken up with the denunciation of false teachers, and it is perhaps significant for
the date of the epistle that the author in the rôle of Peter
first proclaims that they will arise (ii 10 ff.).   While much
of what is said is borrowed from the epistle of Jude, there
are important differences.   The denunciations of Jude are
primarily against unworthy Christians whose lives are a
denial of Christ (verse 4), while in this epistle the condemnation is of false teachers (ii 1), who not only live evil lives,
but deny the coming of the End (iii 4).   It would be too
much to say that this is a conclusive proof of a second-
century date, when Gnostic heresies often combined false
doctrine and immoral practice, but it is at least compatible
with a time when such heresies were rife.   It is impossible
to give a precise date or location to the epistle.   That it was
composed not earlier than the close of the first century A.D.
is clear from its references to 1 Peter and the Pauline epistles
and from the curious passage where the author speaks of
' the day that the fathers fell asleep ' (iii 4), an apparent
allusion to the passing of the first generation of Christians.
A date somewhere in the first half of the second-century is
perhaps as near as we can safely guess.   There is some
evidence to suggest that the epistle was for a time associated
with the Apocalypse of Peter in some circles in the early
Church, and this, like the use of 1 Peter, would favour an
origin in Asia Minor.

CHAPTER XXII

THE JOHANNINE EPISTLES

AUTHORSHIP

THE connection of the first epistle of John with the Fourth Gospel in thought and language is so close as to make it certain that they are by the same author or that the epistle was written, probably with a knowledge of the gospel, by a disciple of the author of the gospel. It is difficult to weigh the admitted similarities against the differences that also exist, e.g. the absence in the epistle of any Old Testament quotations and of a large number of words typical of the evangelists, and the more primitive tone of the teaching of the epistle on the nearness of the End, the Atonement, and the Spirit; yet the claim of the author of the epistle to pass on what he has seen and heard (i 3), with its similarity to Jn. i 14, tells in favour of the identity of authorship, and is perhaps sufficient to tilt the balance in favour of this view.

Early in the second century Papias of Hierapolis is known to have used the first epistle, and Polycarp of Smyrna shows knowledge of the teaching of the first epistle and possibly of the second epistle as well, so that all three can be assumed to have been written in or near Ephesus before the end of the first century.

That 2 and 3 John are by the same hand as 1 John is generally admitted on grounds of style and language. From this it may be deduced that the author is ' the Elder ' (2 Jn. 1, 3 Jn. 1), though it will be seen from the discussion on the author of the Revelation, who was certainly not the same man, that there are obstacles to assuming that the Elder's name was John. The reasons for the growth of this tradition are discussed in the treatment of the gospel (pp. 82-89 above).

THE EPISTLES IN DETAIL

1 John

CIRCUMSTANCES OF WRITING

There is nothing in the ' epistle ' to suggest that it was written as a letter, except for the ' I write unto you ' of ii 1, 12, 13 ; it lacks both the name of its author and any greetings at the end, and may well have been written originally as a treatise or sermon. The purpose of the epistle, although the sequence of thought is often obscure, is clearly to build up the faith of a community well-known to the author in view of the activities of heretics (iv 1-5) whose appearance is a sign that the last hour has come (ii 18).

These heretics had separated themselves from the Church (ii 19), and denied ' that Jesus is the Christ ' (ii 22). They spoke in the spirit, but the spirit of the antichrist, and did not confess that Jesus Christ is come in the flesh (iv 1-3). From these references it is clear that the heresy which is attacked is the Docetic one, which denied the reality of the Incarnation by refusing to admit that the divine Christ could in any true sense ' come in the flesh ', suffer, or die. The Docetic heretics conceived of Christ as appearing in human shape, but neither being born nor dying, and their doctrines, which fitted the Gnostic conception of redemption better than the historic facts of Jesus' life on earth, had a wide vogue in the second century, especially in Asia Minor, where Ignatius denounced them *c*. A.D. 110.

THE TEACHING OF THE EPISTLE

Against such teaching the writer of the epistle sets forth the true Gnosis, or knowledge of divine things (ii 3), which comes from keeping God's commandments, in particular ' that we should believe in the name of His Son Jesus Christ, and love one another ' (iii 23).

While the language of the epistle is continually reminiscent of the Fourth Gospel, e.g. in the antithesis of light and darkness, life and death, the believers and the world, some

aspects of the teaching in the epistle find little or no confirmation in the gospel.   Thus Christ is twice spoken of as
' the expiation for our sins ' (ii 2, iv 10.   This translation
adopted in the American Standard Revised Version, is
better than ' the propitiation ' of the Revised and Authorised
Versions), and there are references to the coming of antichrists as a sign that it is the last hour (ii 18), as well as to the
day of judgement (iv 17 cf Jn. v 28-29).   These differences
between the teaching of the epistle and that of the gospel
have been taken by some critics to indicate difference
of authorship (see above), but they may well represent
concessions on the part of the Elder to the beliefs of the
community.   We know from Revelation and from other
writings that were probably in circulation in Asia at the
close of the first century that the eschatological beliefs of
many Christians were still similar to those taught by Paul to
the Thessalonians (cf. pp. 251-252 below), and the Fourth
Gospel itself at times puts teaching of such a kind into the
mouth of Jesus (cf. p. 255).

In writing to his ' little children ' (v 21), therefore,
the Elder may have felt it necessary to make use of terms and
ideas which he had himself outgrown, and which were
sometimes inconsistent with the general ' Johannine '
tenor of his teaching as a whole.

The Second Epistle of John

This short note is written to ' the elect lady and her
children, whom I love in truth ' (1) to establish them in
their faith and prepare them for a visit from the Elder (12).
The ' lady ' is almost certainly a church (cf. 1 Pet. v 13), and
the greetings from ' the children of thine elect sister ' (13).
It contains a warning against Docetists (7), and gives a
strict warning against giving hospitality or even greeting to
anyone who holds heretical views (9-11).

There are a number of striking parallels between the
language of 2 John and that of the Fourth Gospel, e.g. in the
references to truth in 1 and 2, which add an appreciable
argument in favour of the identity of authorship.

The Third Epistle of John

Although we do not know anything about Gaius, the individual to whom this letter is addressed, the letter as a whole is of great importance. The Elder complains that he has written a previous letter to the Church, but that ' Diotrephes, who loveth to have the pre-eminence among them, receiveth us not ' (9). The previous letter seems to have been brought by brethren of the Elder's own community, who acted as missionaries and relied for their support and lodging on the hospitality of Christians (7) ; Diotrephes had refused to allow members of the Church over which he presided to entertain them, and had expelled Gaius from the community for receiving them (6, 10). The Elder now sends a letter by the same brethren, asking Gaius to ' set them forward on their journey worthily of God ' (5-6), and commending especially one of their number, Demetrius (12). He threatens himself to come and expose Diotrephes shortly (10,14).

The significant feature of the epistle is that a church-leader, against whom the Elder makes no charge of heresy, could defy the authority of the Elder and reject his letter. While the reasons for this may have lain, as the Elder states, in the vanity of Diotrephes, the success of his repudiation of the Elder's authority suggests that the Elder can hardly have been one of the original apostles, and that his authority was comparatively limited outside his own community. If the Elder was indeed the author of the fourth gospel (cf. pp. 87-89 above) the importance of this is clear.

CHAPTER XXIII

THE TEACHING OF THE CHURCH

APOSTOLICITY AND DEVELOPMENT

CHRISTIAN doctrine and practice both rest upon the belief that the Word of God is to be found in the New Testament. When Christians differ, as they do, on important questions of doctrine or conduct, e.g. on the significance of baptism or on the issues of wealth and pacificism, their differences go back to different interpretations of New Testament texts or to different evaluations of parts of the New Testament.

As far as Christian conduct is concerned the questions that arise are for the most part connected with the interpretation of the words of Jesus : sufficient of his teaching has been preserved in the gospels to serve to-day, as it served in New Testament times, for a complete guide to conduct, in the sense that the principles laid down by Jesus need only application to our particular circumstances. Occasional difficulties arise as to which gospel texts represent what Jesus actually said, and the ethical teaching of the rest of the New Testament is often of great value for illustrating the way in which Jesus' words were understood in the earliest Church and for furnishing examples of their application to the needs of the first converts. The development of Jesus' moral teaching, however, in the New Testament Church is not of such a kind as to raise many fundamental problems for the Christians of to-day.

In the case of Christian doctrine the case is different. Whereas Jesus' teaching on conduct was openly given and dealt largely with subjects which concerned men's everyday life, the keeping of the Law, marriage, and the use of property, his teaching about the significance of his life, death, and resurrection was for the most part in private and often in veiled terms ; much of it was strange and new and was very imperfectly understood when it was given. It is, moreover, extremely difficult to decide how much of Jesus' teaching about himself that is recorded in the gospels is authentic and how much is the later invention of pious Christian tradition (cf. pp. 100-101). Finally Jesus' teaching about himself was incomplete; the significance of his work could only be understood afterwards in the light of the experience of the Holy Spirit which the disciples were to have at Pentecost and afterwards. The saying in the gospel of John

> But the Comforter, even the Holy Spirit, whom the Father will send in my name, he shall teach you all things, and bring to your remembrance all that I said unto you (Jn. xiv. 26)

may not, as it stands, be an actual word of Jesus, but the truth which it expresses is a real one.

A few Christian scholars have felt the task of establishing what Jesus taught about himself to be so impossible of achievement that they have sought to transfer the authority on which Christian faith should rest from Jesus to the Apostolic Church's experience of the risen Christ. This is a desperate remedy, for the apostles were not perfect men, as some Christians at least may still 'salva conscientia' maintain Jesus to have been both perfect man and Son of God. There is the further difficulty that 'Apostolic Christianity' needs further definition than it has sometimes received. It is clear that a process of expansion went on as the apostles themselves grow older and the Christian message had to be made intelligible to men of widely differing religious backgrounds; the epistles of the New Testament give us only the personal expression of their faith by a handful of individuals, only one of them a member of the Twelve, at particular moments in their lives. There is, it is true, a unified pattern of theology that underlies most of them (the epistles of James and Jude are important exceptions) which has been given a particular personal development in each case, but the differences are considerable, and raise the important question of the authority

15

that is to be attached to each personal theological interpretation.   To assess the relative value of such interpretations
demands in turn a knowledge of the main steps in the
progress of New Testament doctrine.

THE CHRISTIAN LIFE

Although the epistles rarely appeal to the words of
Jesus to support their teaching on conduct (yet cf. 1 Cor.
vii 10, ix 14) the memory of what Jesus had said was from
the first the formative force that shaped the pattern of this
teaching.   The influence of the words of Jesus on the epistle
of James has already been noted (p. 167), and the preservation in the gospels of so great an element of teaching
matter affords proof of the value set on it by the Church.
There can be no doubt that the retailing of Jesus' sayings
played an important part in the instruction of converts, and
that the circulation of such handbooks as Q (p. 50) reflects
the importance which was attached to the words of him who
was now acknowledged as Christ and Lord.

On the other hand, Jesus had not attempted to lay down
a code that would cover every part of men's conduct.
He had shown what were the great principles that were to be
applied by men to their lives, and had only illustrated by
occasional parables and sayings the motives which should
govern men's actions.   To the leaders of the Church fell
the task of initiating believers in the implications of these
principles for everyday life.   They started with the great
advantage that for all Jews the Law provided a magnificent
code of conduct, which Jesus himself had seen needed only
to be interpreted with the right motives and in its deepest
sense.   The power of the Spirit in the earliest Christian
community showed itself at once in a spontaneous sharing of
goods and in the creation of an atmosphere of joyful goodwill
(Acts ii 45-47).   The practical problems that inevitably
arose seem at first to have been dealt with by the guidance
which the community received from the Spirit and not by the
application of any rigid set of rules (Acts iv 29-35).   Yet the

growth of a specifically Christian 'code' was perhaps inevitable, to guide the convert as to what were the fruits of
the Spirit by which he could recognise his own progress.

When Gentiles began to be admitted into the Church the
need for such guidance became urgent.   Brought up for the
most part with very defective ideas of morality, they had
to be instructed in the essential ethical parts of the Law
before they could understand the Christian interpretation
of these commandments.   It is probable that the Christians
adopted a method of instructing converts and catechising
them at their baptism from the similar methods which the
Jews seem to have employed at this time for receiving proselytes.   The content of such instruction may well have varied
in individual cases, but a study of the epistles reveals a
certain agreement in the general pattern of ethical teaching
which may reflect the existence of a common form of cate-
chism.   A feature of this teaching is the apparent influence
of Jewish models, and the comparative absence of material
drawn direct from Jesus' words.   Yet the teaching of Jesus
himself, as can be seem from the epistles, continued to
dominate the moral demands of Christian missionaries to
Gentiles, and to give a new meaning to the lists of virtues
and vices that they drew up (Gal. v 17-24, Eph. iv 2, vi 14-
17, 1 Pet. iii 8-9).

As the Church continued to grow the problem of order
within the Church became more serious.   Cases of unworthy
living (e.g. 1 Cor. v 1 ff., Jude 16) and of heresy (e.g. 1 Tim.
iv 1-3, 2 Jn. 7) increased, and the tension between the need
for discipline and the love enjoined by Jesus became at times
extreme.   The adoption of rules and regulations tended to
increase (e.g. 1 Tim. *passim*) and the spirit of Jesus' teaching
was sometimes only partially remembered, as in the Revelation (cf. p. 245).   Yet Christian experience of the Spirit,
and the constant reminder of Jesus' teaching at hand in the
stable tradition of the words which he had used, preserved
for future generations the essentials of what had been the
teaching of the apostles without serious change.

CHRISTIAN DOCTRINE

The appearance of Jesus after his resurrection and the manifestation of the Spirit at Pentecost gave to the apostles a new understanding of the meaning of Jesus' life and death. In the light of their experiences they recalled the words of Jesus which they had found so hard to comprehend during his ministry and which they now saw to have been confirmed by what had happened.   When they began in turn to spread their faith and to proclaim the significance of what had happened, their interpretation was along the lines which Jesus had himself laid down in his own explanations of the purpose of his coming.   Yet their preaching about Jesus was no mere continuation of Jesus' own preaching about himself : they considerably expanded what Jesus had taught them and in thus developing his message they unconsciously incorporated some elements which sprang from their own expectation and not from Jesus' own teaching.

The available evidence for determining the nature of the earliest apostolic preaching is not great.   Besides the early epistle of James (pp. 167 f.) and Luke's record of the speeches of Peter (p. 138) there are the epistle to which Peter gave his ' imprimatur ' in later life (pp. 169-175) and the traces in Paul's epistles of primitive beliefs which he had received from the Church (e.g. 1 Cor. xi 23 ff. xv 3 ff., and possibly Rom. i 1-4, viii 31-34, Phil. ii 6-11) (p. 139) ; it is also permissible to draw conclusions from the epistles, not only of Paul, as to the earlier preaching which they presuppose, and to attribute certain features of the gospels, especially Mark, to the influence of early Christian preaching upon the tradition of Jesus' words and acts.

Such evidence can only be used with caution, but some features of the early Christian preaching stand out which can fairly claim to be apostolic.   There is first of all a remarkable ' variety in unity ' :   thus different titles are applied to Jesus, who is ' the Servant of God ' (Acts iii 13), the Holy and Righteous One (Acts iii 14), ' the Prince of Life ' (Acts iii 15) in Peter's earliest speeches as well as ' Lord and Christ ' (Acts ii 36), and is ' Son of Man ' and ' Lord Jesus '

(Acts vii 56, 59) to Stephen, and ' Son of God ' (Acts ix 20) to Paul. There is nothing surprising in this, for Christians agreed in finding that Jesus was the fulfilment of ' all that the prophets have spoken ' (Lk. xxiv 25), and such a united belief inevitably found expression in all sorts of different ways. Yet this use of the Old Testament was not without its dangers for men whose minds were steeped in current interpretations of its prophecies. It seems probable, for example, that the prominence of apocalyptic imagery in even the earliest teaching of the Church was due far more to conceptions of the Messianic Kingdom and the Judgement derived from contemporary expectations than to the restrained and spiritual teaching of Jesus himself. (This subject is discussed in more detail on pp. 250-251).

The core of the earliest Christian kerygma (cf. p. 30) consisted in the proclamation that Jesus had by his life, resurrection, exaltation, and pouring forth of the spirit been proved to be from God (Acts ii 22, 30-36), that he would return in judgement (Acts x 42), and that salvation was offered to those who repented and received baptism in His name (Acts ii 38). Proclamation involved also explanation and Christians had to show HOW these things were so, and to relate these simple tenets of faith to the existing beliefs first of Jews, and then, in course of time, of Gentiles also.

The speeches of Acts and the epistles of the New Testament are largely directed to this task of working out a theology intelligible as well as challenging to men with Jewish and Gentile backgrounds. The development of Christian thought was gradual and followed many different paths : the Pauline epistles are sufficient indication of the way in which even an experienced Christian missionary could vary his intellectual interpretation of his faith over a mere dozen years. All that is attempted here is to indicate very summarily a few of the needs which compelled a development of Christian doctrine and some of the changes of emphasis in Christian preaching which resulted.

The great majority of the Jews looked forward to God's intervention in history, perhaps through an intermediary, as they expected also the pouring forth of the Spirit, and they accepted the need for repentance ; they were, however, convinced that the Law, and the Temple were permanent elements in God's revelation, and that God's acceptance of the Gentiles could only be through bringing them under the Law.   The Christians, in presenting the good news to their fellow Jews, therefore made great use of the arguments drawn from Old Testament prophecy (e.g. Acts ii 25-31, iii 22-26) and were enabled to employ many of the already existing conceptions of e.g. the Messiah, the Judgement, in support of their views.

The preaching of Stephen, however, marked a decisive development in Christian thought. The majority of Jewish Christians had held to their observance of the Law and the Temple worship as bound up with repentance, and they continued after Stephen's time to follow this practice.   Stephen seems to have represented a section within the Church whose interpretation of the nature of repentance had led them to see that neither the full Law nor the Temple were essential (Acts vi 14, vii 48 ff.).   The precise connection of Stephen's teaching with the admission of large numbers of Gentiles into the Church at Antioch that followed is uncertain (Acts xi 19 ff.), but henceforth the Church was faced with the double task of explaining its faith to Gentiles who had a very different background from the Jews and the Christian missionaries themselves, and of justifying its action to the Jews.

The first of these tasks involved the working out of a complete theology. The Gentiles needed instruction as to the nature of God and the relation of Jesus to God, the place of the Spirit in the scheme of salvation and what was implied by salvation, how Jesus had won salvation for men, and what were the purposes of Baptism and the Eucharist. Some of these themes must already have been dwelt on in the Christian mission to the Jews, but the new situation called for the transformation of the gospel into a comprehensive system of belief that took into account the Gentile lack of understanding of what was self-evident for Jews.

The working out of such a system was the work of generations, and as men's beliefs about the world have changed,
some of the work has had to be done over again.   But
within a comparatively few years the foundations of Christian
theology had been well and truly laid.   The nature of
God and man, the relation of Christ and the Spirit to God
the Father, the meaning of Jesus' life, death, and resurrection,
the nature of the Church and the meaning of Sacraments—
the classical Christian doctrines still follow the lines laid
down in the epistles of Paul and John, 1 Peter, the epistles
to the Ephesians and to the Hebrews, and all these epistles
were written within the span of half a century.   The
question of the relationship of these epistles to each other is
an intricate one which can never finally be solved.   They
share certain basic presuppositions and yet often follow
different lines of argument, e.g. the interpretations of the
meaning of Christ's death given by Paul and by the author
of the epistle to the Hebrews (pp. 198, 213).   The Pauline
epistles are the earliest, and the influence of Paul's thought
appears to be present in a greater or less degree in the other
epistles, but Paul himself owes much—how much we cannot
tell—to his predecessors and fellow-workers in the Church.

One aspect of Paul's theology among many that are of
special importance for the development of later Christian
thought may be noted here.   Paul makes a real attempt to
justify to Jews the Christian mission to the Gentiles : his
arguments (Rom. ix-xi) presuppose the present rejection by
God of his ancient people for their ultimate salvation,
but they are connected with Paul's claim that the Christians
and not the Jewish nation are the true heirs of the promise
to Abraham (Rom. iv 13-25).   Paul's efforts to convert the
Jews to his point of view were seldom successful (e.g. Acts
xxviii 23 ff.), but his stress on the Christian Church being
the true Israel of God (Gal. vi 16) and his annexation of the
Old Testament as belonging to Christians were of tremendous
importance for the future of Christianity.   A time was to
come when the cleavage between Christians and Jews was
absolute (cf. the presentation of ' the Jews ' in John vii 13,

xi 8, and Revel. ii 9), but the Christians were still to maintain that the Old Testament was their book and that they were its true inheritors (Heb. i 1-2, xi 1 ff.).

This acceptance of the authority of the Old Testament, which was shared by Jesus himself (p. 116), although often open to criticism as eclectic in its choice and interpretation of texts, preserved the Church in later New Testament times from the complete subjugation of its theology by its Gentile environment. This danger was a very real one. The rites of Baptism and the Eucharist, for example, had parallels in the popular religions of the time, especially in the initiation rites and sacred meals. of the Mystery-Religions. We read of the practice of such rites in the first century A.D. in Greece, and some of Paul's Corinthian converts may have witnessed them and have attributed to them a similar significance to that of Christian sacraments; Paul rejects such rites as diabolical (1 Cor. x 21), and draws out the meaning of the Christian rites from Old Testament 'examples' (1 Cor. x 1-7). The Colossians again seem to have known a heresy which sought to incorporate Christ as one of many instruments of God's redemption of man (Col. ii 8 ff.), and Paul's refutation of this heresy is solidly based on Old Testament conceptions as fulfilled in Christ (Col. ii 8-15).

On the other hand the influence of Hellenism upon the form of Christian doctrine was very considerable even in New Testament times; to a great extent this was due to the Hellenistic background of many of the Christian missionaries who, Jews themselves, had grown up in the Jewish 'dispersion', where Judaism had often undergone considerable superficial modification to make it attractive to Gentile converts. In Alexandria, for example, many elements of Greek thought had been adopted by such Jews as Philo (*ob. c.* A.D. 42) in their theological expositions, and the prologue of John, with its setting forth of Jesus as the pre-existent Word (Greek, *Logos*) of God, stands in such a Hellenistic Jewish tradition. Another influence which was to be of great importance in later times, but which is not

much in evidence in the New Testament books, written
as they were for the most part by Jews, was the unconscious
effect of Greek ideas upon Christians who came from
educated Gentile circles, to whom the Old Testament was a
sacred book but had never been a complete basis of religion
in itself.   Whatever authority we may give to the particular
developments of Christian doctrine that are set forth in the
epistles, it cannot be denied that the underlying unity of
New Testament doctrine rests upon the firm memory of what
the Jesus of history had done and taught and the fruitfulness
with which Jesus' attitude to the Old Testament was
followed in essentials by the early Church.

PART V

THE REVELATION OF JOHN AND CHRISTIAN APOCALYPTIC

CHAPTER XXIV

THE STUDY OF THE REVELATION

No New Testament book is so difficult for the Christian of to-day to understand as the Revelation. Its fantastic imagery and lack of clear order are formidable obstacles to the grasp of its meaning. Yet as the only book of Christian prophecy which was accepted into the New Testament it has a special significance for the understanding of certain aspects of early Christian religion. It is only when the student has read the Revelation and comprehended the way in which a Christian prophet could cast his message into such a form that he can assess the influence of such a type of faith on the moulding of Christian tradition.

The apocalyptic passages in the gospels and the epistles raise fundamental questions as to the place which such teaching had in Jesus' mind. Was the eschatological expectation of Jesus expressed in the crude material forms of contemporary Jewish apocalyptic, or do such passages in the gospels represent the distortion of his original message under the influence of Christian prophecy? How are the contradictions between apocalyptic and spiritual interpretations of the End in Paul and John to be resolved? To answer these questions a right understanding of the Revelation is essential.

BOOKS FOR READING

The best short introduction to the Revelation is perhaps E. F. Scott, *The Book of Revelation* (S.C.M.). Among larger works the recently published work of A. M. Farrer, *The Re-birth of Images*, makes difficult reading, but contains much that is helpful for the exegesis of the book. Of commentaries for the reader who knows no Greek those by M. Kiddle (Moffatt) and by A. Hanson and R. Preston (S.C.M.) may be mentioned.

For the study of the apocalyptic element in the New Testament as a whole, BURKITT, *Jewish and Christian Apocalypses* (Oxford) and the larger work of CHARLES, *Eschatology : Hebrew, Jewish and Christian* (Black) are helpful, as are two recent books, H. A. GUY, *New Testament Prophecy* (Epworth Press) and T. F. GLASSON, *The Second Advent* (Epworth Press).

CHAPTER XXV

THE REVELATION OF JOHN

AUTHORSHIP

THE author of the book gives his name as John (i 1, 4). Tradition from the middle of the second century identified him with the apostle, although there is evidence that this tradition was disputed in the second half of the second century by Christians who found distasteful the teaching of the book on the thousand-year reign of Christ on earth before the final judgement (xx 3-6). Criticism of the tradition was renewed in the third century by scholars who were conscious of the contrasts in style which separate this book from the Fourth Gospel, also traditionally attributed to the apostle.

The great majority of modern critics agree that the John who wrote the Revelation cannot also have written the gospel or the epistles. There are a number of curious verbal coincidences, e.g. the frequent occurrence of ' witness ' and of ' keeping the commandments ' of Christ or God, but these are probably due to the common Asian provenance of the books. Between the general thought, vocabulary, and style of the gospel and epistles on the one hand and those of the Revelation on the other, there is a wide gulf. In the Revelation God's love is mentioned once (xx 9), his fatherhood not at all, and the material imagery of the Revelation is in sharp contrast to the mysticism of the gospel. Many of the specially characteristic words of the gospel are absent from the Revelation, e.g. truth, or used in a different sense, e.g. light, only with a physical meaning; different Greek words are employed in the two books for ' the Lamb '. The style of the Revelation is barbarous, and only consistent with a very imperfect knowledge of Greek grammar.

While such a poor knowledge of Greek is perhaps consistent with authorship by the apostle—and we have seen that many scholars refuse to connect the gospel with the apostle John—there is nothing in Revelation to indicate such authorship, and the statement in xxi 14 that the twelve foundations of the wall of new Jerusalem had 'on them twelve names of the twelve apostles of the Lamb' is hardly consistent with it. The writer shows no interest in the earthly life of Christ apart from his birth (xii 1 ff.), his Davidic descent (v 5), and his death by crucifixion (i 7, 18, xi 8), but the very nature of his work leaves little place for mention of the earthly life of Christ.

Beyond his name, the fact that he was a prophet (xxii 6-7), the place of his vision (i 9), and his acquaintance with some of the Asian churches, the Revelation tells us little about its author. His knowledge of the Hebrew Old Testament and of Jewish apocalyptic thought suggests that he was a born Jew, and the Hebraic solecisms of his style that he was not brought up in the Asian dispersion which used the Greek language in its everyday life, but that he may have come there from Palestine. Of the attempts to identify the author more closely only one deserves serious attention. The historian Eusebius (c. A.D. 320) drew attention to the fact that an earlier Christian writer, Papias (c. A.D. 120), had given in his list of authorities two Johns, one the apostle and one 'John the Elder', and thought that the latter might have written the Revelation. There is much to be said for this view, though it can never be more than a conjecture. The little we know of him suggests that this John was a well-known figure in Asia, and the one passage in the surviving fragments of Papias' work which is directly ascribed to a reminiscence of John the Elder puts into the mouth of Jesus a description of the miraculous fruits of the age to come in terms akin to those used in a first-century Jewish apocalypse (cf. p. 254).

DATE AND CIRCUMSTANCES OF WRITING

Irenaeus (c. A.D. 185) speaks of the Revelation as seen 'not long ago, but almost in our generation, at the end of

Domitian's reign (i.e. *c.* A.D. 95) '. There are grounds for believing that Irenaeus is here quoting from Papias, who himself knew the Revelation, and this date may well be correct. The church in Ephesus has had time to leave its first love (ii 4), that in Laodicea to become lukewarm (iii 16). Domitian seems to have been the first emperor to take emperor-worship seriously, and persecution of Christians seems to have become widespread, if sporadic, in his reign, although the evidence is scanty. Earlier dates have been suggested, but on insufficient grounds. A date in the last years of Nero's reign (54-68) is ruled out by the references to the legend of Nero's return (xvii 8-11), and the verses (xi 1 ff.) which are sometimes claimed as indicating that the temple was still standing seem to draw their significance from Old Testament prophecy (especially Ez. xl) rather than from any contemporary historical situation. A date under Vespasian can be supported by a strict interpretation of xvii 10, but such an interpretation is far from binding in an apocalypse.

How the book came to be written is explained in i 1-3, 9-20. John received a command from Christ (18) when he was ' in the Spirit on the Lord's day ' to write what he saw in a book and to send it to the seven churches. It is permissible to speak of the occasion of the book as the need to exhort these churches, and to reassure them of the reward soon to come (i 1, 3), but the impelling force that led to its writing is the consciousness of the Christian prophet that he has been commanded to proclaim his vision of the future (i 1, iv 1). How far the contents of the book correspond to the actual experiences of the ecstatic vision, and how far the author has sought to expand and interpret his vision, we have no means of learning. What *is* certain is that the form both of his vision and of his presentation of it show the great influence exerted upon his mind by his study of the Old Testament and Jewish apocalypses; there are continual echoes of Isaiah, Ezekiel, 1 Enoch, and, above all, of Daniel. The Revelation illustrates in a remarkable fashion the way in which early Christian prophets drew from Jewish literary sources the language and imagery with which they strove to express their own spiritual experiences and the meaning of the new and final revelation in Jesus Christ.

The letters to the seven churches (ii-iii) tell us a little about the situation of Christianity in Asia when the book was written. There is persecution from without; the imprisonment of some at Smyrna (ii 10-11) and the death of Antipas at Pergamum (ii 13) seem to indicate the hostility of the authorities. The antagonism of the Jews is referred to in ii 9, iii 9. Internal troubles also are plaguing the churches, and we hear of false apostles at Ephesus (ii 2) and of heresies there and elsewhere. We are not informed of what the Nicolaitans taught (ii 6, 15), but the teaching of Balaam (ii 14-15) and Jezebel (ii 20-21) involves fornication and idolatry. The churches are clearly in need of encouragement, and in some cases, of reproof.

THE MESSAGE OF THE BOOK

There is no ' teaching ' as such in the Revelation, and the word is used only of heresies, e.g. ii 15, 20. Even in the letters to the churches it is not teaching which is given, but commands from the Spirit, and the main purpose of the book as a whole is the revelation of the future. The plan of the book is simple, a prologue (i 1-8), the account of a vision of Christ (i 18) commanding John to write what he sees to the seven churches (i 9-20), special messages to each of the churches (ii-iii), the heavenly visions which comprise the main part of the book (iv 1-xxii 5), and an epilogue (xxii 6-21). What makes the understanding of the author's original meaning hard for the reader is the difficulty of divining a consistent and consecutive course of events from the series of visions narrated in the main body of the book. Thus the great day of God's wrath upon the people of the earth is described at the end of chapter vi, and is followed immediately by the sealing of the elect and a description of

their service before the throne of God ; yet the armies of the
kings of the earth are destroyed again, after a whole series
of intervening disasters, in xix 21 ; even after the second
death of all who were not found written in the book of life
(xx 15) there are still evildoers to be found outside the holy
city (xxii 15).

Attempts have been made to explain this disorder of
thought by supposing that the sheets of the original MS.
have been accidentally transposed, that the original book
has been clumsily redacted, that earlier literary sources have
been incorporated by John into a framework inconsistent
with them, or that the series of seals, trumpets, bowls, etc.,
are to be understood not as following one another but as
different ways of presenting the same actions.   None of the
explanations have commanded general assent, however,
although it is clear that John has a wide knowledge of
earlier apocalyptic writings, and that some theory of recapitulation is necessary to produce a logical sequence of
events in the book ; the most probable solution of the confusion of the Revelation lies in the confusion of the writer's
own thought and his lack of concern about strict consistency.
His mind was soaked in apocalyptic imagery drawn from
various sources and not always mutually consistent, and
he wrote, as he believed, under the direct guidance of the
Spirit ; the combination of these two influences enabled
him to write passages of tremendous power and religious
significance, but not to achieve a consistent whole.

The reader will find his way more easily through the
maze of visions if he bears in mind the general scheme of
eschatological expectation that underlies 1 and 2 Thessalonians, 1 Cor. xv, and the apocalyptic chapters Mk. xiii,
Lk. xxi, and Matt. xxiv.   The end is conceived of as
coming in three stages, a period of catastrophe in the
earth and heavens, the coming of Christ to destroy the
power of evil, and the entering of the faithful into their
reward.   This simple pattern has been embroidered and
developed by each writer in a number of ways.   Paul, for
example, writes of ' the lawless one ', whose revelation is

delayed by a restraining force, but whose final appearance will bring on the events of the End (2 Thess. ii) : the dead in Christ are to be raised at Christ's coming and to join those who are left alive to be ever with the Lord (1 Thess. iv); in 1 Cor. xv 23-28 there appears even to be a reference to a temporary Messianic kingdom until the final conquest of death and Christ's deliverance of his kingdom to God the Father.

In the Revelation the general scheme is not fundamentally different from that of Paul, but it has been so developed and overlaid with an abundance of apocalyptic detail and the repetition of events that the connecting thread is hard to follow.

For the history of the Church two sections of the book have had a special importance, the judgement on Rome (xii-xviii) and the account in xx of the Millennium, i.e. the thousand-year reign of Christ on earth (from the Latin mille = 1,000 annus = year).

John's denunciation of the Roman power and her rulers is cast in symbolic language, but there can be no doubt that he regarded the Roman Empire as the instrument of Satan. Hatred of Rome had grown among the Jews with their subjection to Rome and with the failure of the Jewish revolt and the destruction of Jerusalem and the Temple in A.D. 70, but for a Christian of the age of Domitian it was the claim of the emperor to be worshipped that was the supreme offence against God (xiii 6-8). The interpretation of the great harlot as Rome (xvii 3, 18) and of the seven heads of the scarlet beast on which she sits as Roman emperors (xvii 3, 10) is certain. Unfortunately the interpretation of the book has too often proceeded from attempts to show the relevance of its symbols for each passing age, and the challenge of xiii 18 to deduce the name of the beast has been answered with names as different as the Pope and Hitler.[1]

John's account of the Millennium owes much, directly

---

[1] The author was prevented from preaching in a prisoner of war camp in Germany in 1940 because this latter identification had been made in a previous address by a British sergeant-major.

or indirectly, to the belief which can be traced in some Jewish apocalypses (cf. p. 122) that God's Messiah will reign on earth for a period of time before the final judgement. The authority of the Revelation was in turn to persuade many Christians to accept ' Chiliasm ' (Greek *chilioi* = 1,000), and the revulsion of other Christians against this material conception of religion delayed the recognition of the Revelation as canonical for centuries in the East.

THE VALUE OF THE REVELATION

The preceding paragraphs have inevitably concentrated upon the defects of the book, with its one-sided interpretation of the meaning of Christ's message to men. The absence of the ideas of God's fatherhood and love of men, and the comparative subordination of the moral and spiritual side of the Christian gospel to an apocalyptic often at variance with it, are serious failings. And yet, with all its imperfections, the Revelation remains the greatest of Christian prophecies because of its power to fire men's imaginations in times of persecution and crisis with the majesty of God and the hope of glory to come. Its deficiencies are supplied by other books of the New Testament, and, when it is read and studied in conjunction with them, it more than bears out Paul's promise (1 Cor. xiv 3) ' he that prophesieth speaketh unto men edification, and comfort, and consolation '.

CHAPTER XXVI

THE PLACE OF APOCALYPTIC IN THE TEACHING OF JESUS AND OF THE EARLY CHURCH

A RECURRING theme in the New Testament is the expectation of the imminent end of the present world age and of an approaching judgement, accompanied at times by a graphic and material depiction of the events that are to herald and accompany the end. The expectation was not fulfilled and many earnest Christians throughout the centuries have echoed the words of the ' mockers ' in 2 Pet. iii 4 ' Where is the promise of his coming ? for, from the day that the fathers fell asleep, all things continue as they were from the beginning of the creation.'

It cannot be contested that the primitive church as a whole, and even the apostles, held firmly to a mistaken view of the nearness of the End. James' message (v 8) that ' the coming of the Lord is at hand ' is repeated by Peter (1 Pet. iv 17) ' The time is come for judgement to begin at the house of God ', and Paul tells both the Thessalonians (1 Thess. iv 15-17) and the Corinthians (1 Cor. xv 51-52) that some of them will still be alive when the end comes. The teaching of 1 John (ii 18) is that ' it is the last hour ' and of Revelation (xxii 10) that ' the time is at hand ',

THE TEACHING OF JESUS

Even Jesus himself, according to the Synoptic Gospels, had taught during his early ministry of his early return in glory and in judgement. In Mark viii 38-ix 1 we read :

> ' For whosoever shall be ashamed of me and of my words in this adulterous and sinful generation, the Son of man also shall be ashamed of him, when he cometh in the glory of his Father with the holy angels.' And he said unto them ' Verily I say unto you, there be some here of them that stand by, which shall in no wise taste of death, till they see the kingdom of God come with power.'

246

Again, towards the close of the little apocalypse of Mark xiii, with its detailed description of the signs of the end, Jesus says (xiii 30), ' This generation shall not pass away, until all these things be accomplished '.   When the high priest asks him at his trial if he is the Christ, Jesus replies (Mk. xiv 62),

' I am : and ye shall see the Son of man sitting at the right hand of power, and coming with the clouds of heaven.'

These passages from Mark can be paralleled by others from Matthew e.g. x 23 ' Ye shall not have gone through the cities of Israel till the Son of man be come ', and from Luke, e.g. xxii 34-36.   In the face of such evidence it must either be accepted that Jesus is rightly recorded in the Synoptic Gospels as having taught of his early return in glory and the accompanying judgement—and that he was mistaken, or it must be shown that his teaching was from the earliest days misinterpreted and transformed.   There are strong reasons for rejecting the former alternative, and accepting the challenge of the latter.   A close study of the gospels shows that the dominant themes of Jesus' teaching imply no such early end of the world, but are in fact inconsistent with it, and that the ' apocalyptic ' sayings bear many signs of editorial distortion both on the part of the final gospel-authors and of the earlier traditions.

It is clear that the teaching of Jesus was eschatological in the sense that life is to be lived in expectation of the judgement and the coming of the kingdom, and his acceptance of the titles Son of man and Messiah implied a claim that the Kingdom of God had already come or was about to begin.   All these terms, Son of man, Messiah, Kingdom of God, had for his hearers a connection with the apocalyptic expectation of the time, based largely on the teaching of a number of current apocalyptic books, such as the Books of Daniel and Enoch, and exemplified in the teaching of John the Baptist that one mightier than he was about to come,

' Whose fan is his hand, throughly to cleanse his threshing-floor, and to gather the wheat into his garner ; but the chaff he will burn up with unquenchable fire.'   (Lk. iii 17).

The general tenor of Jesus' own teaching, however, indicates that he used these symbols, in interpretation of his own mission, in a sense quite different from that given to those of his contemporaries. This is brought out very well in the consistent picture of the teaching of Jesus given by the source Q. While, according to Q, Jesus claimed to be Son of God (Mt. xi 27, Lk. x 22) and to bring the Kingdom proclaimed beforehand by John (Mt. xi 11, Lk. vii 28), the Kingdom, whether thought of as present (e.g. Mt. xiii, 31-33, Lk. xiii 18-21, Mt. xxiii 13, Lk. xi 52) or as future (e.g. in the Lord's Prayer) is primarily spiritual, although in the latter case Jesus seems sometimes to have used material and traditional metaphors, e.g. of a Messianic banquet (Mt. viii 11-12, Lk. xiii 28-29). When he speaks of the coming of the Son of man, he emphasises its suddenness (Mt. xxiv 43-44, Lk. xii 39-40) and universality (Mt. xxiv 28, 39, Lk. xvii 24, 30), but refuses to name a place (Mt. xxiv 28, Lk. xvii 37) or time (Mt. xxiv 44, Lk. xii 40) for it. The general truth of the Q version of Jesus' teaching is confirmed by a significant number of passages from other strata of the gospels,[1] and although there are many problems that admit of no certain solution, e.g. the difficulty of reconciling passages where the kingdom is spoken of as present with those where it is spoken of as future, there is at least sufficient evidence for reconstructing the main lines of Jesus' authentic eschatological teaching.

When the passages in the gospels which give to Jesus a materially apocalyptic outlook are compared with these others, their secondary nature becomes apparent. In many cases the processes of alteration and distortion can be traced fairly easily, although in other cases we can only guess at the original context of the words or how they came to be put into Jesus' mouth. In the passage already quoted from Mark viii 38-ix 1 we have two genuine sayings of Jesus, one of the judgement that will accompany his second coming,

[1] E.g. for the spiritual conception of the kingdom Mk. iv 26-29, Mt. v 3, xiii 44-45, Lk. xvii 20-21 ; for the suddenness of the coming of the Son of man Mk. xiii 34-35 ; for the refusal to name a time Mk. xiii 32-33.

one of the coming of the kingdom with power in the lifetime of his hearers. The original meaning of the second of these sayings may have had reference to the coming of the Spirit (cf. the possible original meaning of the saying in Mk. xiii 30) or, as some scholars think, to the Transfiguration which follows almost at once in the Marcan narrative; it is only the editorial juxtaposition of the two sayings, falsifying their original contexts, which turns the whole passage into a prophecy of the return of the Son of man within a generation.

'The Little Apocalypse' of Mark xiii illustrates the results of such editorial manipulation on a larger scale. There is no reason to doubt that many genuine sayings of Jesus are embedded in this chapter, and that they include a prophecy of the destruction of the Temple, prophecies of persecution, of false Christs, and of the suddenness of the return of the Son of man; but the genuine sayings of Jesus have been so transformed and robbed of their original contexts in the process of forming a long and confused series of prophecies of the End, many of whose elements are derived from other sources, that the final result is very different in spirit from the original teaching of Jesus. Lk. xxi 34-36, with which Luke closes his parallel apocalyptic discourse, is so reminiscent in its vocabulary of Paul's epistles as to suggest that here also words have been put into Jesus' mouth that in fact represent the belief of early Christians. A similar explanation may account for Mt. x 23, though in this verse some scholars see a genuine word of Jesus whose original meaning had reference only to a proposed 'follow up' by Jesus of his disciples' mission, and for the present form of Mk. xiv 62.

The apocalyptic element in the teaching of Jesus, if such a view of the gospel evidence is accepted, is reduced to small proportions. He spoke of the end of the world and of a final judgement, but refused to name a time for them, and he at times employed in connection with the kingdom that will be at last established, metaphors of the Messianic banquet and of thrones of judgement (Mt. xix 28, Lk. xxii 29-30). At the same time he spoke of the kingdom, already present and growing and being entered, in such a spiritual sense as to illuminate the dominant significance which he attached to these terms.   He charged with a new spiritual significance the existing conceptions of Messiah and Son of man, of the end of the world, and of God's Kingdom.

WHY THE DISCIPLES MISUNDERSTOOD
THE TEACHING OF JESUS

That his apostles, however, should have misunderstood Jesus' teaching to the extent of expecting his return in their own generation is not surprising.   It is clear from Mark's account of the Confession of Peter at Caesarea Philippi that even in recognising Jesus' Messiahship he misunderstood its true nature.   When Jesus spoke of his forthcoming death, and Peter began to rebuke him (Mk. viii 32), it was because Peter, like James and John (Mk. x 35-37) shared in the common belief that the Messiah would come once, and initiate the New Age which was to see God's rule fully established.   When one misunderstanding—that the Messiah would not die—had been removed, it was replaced by another, that his departure was only for a short while and that the establishment of the kingdom was to be on the lines expected by the apocalyptists.   It is significant that Luke represents the apostles even after the resurrection as asking ' Lord, dost thou at this time restore the kingdom to Israel ' ? (Acts i 7), and although the interpretation of the Kingdom of God as a present reality is not absent from the New Testament outside the gospels (e.g. Col. i 13), James (ii 5) and the author of Hebrews (xii 28) use the term only, and Paul (e.g. 1 Cor. xv 50, Gal. v 21) mainly of the kingdom that was shortly to appear.

THE DEVELOPMENT OF APOCALYPTIC IDEAS

Two influences especially confirmed the early Christians in their error, their study of the Old Testament and the apocalyptic writings, and the rise of Christian prophecy.

The use of scriptural proof texts necessarily involved references to 'the last days' (Joel ii 28, cited Acts ii 17) and the nearness of the judgement (Deut. xviii 19, cited Acts iii 23), and to cosmic catastrophes connected with the end (Joel iii 30-31, cited Acts ii 19-20). The very confusions and inconsistencies of much of Christian apocalyptic reflect not only the differences between the teaching of Jesus and that of Jewish apocalyptic, but also the wide variations in the apocalyptic conceptions that existed within contemporary Judaism. While Jewish apocalypses are only rarely quoted directly in the New Testament (yet cf. Jude 14-15), the reading and interpretation of them, in the light of Jesus' Messiahship, exercised a widespread influence in still further adapting Christian teaching on the End to current Jewish conceptions. To such an influence are due the introduction of the figure of Antichrist (1 Jn. ii 18 cf. 2 Thess. ii 3-8), and probably of Daniel's 'abomination of desolation' (Mk. xiii 14), the accumulation of signs and portents before the end (Mk. xiii, Mt. xxiv, Lk. xxi) and some of the accompaniments of the end itself (e.g. the trump of 1 Thess. iv 16 and Mt. xxiv 31). The process of distortion was accelerated by the activity of Christian prophets. The gift of speaking 'in the Spirit of God' (1 Cor. xii 3) was one which greatly enriched Christian life and was of great service for edification (1 Cor. xiv 4) ; at the same time, because of its recognised authority and its freedom of utterance, it was peculiarly fitted to spread in the Church a confusion of ideas about the coming End ; the individual prophet, like the seer of the Book of Revelation, sometimes spoke from a mind charged at once with the teaching of Jesus and with confused memories of apocalyptic writings and utterances ; his words, in turn, were received as authoritative and passed on.

PAUL

Two examples will show the working of such influences in the New Testament. Paul, writing to the Thessalonians in A.D. 50, reminds them of the teaching he has given them about the End (1 Thess. v 2, 2 Thess. ii 5). In his first epistle (1 Thess. iv 15-v 3) he refers explicitly to 'the word of the Lord' that the coming of the Lord will be in the lifetime of at least some of them, a clear indication that the misunderstanding of Jesus' teaching goes back to those who had themselves heard him. He reminds them that they already know that the day of the Lord will come 'as a thief in the night' and that it will be accompanied by sudden destruction on those not expecting it; here his teaching echoes genuine sayings of Jesus. The end itself is pictured in terms drawn from Jewish apocalyptic; the Lord will descend from heaven with a shout, with the voice of the archangel (cf. The apocalypse of Moses xxii), and with the trump of God (cf. 4 Ezra vi 23); those that are alive and the risen dead are to be caught up in the clouds to meet the Lord in the air (cf. Dan. vii 13-14), 'and so shall we ever be with the Lord'.

In his second epistle (2 Thess. ii 3-12) Paul adds further details, some of them inconsistent with the sudden and un-expected coming of the end, which show not only the influence of old Jewish apocalyptic ideas, but also the development of new and perhaps specifically Christian ideas under the stress of contemporary events. The conception of the 'man of sin', who is to set himself forth as God to sit in the temple of God and finally to be destroyed by the breath of the Lord Jesus, owes much ultimately to Jewish apocalyptic, notably to Dan. vii, viii and xi, but the Christians have adapted the conception to their own expectations and have developed a whole series of accompanying ideas, e.g. 'he that restraineth' (ii 7). We can only guess at some of the reasons which led to this particular formulation of an apocalyptic scheme; the attitude of Christians to the policy of individual Roman emperors may well be counted among them, especially if those scholars are right who see in Caligula's attempt in A.D. 40 to introduce his statue into the Temple an event which gave to Christian as well as other Jews a new and contemporary interpretation of Daniel xi 31.

THE ABOMINATION OF DESOLATION

A similar mixture of apocalyptic elements drawn from different sources is to be found in ' the little Apocalypse ' of Mk. xiii. One of the sections of this apocalypse (14-20) deals with the sudden appearance of ' the abomination of desolation ' (Dan. xi 31) and an accompanying tribulation in Judaea. In its present form this passage has been linked up rather awkwardly in a general series of events presaging the end of the world, but it may well once have been an independent oracle on the approaching doom of Jerusalem like that oracle which, Eusebius [1] tells us, ' was vouchsafed by way of revelation to approved men ' of the Church at Jerusalem before the Jewish war of A.D. 67, and which commanded them to depart from the city before the war, and to take up residence in Pella, a small town on the other side of the Jordan.

Jesus' prophecy of the destruction of the temple implied that Jerusalem would also be destroyed, but the form of the Marcan oracle suggests that on the basis of this simple prediction was developed, in the light of Old Testament prophecy, and first-century prophetic experience, a much fuller and more ' apocalyptic ' oracle. This in turn could eventually be put mistakenly but in good faith, into the mouth of Jesus, and its meaning further changed by being made significant for the approach of the end of the world.

THE MILLENNIUM

The Book of Revelation must be read and understood in the light of two generations of such development, and of the special impetus given to apocalyptic by the actual fall of Jerusalem and destruction of the Temple in A.D. 70. That the same kinds of influence remained at work is shown by the continued popularity in some Christian circles of the Millenarian view of the Messianic kingdom. Some of the Jewish apocalypses current in the first century A.D.

---

[1] H.E. III 5, 3.

described a temporary reign of the Messiah on earth before
the final judgement (4 Ezra vii 28 ff., 2 Baruch xl 3).   It is
possible that Paul refers to such a view (in 1 Cor. xv 23-26),
although there is no trace of it in the synoptic apocalypses,
and in the Book of Revelation (xx 1-10) there is explicit
mention of a thousand-year reign of the saints with Christ
on earth.   A curious passage from Papias (c. A.D. 120) has
been preserved in the writings of Irenaeus,[1] in which it is
said that the elders who saw John, the disciple of the Lord,
recalled some of his words.   John asserted that the Lord
had taught about the times to come that the earth would be
miraculously fertile, and that amongst other wonders

> ' vines shall grow, each having 10,000 shoots, and on each
> shoot 10,000 branches, and on each branch again 10,000 twigs,
> and on each twig 10,000 clusters, and on each cluster 10,000
> grapes, and each grape when pressed shall yield 25 measures
> of wine. . . .'

It is clear from the fantastic nature of this description and
from a comparison of this with a similar passage in 2 Baruch
xxix that Jesus is here mistakenly credited with teaching
derived from Jewish apocalyptic sources.   Fortunately the
appearance and growing authority of the gospels, although
they often seriously misrepresented the teaching of Jesus,
prevented the further growth of such accretions.

THE FOURTH GOSPEL

Side by side with this interest in the apocalyptic interpretation—and misinterpretation—of Jesus' teaching there
seems to have persisted a truer and more spiritual comprehension of his words.   For a time this understanding of
the nature of the kingdom was in part accommodated to the
apocalyptic conception, and in Paul's teaching there is an
unresolved inconsistency between his apocalyptic view of the
coming kingdom and such passages as Romans xiv 17.

> For the kingdom of God is not eating and drinking, but
> righteousness and peace and joy in the Holy Spirit.

[1] *Adversus Haereses* v 33 (A.D. 185).

It is noticeable, however, that in his epistles written after A.D. 55 Paul makes only fleeting allusions to the nearness of the End (e.g. Rom. xiii 11-12), and his thought seems to have outgrown his earlier eschatological beliefs.

In the Johannine writings a stage is reached where the apocalyptic conception has largely, but not altogether disappeared and the spiritual aspect of the teaching of Jesus is once more dominant. While in his first epistle (ii 18) John speaks of the coming of many antichrists as a sign that it is the last hour, and of the coming of the day of judgement (iv 17) and there are vestigial traces in the gospel of Jesus' prophecies of the destruction of the Temple (ii 19, iv 21) of his heavenly kingdom (xiii 36, xiv 2-3), of his second coming (v 28-29, xxi 22), and of the judgement of the last day (vi 39, xii 48), in the gospel at least these sayings are given a new significance. The kingdom is a spiritual one (xviii 36), and entrance into it means the possession of eternal life that comes from belief (vi 47); for a future judgement and resurrection are in effect substituted the judgement that attaches to present disbelief (iii 18) and the life that springs from present belief and will continue in spite of physical death (xi 25). It is the supreme achievement of the author of the fourth gospel to have pierced through the confused and distorted tradition of the words of Jesus which was available to him to a truer understanding of the essential nature of the kingdom which Jesus proclaimed.

17*